The Altar-top of the Holy Royal Arch (top) with the letters arranged in the words JE-HO-VAH, JAH-BUL-ON. (Below) The letters are scrambled before the Chapter is closed. For the explanation of these words, and of the three Hebrew characters, see pp. 180-182.

These articles were purchased at a recognised Masonic outfitters in London, and assembled in accordance with a diagram put out by a member of the Aldersgate Chapter of Improvement, No. 1657.

DARKNESS VISIBLE

A dungeon horrible, on all sides round,
As one great furnace flames, yet from those flames
No light, but rather darkness visible
Served only to discover sights of woe.

(Milton, *Paradise Lost*, Book I)

Of darkness visible, so much be lent
As half to show, half veil, the deep intent.

(Pope, *The Dunciad*, Book IV)

The light of a Master Mason is darkness visible.

(*Masonic Ritual, Ceremony of Raising
to the Third Degree*)

Copyright 1952

*First Edition, June 1952. Second, July 1952. Third, Sept. 1952.
Fourth (reset), Nov. 1952. Fifth, April 1953. Sixth, Dec. 1953.
Seventh (reset), May 1954.*

PRINTED IN ENGLAND AND PUBLISHED BY
AUGUSTINE PRESS - 74 PRINCEDALE ROAD - LONDON, - W.11

DARKNESS VISIBLE

A Revelation &
Interpretation
of Freemasonry

BY
WALTON HANNAH

LONDON
AUGUSTINE PRESS
MCMLIV

To LIONEL - *an operative stonesquarer*

AUTHOR'S PREFACE

THE general argument of this book first appeared in an article "Should a Christian be a Freemason?" in the January 1951 number of *Theology*. Although I have not consciously quoted verbatim from this article, I am indebted to its Publishers, the Society for Promoting Christian Knowledge, for their permission to re-use this material.

That article excited considerable controversy, and I am also greatly indebted to the many hundreds of people from all over the world who kindly took the trouble to write to me both in support and in criticism, particularly for the courtesy and forbearance (with certain unpleasant exceptions) of the latter. This correspondence was very valuable in helping me to see further into the spirit of Masonry, and to assess the validity and importance of certain arguments, and the comparative irrelevance of others. It enabled me, too, to correct a few inaccuracies which crept in.

In a book of this nature, however, complete accuracy is difficult if not impossible to achieve. The reasons for this are clearly expressed by one of my (Masonic) correspondents whom I quote by permission. He wrote :—" You will never achieve 100% accuracy in the book you are contemplating. because the accuracy you are striving for *simply does not exist*. Variations between the different workings may consist only of verbal trivialities and ceremonial differences, yet even amongst Lodges professing to work Strict Emulation such deviations occur. A Mason who does not visit extensively (as I have) may find some phrase or direction unfamiliar, and in fairly good faith pounce on it avidly in order to stigmatize the book (as he will be only too anxious to do, believe me!) as 'full of inaccuracies.' But the really honest Mason will in his heart know better, and keep silence."

I have tried to take into full consideration every relevant argument that has been urged by my correspondents on behalf of the Fraternity. But the fact that no adequate or convincing reply has yet been made to the theological objections to the Craft either in the columns of the Church press (including *Theology*), in my personal correspondence, or in the Church Assembly debate in June 1951 (which body was not in any case competent to deal with theological issues) has strengthened my conviction that sooner or later the Church of England, if she is to preserve the integrity of her Christian witness, will have to face the issue and modify, or least define her attitude to Freemasonry. I have been urged to write this book by many who are puzzled and perplexed, and also by some who have recently resigned from their Lodges and Chapters. It is my hope that this reproduction of the Masonic workings will provide a basis of information not always readily available without considerable research, on which others far better qualified than I can base their observations and form their own conclusions. It is obviously wrong (as the Rev. C. E. Douglas pointed out in the Church Assembly debate) to base any case merely on extracts taken from their context. Hence in fairness to Freemasonry it seems only just that the entire context should be published and made freely available. If this small contribution to the literature on the subject exerts even a trifling influence, it will not have been written in vain.

The quotations from Lewis Carroll and others which appear at the chapter heads are for the benefit of those who might otherwise feel that I have treated a turgid and nonsensical ritual somewhat too ponderously. They are not to be taken as any indication that this book is not very much in earnest.

My thanks are due to Dr. V. A. Demant, of Christ Church Oxford, for his kindness in contributing an opinion on the Masonic oaths, and for reading the chapter which deals with that subject; to Dr. Paul M. Bretscher of Concordia Seminary, St. Louis, U.S.A. and to Canon A. Abraham of London, Ontario, for information and literature from America. Also and especially to Dr. H. S. Box for invaluable assistance and advice at every turn, and to Fr. Krivoshein of Oxford for information on the Greek Orthodox attitude. I am most grateful, too, to a certain Bishop and Past Grand Chaplain whom I will not embarrass by naming, for his sympathetic understanding and courtesy in giving a morning of his much-occupied time to trying, at my request, to persuade me to a different opinion on Freemasonry. He succeeded abundantly in convincing me of the personal sincerity of the individual Christian Freemason, which nowhere in these pages do I wish to impugn.

WALTON HANNAH

CONTENTS

PART I—ABOUT THE RITUAL

PART II—THE RITUAL

CONTENTS—*continued*

ILLUSTRATIONS

I

HOW KNOWN

*" Now I declare that's too bad ! " Humpty Dumpty cried, breaking
into a sudden passion. " You've been listening at doors—and behind
trees—and down chimneys—or you couldn't have known it ! "
" I haven't indeed ! " Alice said very gently. " It's in a book."
" Ah, well ! They may write such things in a book," Humpty
Dumpty said in a calmer tone.*
                                    Lewis Carroll, Through the Looking-Glass.

THERE are over six thousand Masonic Lodges under the
jurisdiction of English Grand Lodge, and on an average
nearly a hundred new Lodges are consecrated each year.[1]
As Freemasons are drawn almost exclusively from the
economic middle and upper classes (if these terms still have
any meaning) it will be readily appreciated that they represent
a very powerful and well-organized influence.

The scope of these chapters is not to analyse that influence
on the political and social life of the nation, still less to discuss
the influence on the craft of Templarism or Rosicrucianism, or
to attempt a history of Freemasonry in its development from
the Catholic guilds or lodges of operative stone-masons in the
Middle Ages through the speculative and Deistic seventeenth
and eighteenth centuries to the pan-religious non-Christian
universalism which the Craft upholds to-day. As Freemasonry
very considerably overlaps with the non-Roman Churches,
particularly with the Church of England, my concern is rather
to examine the extent to which this overlap is morally and
theologically justified. In other words, to inquire whether
Freemasonry is compatible with the Christian faith.

In any such investigation one is faced at the outset with the
apparent dilemma that authentic information is impossible
to obtain because those inside the Craft refuse to divulge the

---

1. *Statistics Fraternal Societies*, 57th edition, 1951 (Fraternal Monitor,
   Rochester, N.Y.) gives the number of Masons in England and
   Wales as 550,000 ; in Scotland, 400,000 (?) ; in Ireland 47,000 ; in
   Canada, 218,000 ; in Australasia, 300,000 ; in the United States,
   3,597,810. The total Masonic membership in the world is about
   5,200,000.

secrets, and those outside can therefore know nothing about it. This is the legend that Freemasonry has spread about so successfully that not only is it generally accepted by those outside, but in all sincerity by most Masons as well.[1]

There is, then, only one Masonic secret that has been tolerably well kept, especially from Masons. And this secret is the fact that there is no such thing as a specific Masonic secret.

What passes for secrecy is in reality a mixture of bluff and an assumption that the non-Mason is not sufficiently interested to investigate. So complacent are they on this latter point that they have imposed no effective check on the public sale of printed rituals (and Masonic publishers, like any others, are run on a profit-making basis).[2] Were I to become Grand Secretary I would be tempted to move heaven and earth to introduce legislation to ensure that Freemasons could obtain printed rituals only through their Lodge secretaries or from the Tyler, and then denounce as pirated and highly unofficial such products as outside publishers continued to produce. It is probably too late now, and even were such a step to become effective it would not deal with the problem of the Masonic effects of a deceased Brother finding their way to the second-hand market through the agency of an unsympathetic widow.

Another objection, probably insuperable, to this course of action is that it would imply the sanction of an ' official ' printed ritual, and strictly speaking there is at present no such thing. Until fairly recent times there were no printed rituals at all ; workings were learned by heart and transmitted orally. As was to be expected variations crept in, and when

1. A. E. Waite, on the other hand, in his *New Encyclopaedia of Freemasonry* (1925) admits that it is common knowledge that the secrets " have been betrayed times out of number " (Vol. II, p. 208) and is too honest to insert the usual Masonic qualifications of ' alleged ' or ' supposed ' disclosures. What Waite (together with most enlightened Masons) claims to be the *real* secret of Masonry is not a secret at all, but rather a ' mystery ', verbally incommunicable to the outsider and Mason alike—the Masonic life based on moral symbolism and allegory which the initiate, having been given the ceremonial key, must discover for himself.

2. This public and indiscriminate sale of rituals on further investigation is I think mainly confined to London. I have toured bookshops extensively in certain provincial cities, and friends have done so for me in others, without any success.

printed manuals were tolerated to stabilize the ritual and to ease the burden of committing it to memory, several distinctive workings had evolved — such as Emulation (generally regarded as the norm) and Stability, Oxford, Bristol, and many other treasured local variants.[1] As long as the ' ancient landmarks,' the signs, grips, words, and the general structure of the ritual are preserved and remain constant, trivial verbal and ceremonial variations are allowed, and Grand Lodge has consistently refused to pronounce any working as ' official.' As printed rituals are not allowed inside the Lodge at all, therefore, they are merely tolerated as guides to the various usages in the Lodges, and as aids in committing them to memory. That is their only status.

It can be safely assumed, however, that authentic Masonic publishers do not spend money on printing deliberately bogus rituals with the purpose of putting the public off the scent, and that gentlemen seen committing them to memory in trains and restaurants are not deliberately wasting their time. These manuals, rightly interpreted, do, therefore, give a reliable guide to Lodge workings.

Here, then, is the first source of information.

But of course it is not as easy as all that. These manuals are printed in a manner supposedly " intelligible only to the Craft," and have their gaps (" the sign is given by etc."). Many operative words (as well as some quite inoperative ones, to heighten the mystery) are indicated either by initials or by complete blanks. But this process is extremely clumsily done, again apparently on the assumption that no outsider will bother to study it with the same intelligence and assiduousness that he might devote to a *Times* cross-word puzzle. Different editions of, say, Emulation workings will vary in the words which are initialled and those that are printed in full, so that by comparing several books many of the gaps can be filled at sight. And even where this does not apply, I submit that, given a general idea that the Masonic legend is in some way connected with King Solomon's Temple, such

1. This is perhaps an over-simplification of a very complicated subject. Some distinctive features of local provincial workings probably date from pre-Union times, and survived the attempt of the Lodge of Reconciliation of ' Ancients ' and ' Moderns ' to establish a uniform rite which would please both.

passages as the following (describing the Word of the first degree) can be readily de-coded with a fair degree of probability even without reference to I Kings VII, 21 or Ruth IV, 13 and 17 :—" This.... is derived from the l.h.p. at the p.... way or entrance of K.S.T., so named after B...., the G.G. of D., a P. and R. in I."[1] Other manuals of Masonic instruction on the meaning of the ritual will quite shamelessly and in the clear context of the Temple and even of the Words talk about " the two pillars B. & J." Obviously then there is no great secret about the first degree Word—or of that of the second degree either. And again, even had I omitted the secret pass-word SHIBBOLETH from the Tracing Board Lecture of the Second Degree, the context of the Lecture gives it away completely.[2]

And that brings me to the second source of information, the spate of Masonic commentaries, periodicals, ceremonial guides, and even histories which are unwittingly spattered with clues. Such an excellent, reliable, and usually discreet book as Bernard E. Jones's *Freemasons' Guide and Compendium*, for instance, mentions that Tubal-Cain (printed in full) appears in a certain degree. So he does. In many rituals the pass-word to the third degree is actually given as T.C., the first A. in M., and Genesis IV, 22, confirms that he was the first artificer in metals.

I have left as third and last the most obvious source of information, namely published disclosures. These vary greatly in accuracy and reliability, and the fact that none in this country is altogether up-to-date or dependable is one of my reasons for publishing this book. It would be a lengthy and largely irrelevant task to discuss and evaluate in detail these disclosures, ranging from Prichard and Morgan to the scurrilous badly-printed little pamphlet. One needs to know something of their historical background, the status of the authors and, if Masons, their motives in making such disclosures in order rightly to assess their value and accuracy. One must compare them with each other, for some are merely compiled from earlier disclosures with no reference to contemporary workings, and no fresh information added.

The classic exposé in the United States was that of the unfortunate William Morgan, whose disappearance in

1. See p. 102.　　2. See p. 125.

1826 led to such a popular outcry that Masonry suffered a severe set-back in America which lasted for many years. Amongst the flood of literature of that period was a booklet by the celebrated evangelist, educationalist and ex-Mason, Charles G. Finney called *The Character and Claims of Freemasonry*. In this he stated of Morgan's book "As nearly as I could recollect, it was a *verbatim* revelation of the first three degrees as I had myself taken them." I have mentioned Finney in particular because although of an earlier generation he was a great friend and brother in the Ministry of my own maternal grandfather at Oberlin, Ohio, and his complete integrity, sanctity, and honesty of character made him almost our family oracle. This is one of the *imponderabilia* which naturally carried weight with me in assessing the value of his assertion.

American workings, however, differ considerably from our own. In this country the most reliable disclosure as far as the Craft degrees are concerned is Richard Carlile's *Manual of Freemasonry* which during the past century ran into several editions and can still be obtained. It has never been revised, however, and there are many trifling variations between Carlile and Strict Emulation, including one in the Test Questions which, I believe, has been made use of as a deliberate trap with which to catch the imposter. In the so-called higher degrees he goes more seriously astray — "holy ends" for instance, appears as an absurdly meaningless phonetic rendering of *oriens*. His version of the signs in the Royal Arch is quite different from the way in which they are given to-day. Yet in the three Craft degrees, despite a slight tendency to a greater verbal prolixity than is found in present-day workings Carlile is beyond doubt substantially accurate.[1] Again I have two personal confirmations of this, quite apart from the general

1. E. H. Cartwright, Senior Grand Deacon, in *A Commentary on the Freemasonic Ritual* (Hepworth & Co., 1947) says of this ritual (which he refers to as the "ritual of 1825", and nowhere mentions Carlile's name) "Although as a 'spurious ritual' it is theoretically unreliable, there is no doubt that in some points it does present the contemporary practice of regular Lodges and provide useful evidence in regard to some of the details" (p. 39). He refers to it throughout as a source apparently of equal reliability with other early rituals of more correct origin. The value of Carlile, as he admits, is that it is the earliest post-Union printed ritual. *Historical Analysis of the Holy Royal Arch Ritual* (F. de P. Castells, 1929) also assumes the reliability of Carlile, and discusses when and why alterations have been made in the Royal Arch ritual and signs since 1825.

agreement between this book and authentic modern rituals. A clergyman friend of mine who rather enjoyed his Masonry but refused to take it very seriously admitted frankly in the heat of an argument that the secrecy was largely bluff and cited Carlile as an instance, saying that to the best of his knowledge it was reasonably accurate, and the signs, grips, and words were certainly correct. Secondly, I have a copy in my possession which had folded in it several papers of unquestionable Masonic genuineness—one of those little cards looking outwardly like a cricket fixture list with the Test Questions printed esoterically inside, a Lodge summons, and a receipt for dues paid. It also has certain pencilled comments and corrections which appear to indicate that it had actually been used by a Lodge officer in learning his ritual.[1]

By comparing these various disclosures with the modern authentic rituals of Masonic publishers, and by checking them one against another, one can find the answers to all the blanks and initials with a degree of certainty. There is a common denominator of reasonableness and consistency. When every disclosure for instance, gives an identical account of the first degree Masons' grip, and when a recent ' authentic ' ritual also states that the "G. or Tn. is given by a d.p.o.t.t.o.t.f.j.o.t.h.; this, when regularly given and received, serves to distinguish a Brother by n. as well by d." one can but assume that this grip or token is indeed given by a distinct pressure of the thumb on the first joint of the hand. The only alternative to assuming the transparent truth of these findings is to suppose the existence of a gigantic world-wide hoax in which all Masons join, exceeding in cleverness and consistency any conspiracy yet known to mankind. But of course most Masons are too simple for that. And is it merely coincidence that the ' supposed ' means of recognition are often reciprocated by complete strangers, and even followed up with invitations to visit their Lodges?

I have dealt with this question of the imaginary secrecy of Masonic workings at considerable and perhaps wearisome length in order that the reader may assess at true value the normal and instinctive Masonic reaction to disclosures.

1. I have seen an early copy with an old-fashioned binding containing a lock in the clasp, another indication that it was actually in use by Masons themselves.

" Books purporting to give Masonic secrets "—" what Mr. So-and-So supposes himself to have discovered " are almost stock phrases. The insinuation of doubt or gross inaccuracy is always there. But let us not judge too harshly the apparent near-dishonesty of this means of discrediting an exposé, for Masons have sworn solemnly on the Bible never to reveal.

If you ask a Masonic friend for an opinion on this book, you will either receive a reply in some such terms, or else a complete and evasive silence. What Masons say about it among themselves, however, is a very different matter. Indeed since the first edition of this book appeared, two rumours have become widespread in certain Masonic circles. First, that I was myself at one time a Mason, who was expelled for notorious conduct. Secondly, that I applied for initiation, but was black-balled. There is no shred of truth in either of these stories. At no time have I ever been or thought of becoming a Freemason.

But in conclusion, I can reveal that I have had a final check made on my ritual disclosure. I have two friends living in quite different parts of the country, each of whom I have deliberately kept in ignorance of the other's existence. Both have unquestionably been Masons who have convinced me of the genuineness of their certificates. Both are religious men who have come to the conclusion that *oaths sworn on false pretences are null and void*. Both volunteered for conscience sake and with no prospect of material advantage to look over and correct the manuscript of this book, and the corrections (of an extremely trifling nature), allowing for variations in non-essentials between Lodge and Lodge, in each case agreed.

Now had there been only one, the stock but tendentious Masonic argument that a man who is capable of breaking the Masonic obligation is capable of telling any untruth might conceivably carry weight with a few. But I leave it to the reader to judge whether two people quite unknown to each other could have made me the victim of deliberate deception by telling identical lies on identical trivialities, when both are enthusiastic to establish the truth.[1]

1. The reliability of this book has been further confirmed publicly in a review by D. R. Denman, M.A., M.Sc., Ph.D., writing as an ex-Mason in *The Life of Faith*, Oct. 15, 1952.

II

WHY WRITTEN

" Christopher Robin, you must shoot the balloon with your gun. Have you got your gun?"
" Of course I have," you said, " But if I do that, it will spoil the balloon," you said.
" But if you don't," said Pooh, " I shall have to let go, and that would spoil me."
When he put it like this, you saw how it was, and you aimed very carefully at the balloon, and fired.
" Ow!" said Pooh.
" Did I miss?" you asked.
" You didn't exactly miss," said Pooh, " but you missed the balloon."
" I'm so sorry," you said, and you fired again, and this time you hit the balloon, and the air came slowly out, and Winnie-the-Pooh floated down to the ground.

A. A. Milne, Winnie-the-Pooh.

MY MOTIVE in producing this disclosure is not a desire to irritate my many Masonic friends, nor is it a mere yielding to the temptation to call a gigantic bluff.

There is an increasing number of clergy and devout laity in the Church of England who have their misgivings over Freemasonry, which the necessarily evasive answers of Masons do not altogether allay. They are aware (as indeed is constantly pointed out to them) that many people of the highest distinction and repute both in Church and State are members, but an *illi quoque* argument has no more validity in logic than the *tu quoque*, particularly when it is remembered that these distinguished personages themselves had no previous knowledge of the teaching to which they swore compliance.

There are parochial clergy, too, who realize that although some of their most faithful laymen, possibly Churchwardens and Parochial Church Councillors, are also members of Lodges, there are a great many more who appear to find in Freemasonry a complete and adequate substitute for religion. Those who believe that the Church, and the Church alone, has Christ's authority on earth to teach religious truth and define moral codes openly and fearlessly, may legitimately feel some disquiet at the thought of another and purely human body doing so under a close-tyled Masonic bushel. And again the repeated assurances that Masonry cannot conflict with anyone's religious beliefs do not always adequately allay these misgivings. If churchmen are receiving moral instruction and precept (however innocuous or beneficial) from an outside source, the Church surely has the right, if not the duty, to investigate.

And yet so little information is readily to hand. A straightforward presentation of the ritual itself in the three Craft degrees plus the Royal Arch (the entire Masonic system as recognized officially by Grand Lodge) will therefore enable people who have these misgivings and yet have no time for lengthy researches to judge for themselves.

It is sometimes thought that there is some inner secret imparted verbally to the candidate for initiation, but too esoteric to be hinted at in printed rituals. I can assure the reader, however, from ample personal Masonic confirmation as well as from researches into previous disclosures that this is not so. In toasting the initiate at the Festive Board afterwards it is customary for the Worshipful Master to say a few words on the meaning and privileges of Masonry, but this follows no official form, and the nature of such teaching seldom rises above the platitude, and depends entirely on the Master's own outlook. In an old school Lodge with a fair sprinkling of the cloth the initiate may be told that Masonry is the handmaid of the Church. In a business-man's Lodge the Master may even declare that although he can't answer for everyone, personally he thinks that Masonry is the finest religion in the world.

Only the loyal toast of the Queen and Craft, and the Tyler's toast (" to all poor and distressed Masons ") follow a set form. Official Masonic teachings are contained exclusively in the workings within the Lodge, the lectures and the charges. They may therefore be studied almost in their entirety in these pages. Nothing of value is omitted. The only ' inner secret ' is the Masonic way of life based on this symbolic morality. and the term is equally applicable to the sacramental life of the Church.

It will be seen, then, how utterly without foundation is the Masonic parrot-cry that no one who is not a Mason can possibly form any opinion of Masonic teachings or come to any understanding of what it all means. It is not necessary, after all, to become a member of the Roman Catholic Church in order to understand her teachings. That again is part of the great bluff on which Masons themselves refuse to be undeceived. For after all, no one likes to admit that a solemn oath of secrecy sworn on the Bible is an attempt to protect things which are not secret at all, and that the oath is therefore a meaningless farce.

If it be objected that in giving the signs, grips, and words in full I am merely causing needless offence by publishing matters quite irrelevant to the real meaning of Masonry I can only reply that I do so for two reasons. First, to prove my contention that there are no secrets in Masonry and therefore that the Solemn Obligations are farcical and even invalid, and secondly, were I to reproduce the ritual incomplete in these particulars it might be insinuated that it was incomplete in other more important particulars too, and that outside knowledge of it can only be very partial. I am aware that every possible attempt will be made to discredit and suppress this book, and may perhaps be pardoned for wishing to forestall such action in advance.

A supposed secret shared by half a million people in England alone which can readily be discovered on the shelves of any good library cannot be regarded in the same light as a personal or family secret which if discovered by prying or by accident it would be shameful to betray. If to reproduce Masonic esoteria is to be guilty of perjury at second hand, then the researches of many a classical scholar into the secret mystery-cults of the past must come under the same condemnation. The mysteries of Eleusis, for instance, were secret. Admittedly they are dead, and Masonry is not. But suppose, for the sake of argument, it should be discovered that in some remote fastness of the Aegeans these secret rites were still being kept alive to-day. Would that make the researches of the scholar scandalous ?

I am firmly convinced that for a Christian to pledge himself to a religious (or even, to avoid begging the question, to a quasi-religious) organization which offers prayer and worship to God which deliberately exclude the name of our Lord and Saviour Jesus Christ, in whose name only is salvation to be found, is apostatic. I am also quite aware that there are many Christians, and even Archbishops, who are also Masons who do not see it in that light, either because they do not take their ritual very seriously, or because they allow other considerations such as the good works, benevolence, and moral uprightness of the Craft, to outweigh the clearly pagan implications of its formulae. The Englishman is a Pelagian at heart. It is my sincere hope, therefore, that this book may be of service not only in giving information to the non-Mason, but that it may also lead the Christian Mason seriously to re-consider his position. He might well ask himself at the outset, is it morally licit to bind oneself in advance, by a solemn oath on the Bible, to secrecy and fidelity in an organization which concerns faith and morals of which nothing is revealed to him previously ? Here is the first stumbling-block for the Christian Mason who is at all conversant with moral theology.

III

MASONIC OBLIGATIONS

" I see," said the Queen. " Off with their heads !" and the procession moved on, three of the soldiers remaining behind to execute the unfortunate gardeners, who ran to Alice for protection.

" You shan't be beheaded !" said Alice, and she put them into a large flower-pot that stood near. The three soldiers wandered about for a minute or two, looking for them, and then quietly marched off after the others.

" Are their heads off ?" shouted the Queen.

" Their heads are gone, if it please your Majesty !" the soldiers shouted in reply.

" That's right !" shouted the Queen. " Can you play croquet ?"

*   *   *   *

" What is the fun ?" said Alice.

" Why, she——" said the Gryphon. " It's all her fancy, that: they never executes nobody, you know."

Lewis Carroll, Alice in Wonderland.

THE oaths, or Solemn Obligations as they are termed in the ritual, probably give rise to more misgivings among thoughtful Masons themselves than any other aspect of Masonic workings. The full text of these obligations and the context in which they are taken will be found in their respective degrees,[1] and there is no need to give them again here at length.

The Candidate takes them kneeling, with one hand on the open Bible. The Deacons cross their wands above his head. Although the Worshipful Master has declared that the oaths contain nothing which can conflict with his social, moral, or religious duties, the Candidate finds himself repeating, phrase by phrase after the Master, expressions such as he has probably never used before except in jest or profanity. He renders himself liable to shocking tortures and mutilations should he prove faithless. His throat may be cut, his tongue torn out, his left breast laid open, his body severed in two and bowels burned to ashes, his head cut off, his right hand cut off and slung over his left shoulder to wither and die.

Perhaps in his schooldays he made use of such expressions as " cut my throat and hope to die ", accompanied by even the appropriate gesture, thus unwittingly giving the Penal sign of the first degree. But if he was brought up in a Christian

1. See pp. 99, 119, 135, and 164.

household he would surely have had misgivings over swearing these words on his knees with one hand resting on the Bible.

It will be noticed, too, that although the first degree obligation is solely concerned with secrecy, the second and third degree and Royal Arch oaths include also certain moral principles and loyalties, the infringement of which likewise carries the death penalty. The Candidate swears that he will accept a punishment of being severed in two, for instance, if he fails boldly to repel the slanderer of a brother-Mason's good name, or if the position of his daily supplications does not remind him of a brother's need. "*All* these points," he declares, " I solemnly swear to observe, without evasion, equivocation, or mental reservation of any kind, under no less a penalty......"

It must be admitted that on his initiation he is treated more reasonably. An alternative penalty has been inserted (probably a later interpolation) branding him as " void of all moral worth " and so on, but in England and Scotland, at least, this appears only in the Entered Apprentice obligation ; to assume that it applies equally to the penalties in other degrees when it is nowhere hinted that it does so savours of ' equivocation.' The Irish workings are also more reasonable ; they are sworn in each degree " bearing in mind the ancient penalty ..... and binding myself under the real penalty of being branded deservedly as a wretch," etc. This gets over some of the difficulties. But how can the Scot and the Englishman get over theirs ?

The problem bristles with dilemmas.

Either the oaths mean what they say, or they do not. If they do mean what they say, then the Candidate is entering into a pact consenting to his own murder by barbarous torture and mutilation should he break it. If they do not mean what they say, then he is swearing high-sounding schoolboy nonsense on the Bible, which verges on blasphemy.

Again, in the third degree obligation, the Candidate swears that he will respect the confidences of a brother-Mason, " murder, treason, felony, and all other offences contrary to the laws of God and the ordinances of the realm being at all times most especially excepted." This clause, of course, safeguards the oaths from coming into conflict with the law of the land. It removes any suspicion that respectable English Freemasonry could ever be politically seditious. Yet at the same time this very clause which guarantees Masonic respectability makes nonsense of the penalty which follows it. For although it is nowhere stipulated or even hinted who should have the task of exacting the penalty,[1] it is quite obviously contrary to the laws of God and the ordinances of the realm that a man should be severed in two and have his bowels burned to ashes for any offence whatsoever. A Past Master seen in the streets with his right wrist ending in a stump, and the withered and decaying hand slung over his left shoulder would have every right to demand police protection against further grotesqueries.

The simple common-sense answer to these difficulties is of course that no Mason takes these oaths literally. The pledge to secrecy, he will say, is taken very seriously indeed. The penalties on the other hand are purely symbolic, and to be understood in the Irish sense.

But while this is certainly true it does not remove the objections. This symbolic interpretation means that the faithless Mason deserves dire physical penalties even though they cannot and should not be imposed, and Masons themselves would be the first to register horror and shock if they ever were imposed. The one strongly suspected Masonic murder in recent years, that of William Morgan in the State of New York in 1826, led to mass resignations from Lodges, denial of liability, and a general eclipse of the Craft in the United States for some time, whereas logically they should have gloried in it as an act of justice in conformity with their sworn obligations. This in itself shows the unreality of the position. However symbolically interpreted, the oaths imply that an indiscretion leading to the disclosure for instance of the identity of the pillars at the entrance to King Solomon's Temple with the words of the first or second degree deserves a greater and more barbarously un-Christian torture than society imposes for treason, rape or murder. Even a symbolical interpretation, that is, outrages the sense of justice and proportion.

And although a symbolical interpretation of the penalty

1. There is, however, a certain vague tradition that the Tyler is responsible for this duty.

clauses is universally accepted in practice, it is impossible to reconcile it with the express declaration, sworn on the Bible and in the presence of God, that the oaths are taken " without evasion, equivocation, or mental reservation of any kind." This would appear to rule out the possibility of any clause in the obligations meaning other than it says, or being taken in a different sense from that which is clearly expressed.

There is, of course, the argument from antiquity. The oaths are landmarks, priceless survivals from a primeval past less squeamish over the blunt forthrightness of rough-and-ready justice than our own century. But age in itself does not justify, or make wrong right. Logically, the argument could be equally applied to a survival of the excesses of the Roman Bacchanalia.

The Christian may well feel that not only are the penalties out of all proportion to the crime, but that the oaths themselves, taken on the Bible in an atmosphere of religious solemnity, are also out of proportion to the comparative triviality of the secrets thus guarded, and on that score alone are profane. And certainly there are many Masons, Christians among them, who aggravate this profanity by taking the religious side of Masonry lightly. By doing so they may feel that they escape the condemnation of belonging to an alien cult, yet at the same time they only thereby increase in proportion the profanity of their oaths.

If Masonry, which professes to be based on the practice of every moral virtue, claims that these oaths with their bloodthirsty penalties are congruous with Christianity, one wonders whether the Christian Mason would see any incongruity in approximating the Book of Common Prayer to Masonic usages. Suppose, for instance, candidates for Confirmation were asked to swear " do ye here, in the presence of God, renew the solemn promise and vow that was made in your name at your Baptism—under no less a penalty than that of having your throat cut across, your tongue torn out by the root, and buried in the sand of the sea ? " And yet if it is right for the Christian to swear such oaths in a Masonic Temple dedicated to God, why should a similar oath seem blasphemous (however symbolically interpreted) when sworn in a Church dedicated to God ?

The only possible answer is that I am taking these things

far too seriously. But this answer can only mean that it is morally licit for a Christian to swear a solemn oath on the Word of God and in His Holy Name—and yet *not* take it too seriously.[1]

I sent a transcript of the Masonic obligations with their context to Canon V. A. Demant, the Regius Professor of Moral and Pastoral Theology at Oxford University, and asked him for his judgment as to whether they were morally licit for the Christian. His reply (which of course is conditional on the accuracy of my transcript, being that which appears in this book) was as follows :—" Looking at the nature of the vows in general, it does seem very difficult for a Churchman to undertake them without being guilty of either vain (*vanum*) or rash (*temerarium*) swearing. He seems to be initiated into an alien cult. If it is not taken seriously—or taken very symbolically (in contravention of the oath's words : without evasion, equivocation, or mental reservation of any kind) then the oath comes under the heading of vain swearing or profanity. If it is taken seriously then it must be put down as rash swearing, for there is no certainty that the Christian initiate will not find afterwards that he has joined an alien cult."

Another difficulty in interpretation which may arise for the Freemason of sensitive conscience is ambiguity over what is to be considered secret. He promises that he will never reveal " any part or parts, point or points, of the secrets or mysteries" of Freemasonry, yet nowhere is it specifically defined what is secret and what is not. Having taken the oath, the Worshipful Master informs the initiate that the secrets of this degree " consist of a sign, token, and word "—which would seem to indicate, if " consist " be taken to mean what it usually means, that any other matters which the initiate may learn are either not secret, or are covered by the term " mysteries ". On any interpretation the publication and public sale of printed rituals seems a clear breach of the obligation. When even the secret words are indicated by initials, it is difficult to understand in what spirit the Masonic compositors

---

1. " Concerning the oaths and obligations, we may say, cowboys and Indians." (The Rev. W. G. Branch, writing as a Master Mason to the *Church Times*, March 30, 1951.) This attitude is undoubtedly the common one, and indeed extends to the whole Masonic ritual.

and printers working for Masonic publishers promised not to "write those secrets, indite, carve, mark, engrave, or otherwise them delineate...whereby or whereon any letter, character, or figure, *or a least trace of a letter, character, or figure*, may become legible or intelligible." Masons who possess and use these rituals would appear to be accessories to these crimes, and "crimes" is surely not an overstatement, as the oaths clearly state that they deserve the death penalty. In whatever sense the oaths are taken, then, it is obviously not "without evasion, equivocation, or mental reservation of any kind." The fact that there are no real secrets whatsoever in Masonry adds somewhat to the preposterous unreality and insincerity of the oaths. Although the Candidate may be quite unaware of it, he is in reality pledging himself, as far as secrecy is concerned, to maintain a colossal system of bluff.

Any Freemason is entitled to proclaim to the world that British Masonry believes in God, is loyal to the State, and runs a hospital, for these things are altogether admirable and beyond controversy. There is no secret either about Masonry being a system of symbolic morality, for here too it gains the approval of the world. The "secrets and mysteries," apart from the methods of recognition, appear to begin where Masonic teachings and practices deviate from orthodox Christianity. It is not blazoned abroad that a death and resurrection rite is practised in the third degree, that the names of pagan deities are equated with that of Jehovah in the Royal Arch, or that fantastic tortures are attached to violations of the oaths. The average Mason, to do him justice, keeps his oath to the letter by not talking about Masonry at all, and by changing the subject as adroitly as possible. If forced into a defence, however, he will not go far wrong according to Masonic precedents if he freely admits those features on which there can be no disagreement, but keeps as secrets and mysteries such aspects as might incite ridicule, disapproval, or condemnation.

To what extent are the oaths binding in conscience once they are taken? It is difficult to give a precise or universal answer for the member of the Church of England, though there are certain guiding principles.

An oath may be subsequently realised to be " vain and

rash swearing " and hence sinful ; this in itself does not invalidate the obligation if it was taken in good faith with every intention of keeping it.

On the other hand, an oath taken on false pretences is null and void. Suppose, to take an extreme and unlikely example, a man interested in social work swore an oath of loyalty and secrecy to an organization on the express understanding that its aims were to provide holiday homes for tired mothers. After he has taken this oath it is revealed to him that the real aim of the society is to drop an atom bomb on Buckingham Palace. His oath of loyalty to that organization is obviously not binding in conscience, because it was taken on false grounds, and he could not fulfil it without sin. But in this instance, as a loyal citizen, he may well feel that the secrecy, too, is not binding on him ; that it is his duty to inform the police, that he would be guilty of a serious sin of omission were he to fail to do so.

Now the Masonic oaths are taken on the express understanding that they can in no way conflict with a man's social, moral, or religious duties. And without doubt the Worshipful Masters who administer them do so in perfectly good faith, and themselves see no possibility of such a conflict. The majority of Masons who take them, even good Christian Masons, do not appear to be aware of any conflict, largely, I think, because they have never had any cause to reason the situation logically in the light of their faith. Obviously the rank and file of the Brethren cannot possibly be expected to be moral theologians, and although the gruesome penalties often jar on their natural feelings when first recited, and certain portions of the ritual may seem strangely at variance with what they may hear in Church, familiarity usually dulls misgivings in the course of time. But should a Christian initiate come to realise that Masonry in regarding all Gods as equal, or in offering prayers which deliberately exclude our Lord, or in proclaiming the name of God in terms of heathen deities as in the Royal Arch (things which were not disclosed to him on initiation) does violate his Christian principles, his oath ceases to be binding in conscience. The obligation to secrecy may remain. But if he feels very strongly that Freemasonry is even unintentionally undermining by its subtle universalist heterodoxy from within the supreme majesty due to our Lord and the distinctive and exclusive witness of the Church as devastatingly as an atom bomb on Buckingham Palace might undermine the British constitution, it is surely arguable that he has a clear duty in conscience to speak out in warning.

" If anyone swear rashly with his lips to do evil, or to do good, whatsoever it be that a man shall utter rashly with an oath, and it be hid from him ; when he knoweth of it, then he shall be guilty in one of these things : and it shall be, when he shall be guilty in one of these things, that he shall confess that wherein he hath sinned." (Leviticus V, 4-6).

IV

IS MASONRY A RELIGION?

*" Whether the fogs produce the serious people or whether the serious
people produce the fogs, I don't know, but the whole thing rather
gets on my nerves."*

Oscar Wilde, Lady Windermere's Fan.

MASONRY frequently declares that it is not a religion,
yet it claims to be religious.[1] Unofficially one even
hears it stated "Masonry is not *a* religion, it *is* religion."
If Masonry were a new thing, and if the Masonic ritual had
been composed only this year, and submitted to an impartial
panel of Bishops for their judgment, approval, and blessing,
there can be little doubt that it would be rejected with amused
scorn. But while many distinguished clerics vigorously deny
that Masonry is a religion, and expect the outsider to take their
word for it without further investigation, the outsider is sometimes pardonably doubtful and legitimately curious as to how
these clerics would define the word religion, about which, if the
term be denied to Freemasonry, there appears to be some
woolly thinking. For instance, the Rev. Canon E. Paton-
Williams, Past Assistant Grand Chaplain and Assistant Provincial Grand Master for East Lancashire, in a purely pagan
Christmas message to the *Freemason's Chronicle* (Dec. 22nd,
1951) wrote, " It was Plato who said we must now wait for
one, a God or God-like man, who will teach us our duties
and take away the blindness from our eyes. Masonry is
fulfilling that mission in no uncertain manner. Masonry
heralds the *Dies Natalis Solis Invicti*." Any Christmas message from a clergyman which deliberately omits all mention
of Christ may be regarded as a theological curiosity, but it
would be difficult to maintain that Canon Paton-Williams is
not here referring to Masonry in terms of a religion, however

1. This distinction is, however, practically meaningless. It is equivalent to saying that a thing is not an abomination, but it is
abominable. An adjective must refer to a noun. A symbol might
be said to be religious but not a religion, but it is difficult to
apply this to an organization in this context. If Masonry is
'religious', to *what* religion is it related? To Christianity?

pagan. And a Past Assistant Grand Chaplain has surely some authority to speak on the religious nature of the Craft.

How is one to arrive at a fair judgment on this crucial matter ?

Christian Masons obviously cannot assent in as many words to the proposition that Masonry is a religion, for Christianity is an exclusive faith. Even to admit such a possibility would provoke the suspicions and perhaps investigations of those Churches which have not yet pronounced against it. It cannot, it must not, be for them a rival to the supreme claims of Christ. Therefore, regardless of certain clear implications in the ritual and declarations of their own members to the contrary, it *is* not. They prefer to consider it a handmaid of the Church ; a strong moral foundation on which any faith can be practised, but no more a religion than the Mothers' Union or the Boy Scout movement.

Let us be quite fair to this position. In the three Craft degrees of Entered Apprentice, Fellow-Craft, and Master Mason the specific " secrets " are really no more than methods of mutual recognition in certain grips (or handshakes), signs, and words, knowledge of which (together with the Grand Lodge certificate) will prove a man on examination to be a Mason. All this seems perfectly harmless. The rest of Masonry to them is concerned with the symbolism of character-building, and indeed Craft Masonry defines itself as " a peculiar system of morality, veiled in allegory, and illustrated by symbols." Certain events, mainly apocryphal, concerned with the building of King Solomon's Temple form the core of the allegory, and the various implements and working-tools of the operative stone-mason (particularly, of course, the well-known emblem of the square and compass) to which moral teachings are attached, are among the symbols.

" We are organised," said the President of the Board of General Purposes to Grand Lodge in September 1949, " to provide a series of Lodges where Masons can meet in a hallowed atmosphere, where good fellowship can be promoted through a Brotherhood founded on the Fatherhood of God, where we can be happy in a confidence founded on mutual trust, where character can be moulded and strengthened and aptitudes developed, so that our members are thereby better qualified to exercise a wholesome influence as citizens in their private capacities on all matters of public issue."

This, coupled with the spice of mystery, an occasional evening away from the wife, and in some cases an affection for pretentious titles, a love of dressing-up and ceremonial, is the sum total of what the Craft means to the average Master Mason, and perfectly innocent and harmless it all seems to him. He may be aware of various references in the ritual to the crudities of pagan worship, for instance to the " sun at its meridian," but these are looked on as old-fashioned survivals and rather quaint. Most Masons do not take their ritual seriously, and certainly do not read the works of Ward, Wilmshurst or Waite. They would not understand them if they did.

The issue of whether Masonry is or is not a religion is confused by the traditional and Pelagian tendency of many Englishmen to fail to distinguish between religion and morals. The following syllogism, therefore, is typical :—religion exists to help people to lead good lives. Masonry helps people to lead good lives. Therefore Masonry is religion. Blissfully unaware of the fallacy of the undistributed middle and convinced that religion is what any man chooses to make it, the Englishman may go on by arguing that as Masonry teaches morals much more pleasantly and excitingly than the Church, therefore it is a more satisfactory religion. Everybody is going to end up at the same place ; his wife and the parson call it Heaven, he calls it the Grand Lodge Above.

Seen in this light, Masonry is not so much a religion as a parasite on religion, and a rival to the Church as a moral guide.

But there is more in it than this. There are in the Masonic workings distinct elements of religion in a far more supernatural sense of the word, a religion that is entirely non-Christian. And when critics of these elements are accused by Masons of misunderstanding completely the meaning of Masonry, what really happens is that these critics call attention to things which many Masons, Churchmen in particular, have never seen or prefer to ignore.

I have so far resisted the temptation to build up a scissors-and-paste case for this on the testimony of Masonic mystics[1]

1. This has already been done admirably and convincingly by the Rev. C. Penney Hunt in *The Menace of Freemasonry to the Christian Faith.*

as I prefer to base my case on the ritual itself. But there is a passage in a book by Sir John Cockburn (Past Grand Deacon of England, and Past Deputy Grand Master of Australia) called *Freemasonry ; What, Whence, Why, Whither* which will bear quotation because it is in conformity with the ritual, and few Masons could logically disagree with it. He writes :—
" The question whether Masonry is a religion has been keenly debated. But the contest appears merely a war of words. Perhaps the best way of arriving at a conclusion would be first of all to enumerate the points which are common to most religions and then to enquire in what respect Masonry differs from them. Religion deals with the relationship between man and his Maker and instils a reverence for the Creator as first cause. Religions abound in observances of worship by prayer and praise. They inculcate rules of conduct by holding up a God or Hero as a pattern for imitation....It would be difficult to say in which of these characteristics Freemasonry is lacking. Surely it abounds in all. Its ceremonies are elaborate and are unsurpassed for beauty and depth of meaning. They are interspersed with prayer and thanksgiving......If the title of religion be denied to Freemasonry it may well claim the higher ground of being a Federation of Religions. It is a form of worship in which all religions can unite without sacrificing a jot of their respective creeds."

All these facts, except the last, mentioned by Sir John Cockburn can be abundantly substantiated. The ritual is worked in the spirit of a solemn religious ceremony ; it is a frequent custom to sing hymns at the opening and closing of the Lodge, candles are lighted before the three pedestals, and the Bible is always open before the Worshipful Master. The Lodge must be opened and closed with prayer, which is also offered for the Candidate at his initiation, passing, raising, and exaltation. The Grand and Royal Sign is accompanied by the exclamation " All glory to the. Most High ". The places where Lodges meet are customarily known as temples, a word strongly associated with worship and religion. Most Lodges have chaplains and organists who have their regular part to play in the ceremonies.

It may still be argued that Boy Scouts sing hymns and have chaplains who offer prayers which, at least in open troops, can also be vague and pan-religious, and yet Scouts may be devout members of a Church without any incompatibility. Masonry, however, goes very much further than this, even if individual Masons do not.

For Masonry claims to impart to its initiates a spiritual and esoteric light. True, the Candidate must profess a belief in God which implies that his previous darkness is not complete, but the symbolism throughout is clear. He is stripped of money and valuables at his initiation to symbolise his poverty. his blindfold typifies a state of spiritual as well as material darkness, his cable-tow is a sign of humility. He is introduced into the Lodge with the words " a poor candidate in a state of darkness . . . humbly soliciting to be admitted to the mysteries and privileges of Freemasonry ". After he is obligated (a vile phrase, as Polonius would have said—but not mine) he is asked what is the " predominant wish of his heart " and he replies, light. This is the most dramatic moment of the ceremony ; coinciding with a thunderous hand-clap from the assembled brethren his hoodwink is removed, and for the first time he beholds the Lodge. The emblematic Masonic lights are now indicated to him, being six in number ; the Volume of the Sacred Law, the square, the compasses, the " sun to rule the day, the moon to govern the night, and the Worshipful Master to rule the Lodge." Whether the illumination received is sufficient to justify the offensive phrase in the second degree Obligation which stigmatizes non-Masons as the " uninstructed and popular world " is perhaps open to question ; certainly in the third degree this Masonic light shows beyond doubt not only its inferiority to, but its utterly pagan incompatibility with the light which Our Lord shed upon the grave, for we are told that " the light of a Master Mason is darkness visible, serving only to express the gloom which rests on the prospect of futurity ".

And yet Masonry believes in immortality. It believes that death can be trampled under foot and expresses the hope that " when we shall be summoned from this sublunary abode, we may ascend to the Grand Lodge above, where the world's Great Architect lives and reigns forever." But this hope of immortality is not in Christ, but through the example, dramatically re-enacted by the candidate, of a semi-mythical Phoenician brass-founder, Hiram Abiff, who died rather than betray the secrets of Masonry. Here indeed is a type of every pagan dying vegetation cult, and yet it is more than drama. It is presented in the ritual however symbolically as a religious rite ; not only as a moral example but as a quasi-sacramental experience with an *ex opere operato* significance, raising the Candidate, as one of the Lectures expresses it, " from a dead level to a living perpendicular." " It is thus," says the Traditional History, " all Master Masons are raised from a figurative death to a re-union with the former companions of their toils." Of what is this death figurative ? The passage is reminiscent of the phraseology of the Prayer-Book Baptismal service, " being dead unto sin, and living unto righteousness ... as he is made partaker of the death of thy Son, he may also be partaker of his ressurection." The prayer at the beginning of this ceremony for " Thy servant who offers himself a Candidate to partake with us the mysterious secrets of a Master Mason " continues with this passage :—" Endue him with such fortitude that in the hour of trial he fail not, but that, passing safely under Thy protection through the valley of the shadow of death, he may finally rise from the tomb of transgression, to shine as the stars for ever and ever." If (as seems obvious) this refers to the death ceremony shortly to be performed as well as to the Candidate's latter end on earth, it indicates that it is the " mysterious secrets of a Master-Mason " which have robbed the grave of its victory. " But thanks be to God," Bro. Paul would have written in his Communication to the Lodges which are in Corinth, " which giveth us the victory through our Grand Master Hiram Abiff."

The fact that most Masons do not see the third degree ceremonies in this light may completely exonerate them from the sin of wilfully partaking in what the early Fathers of the Church stigmatized in contemporary mystery-religions as satanic parodies of Christian worship, but it does not exonerate Masonry, which after all claims (in the first degree Tracing Board Lecture) that its usages and customs approximate to those of ancient Egypt. Unawareness of an obvious and logical interpretation does not *ipso facto* make the interpretation false.

The question of universalism in Masonry may be variously interpreted. God is presented and titled in such terms that people of all reputable faiths may agree in a lowest-common-denominator deity shorn of all attributes distinctive of any single system of belief. Masonry is presented as a unifying influence because in its Lodges men of different religions can meet together for their common good and for common prayer. But, says the Mason, this represents a minimum of belief—not a maximum or an optimum—on which no disagreement is possible. The Christian will of course know that the Great Architect of the Universe is the Holy Trinity. The Hindu, Brahma, and the Moslem, Allah. In their hearts they pray to him as such.

But even in this supposed minimum or common-denominator conception of God there are grave difficulties. The titles given to the deity are so taken for granted by the Fraternity that their irreverent inadequacy does not seem to be realised. To call God, as in the first degree, a " Great Architect " is derogatory to His creative omnipotence, for an architect only puts together from materials already at hand. He designs, but he does not create, and the conception is frankly Deist. " Grand Geometrician " is even more woefully inadequate, and smacks of the outmoded symbolical mathematics of the Kabbala. The " Great Overseer " of the side-degree of Mark Masonry is tolerable if it refers to the " all-seeing eye " (which is certainly used as a Masonic symbol) but in the context of this working it appears more relevant as a divine type of the overseer or foreman over labour who works under the architect or contractor.

All these epithets may be allowable as attributes of the Godhead, but the fact that God is referred to officially and almost solely under these titles in these respective degrees suggests that they are definitions rather than attributes.

The third degree name, " The Most High " is quite unexceptionable and indeed familiar to the Christian. But in the Royal Arch very grave difficulties arise. For here the secret word is not a Biblical name or catch-phrase, nor a mumbo-jumbo of corrupt Hebrew, but a compound word of quite recognisable origin spelt out on the top of the Altar in separate character of metal, which claims, together with Jehovah, to be the " sacred and mysterious name of the true and living God most High." This word, JAH-BUL-ON, is explained in the

Mystical Lecture as consisting of certain titles or attributes of divinity to which in English no one could take exception. Yet this word is made up (as is also explained) of the Hebrew Jahweh coupled with the Assyrian Baal, so utterly repugnant to the Prophets even as a symbol, and the Egyptian On or Osiris. However happily it may be recited by the three office-bearers Zerubbabel, Joshua, and Haggai, syllable by syllable, their originals in the Old Testament would have been shocked beyond measure. The great Masonic authority Albert Pike Grand Commander of the Southern Jurisdiction of the Supreme Council at Charleston, U.S.A. (a Masonic body which does not include the Royal Arch) was disquieted and disgusted at the introduction of this word. He wrote :—" No man or body of men can make me accept as a sacred word, as a symbol of the infinite and eternal Godhead, a mongrel word, in part com-posed of the name of an accursed and beastly heathen god, whose name has been for more than two thousand years an appellation of the Devil."[1] The fact that Anglican bishops and clergy see no inconsistency in forming groups of three to recite this word almost as an incantation is really staggering.[2] Of course they would say that it is all very symbolic, but Pike objected to it even as a symbol. They also say doubtless that they do not take it very seriously[3] but this implies an attitude to God and to a solemn Bible oath which suggests the unfortunate possibility that another solemn oath to " banish strange and erroneous doctrine " may likewise not be taken too seriously, at least where secret doctrine is concerned. But of this more in the following chapter.

The claim that the Masonic deity is common-denominator again breaks down when the Greater Lights of this degree are indicated, which are the creative, preservative, and annihilative

1. *The Holy Triad*, Washington, 1873.
2. In view of the un-Scriptural nature of this Masonic title for the Deity, one is puzzled by the widespread attitude, expressed by the Right Worshipful Provincial Grand Master of Norfolk (the Bishop of Norwich) to a meeting of the Provincial Grand Lodge at Yarmouth (as reported in the *Freemasons' Chronicle* of July 28, 1951) that " Masonry....was a system of morality that was based on the recognition of, and obedience to, the Volume of the Sacred Law, and this was the full extent, so to speak, of its religious character."
3. Another Masonic Bishop in a personal letter, although admitting that the analogy was far from perfect, drew a comparison between the Masonic ritual and a Punch and Judy show.

powers of the Deity.[1] This is an exact correspondence with the Hindu trinity of Brahma, Vishnu and Shiva, and is not only non-Christian but un-Christian.

Indeed the plea that Masonic workings are not to be considered as religious rites but as dramatised morality breaks down completely in this degree. There is plenty of moral exhortation, yet the contrast between the Craft and the Royal Arch is remarkable. In the former the signs (apart from the Penal signs) are ' casual ' and connected with certain events in the Masonic legend ; the Words are given out, but are quite incidental to the drama and have no particular religious significance. The Royal Arch, on the other hand, is concerned almost entirely with the quest and discovery of the lost Word, and that Word is a pagan and syncretistic name of God. Royal Arch signs are fully explained in the Mystical Lecture as religious signs, exemplifying the relationship of man to his Maker. The full title of this degree is the *Holy* Royal Arch, and the Chapters set up their altars. The Officers represent the functions of ' prophet, priest, and king ', and they are given as their own secret words three Old Testament titles of God—*Jah* for King Zerubbabel, *El Shaddai* for Prophet Haggai, and *El Elohe* for Priest Joshua. Although the custom is tending to die out, there is provision for a foot-washing ceremony at the Installation of Joshua, and for him and Zerubbabel to be solemnly anointed with oil. The use of incense, too, is not unknown in Royal Arch ceremonies. All these things are, by any recognised definition, religious rather than moral symbols, and indeed this degree claims to teach us about the nature of God. It is quite impossible to maintain that " Masonry has no theology "[2] when the second half of the Mystical Lecture which deals with the Altar-top (Jehovah, Jah-Bul-On, and the Baal trinity made of the Hebrew

1. See, however, note 1, p. 175.
2. The late Bishop Crotty actually used this phrase (as reported in the *Freemasons' Chronicle* Aug. 25, 1951) in addressing the Provincial Grand Lodge of Sussex at a Masonic service in the Parish Church of Hove. He added that Masonry " had its own contribution to Man's consciousness of God ", but naturally did not, in a Christian Church, refer to the fact that God the Son is deliberately excluded from this Masonic consciousness. The Rev. J. L. C. Dart, defending Masonry as a Christian priest in *Theology* (March 1951) admitted that Freemasonry has a theology by saying " It would not be true to say that Masonry has no doctrine of God."

characters Aleph, Beth, and Lamed) is sheer theological exposition on the nature and attributes of the Masonic deity.[1]

Invenimus cultor Dei, civis mundi is a motto which appears on every Royal Arch jewel, and is translated in the Jewel Lecture " we have found the worship of God, O citizen of the world ". This translation would merit a beating for any fourth-form schoolboy, but it is theirs, and must be accepted.[2] But again its meaning and implications on the common-denominator no-theology theory are disastrous to the Christian Mason. The believer in a vague first-cause God on being converted to Christianity might exclaim with joy in the words of this motto. But it is puzzling to understand how a believer in the Holy Trinity can claim to have found the worship of God in Masonry when the God whose worship he has found is a minimum belief, a God which totally excludes Christ, his divine redeemer. One can only assume again that he does not take all this too seriously. If he took the claims of Christ seriously, it is difficult to see how he can take to Masonry at all.

But supposing these difficulties can be overcome (or as is more likely, ignored) the question remains whether there is such a thing as a religion behind religions, in which all men agree, and whether it is lawful for the Christian to join in common worship with the Moslem of a common-denominator God specifically of neither faith, whom each in his heart worships as his own God. This issue is fundamental, and no amount of eloquence on the non-controversial benefits of meeting together to promote charity and good works should be allowed to obscure it. In this country the issue in practice arises but seldom, but Masonry stands four-square on the principle that it can and should happen. Many Anglicans have tender consciences over joint service with Nonconformists on the ground that where different bodies mean different things by what they say in their worship, that worship becomes unreal.

1. See pp. 178-83. The seeming approximation of this trinity (Ab, Bal, Father, Lord ; Al Bal, Word, Lord ; Lab Bal, Spirit, Lord) to the Christian Trinity which is often urged by Masons is vitiated by the fact that Bal or Baal was an abhorred term which the Hebrews would never dream of applying to or confusing with Jehovah. It would have sounded as idolatrous to them as, say, Father, Moloch ; Word, Moloch ; Spirit, Moloch, would to the Christian.

2. See note, p. 224.

And yet the differences between separated Christian bodies are trifling compared with the difference between those who do and those who do not accept Christ as the Son of God, their only Mediator and Saviour. Christianity is an exclusive faith. To offer worship to God in forms which reject Christ with the specific intention of including people who likewise reject Christ is an act of apostasy for which no amount of mental reservation can altogether atone. To argue that as there is undoubtedly some measure of truth in all faiths the Christian is at liberty temporarily to set aside what he knows to be the full revealed truth in order to come down to the level of what the non-Christian happens to have in common with him is again apostasy, however charitable the motive.

The Church does not sanction common-denominator worship with other religions. The Christian, therefore, himself a part of the Church yet who claims the right to worship outside the Church in a manner forbidden within it is simply defying her authority, and what is perhaps worse, doing so in secret. For it cannot be admitted that there is one worship of the Church and another of the Temple if there is a vital conflict in principle between the two.

Masonry practised on the mission-field would show clearly this grotesque situation. Although most Christian missionaries to-day recognise in non-Christian cults such elements as reflect a knowledge of God and His holy will, this is quite different from worshipping together with those people they have been sent to convert, in an atmosphere which regards all gods as equal. The missionary in all good faith may not do so personally, but Freemasonry in whose Lodges he so worships refuses to draw distinctions. By all means let him meet his prospective converts socially and co-operate with them cordially in every lawful enterprise for charity or welfare. But to worship with them in this context can only weaken his Christian witness. Again allowing that in practice this situation seldom arises, the very fact that the missionary is a member of a fraternity which allows and encourages such a situation is difficult to explain away.

St. Paul's missionary address to the Athenians on Mars Hill was not, perhaps his most successful effort. But had he met some of his audience later in the day at the Athenaeum Lodge of Antiquity and prayed with them in a common devotion to the Great Architect who equally represents the Father of Christ Crucified and the ' Unknown God ' whom he had castigated them in the morning for worshipping superstitiously and ignorantly, it is open to question whether his converts would not have been even fewer. But in any case it is stretching the imagination to the breaking-point to conceive of St. Paul becoming Bro. Paul under the aegis, say, of an unconverted Galatian Worshipful Master assisted by two unconverted Corinthian Wardens even though all four could express a sincere belief in a Higher Being not unversed in the science of architecture or geometry. Such a belief would be accepted as adequate for initiation by the Grand Lodge of England to-day.[1] The situation is as fantastic as to imagine Elijah seeking some secret formula whereby the followers of Jehovah and Baal might meet in brotherly prayer when no one was looking.

Again if Freemasonry had been practised in the primitive Church of Rome to the same extent as in the present-day Church of England many quite unnecessary martyrdoms would have been spared. Christians in those days were willing to face death rather than cast a few grains of incense to the Emperor or other deities. But had their pagan brethren from Numa Pompilia Lodge claimed the right to visit Lodge Roma Ecclesia the latter would doubtless have discovered that the Great Architect of the Universe to whom they prayed together in brotherly peace and harmony could be equated with Nero and Jupiter quite as legitimately as with the Holy Trinity.[2] Why then deny to the point of death in the Colosseum outside the Lodge what was so inevitably true inside ?

Although Christians may claim that their Masonry is not a religion but an ethical and charitable handmaid to the

1. The Rev. F. de P. Castells, referring to the Impersonal Necessary Being of Spinoza's agnosticism, actually declares " This *Deus Ignotus* accords with the conception presented to us in the modern R. A. Degree." (*Origin of The Masonic Degrees*, p. 307.)

2. Aldersgate and certain other Royal Arch workings abundantly justify this point by including in the ritual the first verse of the Universal Prayer of Pope :—
> " Father of all, in every age
> In every clime adored,
> By Saint, by Savage, and by Sage,
> Jehovah, Jove, or Lord."

Church, Masonry itself nowhere claims to occupy such a subordinate position. On reading the ritual carefully Masonry will be found to present itself as a complete and self-sufficient system of moral and spiritual guidance through this world and the next. It teaches one's whole duty to God and to man, and a way of justification by works which if followed will lead to salvation. Nowhere does it give the slightest hint that anything further is necessary to the religious life. It urges, it is true, the reading of the Volume of the Sacred Law, but as this may or may not be the Bible[1] the inference is obviously that moral precept rather than the doctrines of any particular Church or religion should be the object. One of the Charges (bound up with the Book of Constitutions but usually not with the ritual) declares that whatever a man's religion may be, he is not debarred from the order as long as he believes in the Glorious Architect, and that if he has a faith he is to demonstrate its superior excellence by his conduct. This however does not imply that he should have any other religion, but merely that if he has, it need be no impediment to his becoming a Mason. There is plenty of sound instruction to the initiate to be a loyal and law-abiding citizen, which is uncontroversial. But there is no suggestion that he should be loyal to any Church, which might disrupt the harmony of the brethren. In an organization which claims to be ' religious ' and to have found the worship of God this consideration alone might make the convinced Christian a little thoughtful.

The religious outlook of Masonry strongly echoes the Deism of the eighteenth century in stressing the light of nature as a moral guide, in beginning and ending with man's upward aspirations to God, with man's justifying himself in the eyes of God by his own good works. Although Masonry also echoes Gnosticism in claiming to impart an esoteric light that is *sui generis* it disdains (or at least ignores) any conception of God reaching down from Heaven to save and heal mankind.[2]

1. The Volume of the Sacred Law in a Moslem Lodge, for instance, would be the Koran, and in a Jewish Lodge the Pentateuch. In England it is of course normally the Bible. The New Testament is included, but ignored in all Degrees officially recognised by Grand Lodge.
2. A reference, however, to Freemasonry as a revelation from God may be seen in the second line of the first verse of a hymn by Charles Delafaye ; the fact that it is included in Anderson's Constitutions gives it a certain authority :— (cont. foot of p. 41)

At best, " Freemasonry is to be regarded as a human groping after that very thing which God himself has established in the Christian Church."[1] Masonry teaches much of moral righteousness but almost nothing of sin or repentance. It is a religion of complete uprightness and respectability, of justification by works, but not of holiness or humility. Perhaps that is why the British Empire and America produce many times more Masons than the rest of the world together.

No Mason would attempt to deny that his workings are shot through and through with paganism, pre-Christian mysticism, and elements taken from contemporary non-Christian religions. But, he will argue, as long as these things are in themselves morally unexceptionable, where is the harm in that ? Is not Christianity also full of pagan customs and ceremonies, is not Easter a time-immemorial festival of new life in the Spring, and the reverence paid to the Mother of God but an echo of the Magna Mater of imperial Rome ? Did not other religions have as a saviour a virgin-born demi-god who died and rose again ?

No instructed Christian would attempt in his turn to deny the possibility of a substratum of truth in these assertions, and the student of comparative religions might go even further. But if he is an instructed Christian he will realise that there is for him no analogy or justification whatsoever.

Christianity is a faith revealed by God to man, not a system worked out by man of ascent to God. Before that supreme and final revelation of truth in the Incarnation of our Lord there had of course been partial glimpses and foreshadowings of it, purely human and not revealed, by no means entirely limited to the Jewish nation. There were anti-types indeed of our Saviour in the pagan world. Man's hunger and yearning for God, his aspirations to truth, the fulfilment of his natural religious instincts were of course fruitful of more than mere glimmerings of truth, for man, though sinful and fallen, was

Hail Masonry, thou Craft Divine !
  Glory of earth, from heaven revealed ;
Which doth with jewels precious shine,
  From all but Masons' eyes concealed :
Thy praises due, who can rehearse,
  In nervous prose or flowing verse ?

1. Dr. H. S. Box, *The Nature of Freemasonry*, p. 53.

made in God's image and endowed with an intellect and a conscience. But the Incarnation is the supreme and final revelation in which types and shadows had their ending. And Christianity is not only supreme but complete in its revelation ; whatsoever truth, however partial, had been before guessed or discovered by man's intellect was naturally included and baptised into it. Many customs, symbols, and ceremonies which were of value were adopted. Much else, too, was fiercely rejected. For God had sent His Son into the world to reconcile mankind to Himself, and to lead them, guided by the Holy Spirit, into all truth. And there is salvation in no other name.

No one would be so narrow or so dogmatic as to assert that those who live and die without Christ are bereft of all hope of salvation, if they live according to the light that is in them in good faith, for that would be limiting the infinite mercies of God, who is not bound by His own laws though man is so bound. But if it is blasphemous to limit God's uncovenanted mercies, it is equally presumptuous of man to take them for granted.

For the Christian who accepts this revelation, however, to revert to pre-Christian types and shadows for spiritual or moral light, and in so doing to ignore our Lord altogether and exclude all mention of Him in an unofficial and man-made system of worship and moral betterment is to dishonour the Incarnation by ignoring it and by going behind Christ's back. Those who maintain that Freemasonry is " Christian in all but name " or even compatible with Christianity have all too often no idea that the faith of Christ really means anything more than a standard of decent conduct. Nor do they appear to realise that all worship which deliberately excludes Christ is pagan. " Idolatry," said Archbishop William Temple in *Personal Religion and the Life of Fellowship* " does not consist in bodily kneeling before a material image ; it consists in worshipping God under any other conception of Him than that which is set before us in the Gospels......Idolatry is indeed a deadly thing."

Archbishop Temple, of course, was not a Freemason. *Tempora mutantur.*

V

THE CLERGY AND THE CRAFT

"The White Knight is sliding down the poker. He balances very badly."
Lewis Carroll, Through the Looking-Glass.

IN ADDITION to the theological and moral objections to the ritual and oaths which have been already set out, there are further considerations which make Freemasonry particularly unsuitable and unbecoming to the clergy.

Superficially at least it seems lacking in dignity and propriety that a priest and more particularly a bishop should undergo, usually at the hands of the laity, the rather ludicrous humiliation of the preparation for initiation. That a bishop should, in the name of the Great Architect, be deprived of his episcopal ring and pectoral cross along with all other articles of metal, and be blindfolded, haltered and partially undressed in search of a Masonic light of which the Church in her fulness of grace knows nothing, is an act of humility to a purely human institution which seems to differ not only in degree but in kind from a layman undergoing the same ceremony. One simply cannot imagine the Apostles doing it. And a bishop as successor to the Apostles has not only dedicated his life to the service of maintaining the Apostolic faith and salvation in Christ alone, but is himself, as a member of the episcopate, the *esse* of the Church. And the priest is the representative in the parish of the bishop.

Of course the clergy share with the laity the right to indulge in harmless and amusing parlour games and charades in fancy dress in their moments of leisure. But the Masonic workings certainly have in them too much of the solemn religious ritual to be so easily dismissed.

It has already been stressed that the syncretistic universalism of Masonry is untenable on the mission field. Yet in a sense England, too, is a mission field where unbelief exceeds belief. Anglicanism, it is true, does not provoke the hostility and outright rejection that is accorded in Europe to the Church of

Rome, but indifference may be a more deadly and insidious danger.

Many, perhaps even the majority of decent-living folk outside the ministrations of the Church have a certain belief in a higher being which, however vague, qualifies them for admission to Freemasonry. Yet they could no more be called Christians (even though they may have some traditional respect for our Lord as a good man) than could the lapsed Moslem who also leads a decent life and may also express respect for the teachings of Christ.

Now the motive of many a clergyman in joining the Craft is often the laudable one of seeking to mix more intimately than might seem otherwise possible with influential laymen who are already members of his Church ; and with those who are not, in hopes of bringing them in. As religion may not be discussed inside the Lodge (though perhaps the vicar didn't know that when he joined) he can obviously only do so by making and cementing friendships to be followed up professionally outside. In passing it might be pointed out that (however much it happens in practice) it is considered highly un-Masonic conduct to use Masonry to promote business ends ; by analogy, therefore, it would seem that to use it even indirectly as an organ for proselytism might be considered equally undesirable by Grand Lodge.

But is this motive really desirable or legitimate from the point of view of the Church ? A parson may justifiably visit his Local to seek and to save the sinners and unbelievers of his parish—and probably he will enjoy his half-pint with the saints and believers there, too ! He may join any lawful club where he feels his influence may be felt, and the light of Christ be spread. But the argument that this provides a justification for meeting people in the Lodge at a pre-Christian level as a *preparatio Evangelii* is both deadly and fallacious.

For initiation into Masonry is not merely 'meeting' people at any level at all. It is *joining* them—identifying oneself by solemn oath with those people and with their sub-Christian beliefs. It is praying with them in prayers which deliberately exclude our Lord. And even though it be regarded as a minimum and not a maximum standard of belief (as the Christian Mason must) to join such a system which nowhere claims to be a minimum belief might well appear to sanction it as an adequate belief.

The argument that it is legitimate to meet people at a pre-Christian level would appear equally to justify a Christian priest in undergoing a slight surgical operation and becoming a Jew for one evening a month in order to convert that race to Christianity. It is true that Judaism rejects Christ, whereas Freemasonry ignores Him. But the result is equally non-Christian.

But although Masonry does in a sense represent religion at a pre-Christian level, it also claims to impart a light, spiritual and moral, which shines nowhere else. It claims to have secrets which add to a man's sense of spiritual values, and improve his character. It claims the exclusive possession of certain truths, one of which is the sacred and mysterious name of God. It claims to have found the worship of God.

The ordinary Christian who knows that his vicar is a Mason may therefore be entitled to doubt whether the revelation that is preached from the pulpit is after all complete, if his pastor finds it expedient or even possible to supplement it with hidden mysteries obtainable only in the Lodge.

Furthermore, there are to-day two deadly enemies to the divine supernaturalism of the Church. One of them is humanism. The other is the increasing popularity of a pseudo-mystical occultism which finds expression in spiritualism, theosophy, and other less desirable manifestations. Free-masonry is frankly humanist in tone, and yet at the same time includes a great deal of mystical and symbolic nonsense about geometry and astronomy which no educated Mason in this enlightened age would dream of taking seriously. Can a bishop or priest seem to countenance these tendencies, even in the socially and morally respectable setting of the Lodge, and at the same time run a risk of what might appear a dual allegiance, a religious bigamy?

For this risk is certainly there, as becomes apparent when a bishop finds his episcopal oath and his Masonic obligation in conflict, and when the latter perforce takes precedence.

This is indeed a grave charge, and I am treading on delicate ground in substantiating it, but the matter is important. I can deal with it best if I write personally.

Some years ago a brother priest approached me with a view to my becoming a brother Mason. He kept within the law by not asking me outright, but indicated that it would be a very good thing if I did so, and that he would always be glad to propose me. It really comes to the same thing. I replied that I was extremely reluctant to join any organization of which I was allowed to know almost nothing in advance. To which he answered that if everyone felt that way there would be no Masons at all, for no one outside the Craft could possibly discover its secrets, and what was good enough for the bishops who had become Masons ought to be good enough for me.

It was that reply which interested me in the subject. I remembered a Member of Parliament telling me (long after such a revelation could have been considered indiscreet) that even at the secret sessions of the House of Commons during the war it was considered too dangerous to reveal top secrets of policy and strategy even to some six hundred trusted M.P.'s, and that in general they were occasions for members themselves to discuss such delicate topics as shipping losses and tank deficiencies. Was it then probable or even possible that an organization of some five million people, doubtless including good, bad and indifferent, which had been in existence for over two centuries could really keep the rest of the world in complete darkness as to their secrets? I was intrigued, and started to investigate.

I was surprised at the facility with which information could be unearthed in a manner explained in the first chapter, —and yet increasingly perturbed at the nature of that information. Accordingly I wrote to a Masonic bishop whom I had once met personally setting forth some of these perplexities, mentioning the inclusion of Baal in the secret name of God in the Royal Arch, making it quite clear that I was asking him for guidance as a bishop in a matter which concerned faith and morals.

The reply was more taken up with surprise tinged with indignation that I had discovered supposed secrets than with any anxiety to allay my misgivings. He said very courteously that if I did not like Freemasonry I had better not join, but he was not allowed to discuss these things with any who were not

Masons. To which I wrote in return that I was truly appalled at the implications of this remark. I had made a *prima facie* case (and I then claimed no more) for the Craft being incompatible with Christianity, and appealed to a bishop for guidance. And his reply that he was bound by oath not to refute or even discuss such matters, although they admittedly concerned faith and morals, with any who were not similarly oath-bound to secrecy clearly implied that his Masonic obligation took precedence over his Episcopal oath to banish strange and erroneous doctrine. But there was no reply.

Other Masonic bishops to whom I wrote either were equally evasive, or did not trouble to acknowledge my letters. " Dignified silence " is a phrase much beloved by Masons. One delightful exception, to whom I shall always be grateful, invited me to his house and heard me out with truly Christian patience and charity. But he was equally unable to answer my objections.

My questions to these bishops admittedly were not directly concerned with definitions of the doctrine of the Church. Yet they did concern the teachings of a body which claims to worship the same God as the Church and which overlaps the Church—these bishops being within that overlap. No bishop can be expected to be omniscient even in matters pertaining to God ; had I asked some abstruse question on the adventism of the Irvingites any bishop would be entitled to say that he didn't know and it wasn't his subject. If he thought the question silly he could even answer in terse Anglo-Saxon monosyllables, and I should have no cause to complain. But these bishops refused to answer questions about the name and nature of the God whom they worship as Masons, even though they would of course claim Him to be the same God whom they worship and serve as bishops. Obviously they knew the answers to my serious and perfectly reasonable questions, but they were oath-bound not to give them to any Christian whom they are divinely appointed to guide and instruct unless he was a brother Mason also pledged to secrecy, by an oath quite unrecognised by the Church.[1] This is lamentable and

1. Since the first appearance of this book, however, several ex-Mason clergymen have assured me that the real reason I received no answer is the fact that there *is* no answer. That, of course, was before the publication of *Light Invisible*. (See Appendix D.)

highly disquieting. Surely no bishop or clergyman should expose himself to even the possibility of finding himself in such an invidious and equivocal situation by joining a society possessing secrets of such a nature.

One of two things must be true. Either the implications of my questions were wrong, in which case I myself was in error in believing things that were " strange and erroneous." If this is true, then these bishops were breaking their episcopal vows by refusing to banish my errors, for such terse words as ' nonsense ' when coupled with an inability to refute factually is no refutation of what is, to say the least of it, strong *prima facie* evidence.

The alternative is that the implications of my questions were at least partially true, and the fact that no one has yet refuted the case, and that certain Masons have even resigned their Lodges and Chapters in agreement with me has heightened that possibility. The question of unbanished strange and erroneous doctrine then assumes a context so delicate that I must leave it at that.

Admittedly these Masonic bishops and clergy must defend themselves with one hand tied behind their backs. This, however, can hardly be regarded as an unfair disadvantage, as their Lordships deliberately, securely, and irrevocably tied them there themselves. But is this attitude a dignified one for our Fathers-in-God ?

VI

THE GREAT DILEMMA

" Have you guessed the riddle yet ? " the Hatter said, turning to Alice
again.
" No, I give it up," Alice replied ; " what's the answer ? "
" I haven't the slightest idea," said the Hatter.
" Nor I," said the March Hare.

Lewis Carroll, Alice in Wonderland.

FREEMASONS will probably consider that I am making
a great deal of fuss and bother about certain aspects of
their ritual which certainly do not occur to them at all.
They may agree that it is just possible to read into the ritual
the interpretation that I (and many Masonic writers as well)
read into it, but that as most Masons do not so interpret it,
it is really preposterous to raise the issue.

They will say, too (and the point has been already dealt
with) that certain pre-Christian and pagan elements can be
read into the liturgy and usages of the Church.

The teachings of the Church, however, are public property
which are openly and fearlessly proclaimed before the world.
They have been for centuries examined, criticised, attacked,
subjected to every test and scrutiny known to the scholar,
friendly or hostile. The clergy especially who are the guardians
of the Christian mysteries have trained themselves in
controversy. They have familiarised themselves with popular
objections to creed, sacraments, and service-books, and should
have a clear answer to them. For they know that these things
have stood the test of time, of criticism and investigation.

Freemasonry, on the other hand, although sometimes
denounced, has been comparatively immune from real criticism
and investigation from outside. And indeed it appears to
claim this immunity as a privilege almost by divine right,
even though no other body enjoys or would dream of claiming
such a position.[1] Yet immunity from outside criticism always
tends to have an enervating effect upon self-criticism from

1. The arrogant complacency of this attitude is exemplified in a letter
   from the Grand Master the Earl of Scarborough to Dr. H. S. Box
   (printed in the *Church Times* of Dec. 7, 1951), stating " I can only
   take cognizance of complaints referred to me by a Freemason."

within ; it encourages a sense of smug security. The Counter-Reformation, after all, did not take place until after certain Christians had left the Catholic fold and attacked its abuses.

The average Mason, therefore, in his close-tyled security has seen no necessity to examine his workings critically or to justify them from the Christian point of view to the world outside. Why should he bother to discover answers to questions that he is oath-bound not to answer, and which in any case do not interest him, and are unlikely ever to be asked ? As generally speaking Masonry appeals to the least spiritual layer of the bourgeoisie (I do not say the least moral, or the least respectable) the Masonic conscience, still speaking in broad generalities, does not, even amongst its Christian adherents, instinctively shrink from those aspects of the workings which dishonour the supreme mediatorship of our Lord and Saviour by ignoring it or by providing substitutes. Their Biblical scholarship (again with exceptions which defy explanation) is such that they either do not realise how utterly repugnant to the Prophets of God was any confusion between Jehovah and Baal, or they do not appear to think it matters. They do not seem aware that syncretism, ' natural ' religion, and indifferentism were the deadly enemies of the early Church which Freemasonry has made friends with to-day. If no one outside the Lodge is likely to discover and comment on these aspects of Masonry, why should they bother ? After all, the Grand Principles are " brotherly love, relief, and truth " (principles equally upheld by the Church, but with less concomitant conviviality) and does it matter in what context these unexceptionable principles are upheld and promulgated ?

It seems that those who declare that this interpretation of Freemasonry is preposterous and utterly out of touch with reality do so, not from inside knowledge which comes from investigation and criticism, but from the very lack of these things—from a tendency to take it all uncritically for granted.

However presumptuous, an analogy suggests itself. When in the days of the Oxford Movement the celebrated Tract XC appeared it was met with anger, scorn, derision, and accusations of disloyalty from many people in perfectly good faith who had traditionally taken it for granted that the Thirty-Nine Articles were an impregnable bulwark of Protestantism in the

Church of England. To-day, however, the main thesis of the tract, that the Articles are at least patient of a ' Catholic ' interpretation and were deliberately so drawn up as a compromise is generally accepted by Anglican theologians and Church historians.

There will always be die-hard Protestants who reject this interpretation. Probably, too, there will always be die-hard Masons.

Not every Mason, not even every Christian Mason, could reasonably be expected to be a theologian or perhaps to realise even the possibility of his Craft being at variance with the exclusiveness of the Christian faith. Yet surely anyone capable of clear thinking must realise that in Masonry is an inescapable and insoluble moral dilemma.

If Freemasonry claims to possess secrets the knowledge of which would benefit all mankind in enabling a man to lead a higher and more moral life, it is immoral to keep that knowledge to itself.

If Freemasonry does not possess such secrets, it is equally immoral for it to claim that it does possess them.

And after all, why should any knowledge about morals and the nature or name of God be kept secret ? The Tracing Board Lecture of the first degree attempts an answer, it is true, but an answer which would be scorned as fatuous in an enlightened twentieth century.[1] For this lecture implies that the teachings of Masonry are kept secret for the same reason that higher knowledge was the secret and oathbound possession of the few in ancient Egypt, because it conferred occult powers which might be mis-used in unworthy hands.

But can our democratic and enlightened Masons of to-day think of a better answer ? Their own ritual nowhere suggests one, but it is difficult even after the most exhaustive examination to consider that ritual ' enlightened.' However symbolically the turgid nonsensicalities of its mysteries may be interpreted, this, apparently, must always remain an unexplained mystery. Even to Freemasons.

1. See p. 109.

VII

BENEVOLENCE, BROTHERHOOD, AND TOLERANCE

*" You know the sort of things ministers say in cases of this kind.
A few ordinary platitudes will do. In modern life nothing produces
such an effect as a good platitude. It makes the whole world kin."*
Oscar Wilde, An Ideal Husband.

THE first reaction of a Mason on hearing theological criticisms of the Craft often seems to be " how *dare* you ! Don't you realise the *good* we are doing ? "
The answer is deliriously irrelevant. Papal infallibility is not proved by the selfless labours of the Poor Clares in the slums of Paris, nor is the imperfect Christology of Unitarians justified *ipso facto* by the fact that many of them subscribe most generously to hospitals and are kind to their maiden aunts. Hindus are kind to cows, which is also a most estimable virtue.

But let it be admitted that Masons are indeed generous, with a lavishness which often leaves Christian giving far behind. The Charity Column which circulates at the Festive Board returns with far more paper and large silver in it than the average collection bag at Evensong. Let it be admitted, too, that the Masonic institutions, their hospital for sick Masons, their nursing-home, and their two schools for the children of Masons are well and efficiently run. They have a Fund of Benevolence for the benefit of poor and distressed Masons, their widows and orphans.[1] In addition to these closed-shop charities, the scope of which is equalled by the benevolent and insurance funds of many a trade union, other deserving non-Masonic institutions, Lord Mayor appeals, and so on, are liberally supported by Lodges.

Yet the claim that " no other institution has done more to relieve the poor and heal the sick—" is obviously quite untenable if these Masonic institutions for the benefit of Masons,

---

1. In order to benefit from the Fund of Benevolence it must be proved that the Mason himself or whose widow or children seek relief was a subscribing member of his Lodge for at least five years. This is, of course, a perfectly reasonable requirement, yet a fund so administered savours of insurance rather than of charity.

excellent and above criticism as they are, are compared numerically with the vastly greater number of schools, hospitals, and orphanages sponsored throughout the world by the Church of God. If the claim means that *pro rata* the average Mason gives more than the average Christian, it is probably justified. Undoubtedly they boast more about it. But Masons come mainly from the better-off sections of the people who can afford to pay not inconsiderable fees for their privileges.

When every allowance is made, Masonic benevolence is not to be identified with the ideal of Christian charity. It is not the spirit of the widow casting in her mite, but of rich men (styling themselves Sons of the Widow[1]) giving of their superfluity.

Now there is nothing un-Christian about superfluity, and Christ did not (in that instance) condemn it. He merely said that the other was dearer to His heart and more acceptable to God because she gave till it hurt.

The Masonic ritual with a matter-of-fact business-like common-sense warns against this ideal of Christian charity. The third degree obligation pledges the Candidate to relieve a brother Mason in need only " so far as may fairly be done without detriment to myself or my connections," a phrase which is repeated in various charges and lectures.

The Charity Jewel which may in practice be purchased for twenty pounds and a term of stewardship, and further bars added for ten pounds each, is a piece of Pharisaism so outrageous that the more spiritually-minded Masons themselves have their misgivings and subject it to fierce criticism. Perhaps it is only rubbing unnecessary salt into the wound for outsiders to wish them well.

Undoubtedly the greatest attraction of Freemasonry to most of its adherents is not its ritual or religious implications, nor its supposed advantages in business and certain professions, but the warm fellowship of sincere and genuine friendliness and brotherhood at Lodge meetings and at after-proceedings, a *koinonia* which has to be experienced to be fully appreciated. For Masons admit frankly that they exist for the entirely

1. " On the supposition that all Master Masons are Brothers to Hiram Abiff, who was a Widow's Son." (Ceremony of Raising to the Third Degree.) See p. 148.

laudable purpose of mutual enjoyment as well as for mutual benefit.

No one indeed would wish to level any criticism whatsoever against this were not Masons inclined a little self-righteously to hold themselves up as an example to the Church in claiming to have achieved brotherhood and mutual love where the Church has failed. The Rev. C. K. Hughes, signing himself ' Priest and Freemason ' wrote to the *Guardian* (Feb. 23, 1951) " Proctors in Convocation should ask themselves why so many elements of fellowship, loyalty, brotherhood, charity and the like, which marked the New Testament Church are absent from the Church of England, but supposed to be present in Freemasonry ? If the organised Church provided what Freemasonry provides, there would be no need for the latter."

This attitude implies that the Church and Freemasonry can be compared on similar grounds, and that the latter is successful where the former has failed. That the standard of fellowship and brotherliness in the Church falls far below the ideal set out by our Blessed Lord few would deny, for the Church on earth is struggling in (and against) a fallen and sinful world.

Yet the fellowship of the Lodge is based on something so different from the fellowship of the Church that a comparison is really impossible. It is based on a principle of exclusiveness that makes it, although quite genuine in one sense, yet nevertheless artificial. For the Lodge is made up not only exclusively of men, but of men of similar background, income-group, and interests. In many Lodges they are of the same profession. Controversial matters such as religion and politics are barred for fear of disturbing the harmony. Anyone known to be quarrelsome or uncongenial can be black-balled from initiation. Given these conditions, stimulated by excellent food and drink, a hearty good fellowship which not even the long and usually platitudinous toasts can depress is not difficult to achieve.

Masonic fellowship is quite above criticism once these limitations are appreciated. For of course men (and women too) will naturally and rightly forgather into clubs and associations into which people of like interests, background, and hobbies can temporarily withdraw themselves for mutual profit and enjoyment. But to compare it with the wider fellowship of the Church is deliberately misleading.

For Christ suffered and died on the cross to open the gate of Heaven not only to the respectable business-man, bank manager, doctor, lawyer, officer, parson, and civil servant. He died for the woman and the child too. He poured forth His precious blood for the scandalmonger, the pimp and the prostitute, He suffered scourging to atone for the sins of the bestial and cruel, He endured agonizing thirst for the sots and drunkards, He endured every humiliation in satisfaction for the sins of the proud and the self-righteous. To all mankind, therefore, the Church spreads out her arms in her call for penitence, for a realization of the true and wider brotherhood of man redeemed by the precious blood. She has no blackball and no waiting-list for Baptism, she has no Tyler with drawn sword at her portals to keep away those likely to disturb her peace, for the life of the Church Militant here on earth is not a life of peace and enjoyment, but of constant spiritual warfare. She has it is true the weapon of excommunication, but she ever welcomes back the penitent. She dare not ban controversy within her ranks, for through controversy truth may be established.

Naturally, then, her fellowship here on earth is human and desperately imperfect. But it has a divine reality, and amidst all her storms and stresses she offers, not hearty conviviality, but the true joy that comes from the peace of God that passeth all understanding. What, then, has Freemasonry to teach her ? What merit has the untimely death of Hiram Abiff that can supplement the redemptive sufferings of our Lord, which unite the redeemed into the true Body ?

Another virtue in which Freemasons claim to excel the Church is tolerance. " Let a man's religion or mode of worship be what it may," runs an old Charge, " he is not excluded from our Order, provided he believe in the glorious architect of heaven and earth, and practise the sacred duties of morality." Here, they say, is no bickering over creed and dogma, no wrangling over politics, but an example to the world of how to live and let live.

Apart from a hyper-sensitive intolerance of outside criticism, however, there is one highly significant exception to this genial tolerance of Grand Lodge, which lies in its attitude to other Masonic bodies which it does not recognise.

These fall into two groups. First, there are the Mark Master Masons, the 'Higher Degrees' of the Ancient and Accepted Rite, the Knights Templar, the Royal Order of Scotland, the Allied Degrees, and others with whom, although there is no official recognition, relations are friendly, and Craft Masons are not debarred from joining them.

In the second group come various bodies including the Grand Orients of Europe[1] and certain splinter-groups from them, the 'Eastern Star' and other bodies of Adoptive or Co-Masons. It is these last that deserve attention.

The reason given for the schism with the Grand Orients is that they forsook the ancient and absolutely essential landmark of belief in the Great Architect. Fair enough. But there is in England an organization open to women known as the Honourable Fraternity of Ancient Masonry (derived from Mrs. Besant's theosophical Masonry but now repudiating it) which practises precisely the same Strict Emulation ritual as Regular Masons, with the same signs, grips and words,[2] which has the same moral teachings, and the same belief in the Great Architect. Admittedly it is unimportant and numerically insignificant, numbering its Lodges in tens where Grand Lodge numbers its thousands. But the principle remains. Grand Lodge will have none of it, and claims the right to discipline and expel any regular Mason who visits any Lodge where women are admitted as Masons. It would seem to follow then that the landmark of restricting the moral and spiritual light of Masonry to men only is of equal importance to the landmark of belief in the Great Architect, for women who have seen the same Masonic light and share the same secrets and grand principles are nevertheless scorned and denounced as bogus Masons.

It is often asked why anyone in the Church should seek a measure of condemnation for a body of men as respectable, generous, and God-fearing as Masons when the open Godless-

---

1. There is evidence that the breach between Grand Lodge and the Grand Orients is not quite so complete as is generally believed. See *English Masonic Isolation, a Myth Exploded*, (Britons Publishing Society), which if not quite succeeding in exploding the 'myth' certainly gives some uncontrovertible and disquieting facts.

2. The form of preparation alone varies from Strict Emulation workings in that the shoulder rather than the breast is bared.

ness of Communism is menacing and rampant. One could answer that a subtle heterodoxy from within can be more deadly than the open enemy without. But in any case has the Mason a right to ask that question unless he in turn can explain why Grand Lodge has passed a similar measure of condemnation on a body of respectable, generous, and God-fearing women ?

Every organization has of course a perfect right to impose its own rules and discipline upon its members. But only in a legal sense has every organization the right to boast of its tolerance and universality.

VIII

CONTEXT

" I don't know what you mean by ' glory,' " Alice said.
Humpty Dumpty smiled contemptuously. *" Of course you don't till
I tell you. I mean ' there's a nice knock-down argument for you ! ' "*
" But ' glory ' doesn't mean ' a nice knock-down argument,' " Alice
objected.
" When I use a word," Humpty Dumpty said *in a rather scornful tone,*
" it means just what I choose it to mean—neither more nor less."
" The question is," said Alice, *" whether you can make words mean
so many different things."*
" The question is," said Humpty Dumpty, *" which is to be Master—
that's all. ...... Impenetrability !* That's *what I say ! "*

        *   *   *   *

" Oh ! " said Alice. *She was much too puzzled to make any other remark.*
                                          Lewis Carroll, Through the Looking-Glass.

A FREEMASON usually starts with the assumption, not often challenged, that an outsider can know nothing of what goes on inside the Lodge. Should this be disproved, and a certain amount of knowledge displayed (which of course the Mason can neither confirm nor deny) he can only fall back on the argument that the ritual cannot be understood or rightly interpreted outside the context and atmosphere in which it is worked.

Freemasons have the unquestioned right to interpret their own ritual in their own way, or in any way they please. If they interpret it in a sense that violates, strains, or ignores its clear meaning, however, the onus of proving the validity of their interpretation would appear to rest with them. But ' context and atmosphere ' is the last ditch argument which seems unanswerable, as the outsider cannot disprove it by the simple expedient of visiting a Lodge to see and feel for himself—though gate-crashing is by no means a complete impossibility. A few cases are on record. Others have never been detected. Such is the occasional carelessness of Lodges, particularly in the Metropolitan area.

It would be idle to deny, however, that this argument from context has a superficial force. A simple statement in print, for instance, can often be given two or more distinct and separate meanings according to the vocal stress of the words which a printer objecting to the use of italics would be unable to convey. Yet it would be difficult to maintain that the meaning of a ritual could be seriously misunderstood or misinterpreted in such a way.

Perhaps a better analogy occurs in the worship of the Church of England. The comprehensiveness of this body is well known, and it is certainly true that the Communion office of the Book of Common Prayer in one setting can be made to approximate to the Roman Mass, with emphasis on sacrifice and objectivity, in another setting it takes on the meaning of a simple and rather subjective Protestant commemorative service.

Again, a non-Catholic reading in cold print the Lord's Prayer followed by ten Hail Mary's set out in full repetitiousness in close type, ending with the Gloria, and all repeated five times (supposing that it ever had been so printed) might legitimately feel that the Rosary was a wearisome form of devotion. He might of course continue to think so were he to hear it publicly recited in Church ; on the other hand heard in this context possibly within the framework of Benediction or before the exposed Sacrament he might be carried away by the devoutness of the congregation offering up a great surging billow of prayer made by tiny ripples to the Throne of Grace and see something of the inner meaning of it all which the mere printed words cannot convey.

Without going into the tangled complexities of the Elizabethan Settlement which gave shape to the Book of Common Prayer, it may safely be stated that a deliberate compromise was achieved to make as many people of varying views as happy as possible within the Anglican establishment. The Ornaments Rubric and the Black Rubric both have their place, and if the twentieth-century contrast between the meaning of worship in Margaret Street and Islington, or between Virginia and Fond-du-Lac, was not foreseen it was certainly invited. The history of the Masonic ritual offers no such explanation to justify the difference of interpretation placed upon it by those, Masons or others, who look on it as a separate mystery-religion and those whose first allegiance is to the Church and who see nothing incompatible in being Masons as well. If continuity is to be traced between Freemasonry to-day and the operative trade guilds of medieval and Catholic stone-masons (and the subject is almost as controversial as the continuity between Anglicanism and the medieval Church) it must be admitted that after Grand Lodge was established, Anderson's Constitutions in 1723 completely and entirely excluded all specific references or allusions to Christ and His Church in a way in which the Prayer-Book never completely eliminated medievalism.[1]

The clear intention of the Masonic workings is to provide a symbolical and allegorical system of character-building and morality based on pagan models which cannot conflict with, and may indeed be the basis of a belief in any reputable religion, and to offer prayer and worship to a Most High who can be equated with any deity. The wording of the ritual and every ceremonial act with which it is performed can be reconstructed in detail by the non-Mason. All that the Mason can allege is lacking in the outsider's understanding of it, therefore, is the context, the spiritual atmosphere which inspires and animates the performance. But can this atmosphere really alter the clear meaning and purpose of the words ?

Participation in a public recitation of the Rosary may bring meaning to it and awaken to life what on paper may appear very dry bones. But it does not in any way alter the meaning. Rosary manuals instruct the novice that it is not the words of the Hail Mary which are important but the meditations on the various mysteries to which they form a verbal accompaniment, and to take part in such acts of worship can do no more than convince the inquirer that there may be a spiritual validity and reality in what might be thought monotonous repetition. But the Protestant who is convinced that invocation of the saints is wrong and an infringement of the supreme omnipotence of God will not see a different meaning in the Rosary as recited than in the Rosary as described. The

1. The only clear exceptions of which I am aware are the Christian symbols of faith, hope, and charity (the cross, anchor, and chalice) on the first degree tracing-board and the curious reference in the third degree to the " bright morning star whose rising brings peace and salvation to the faithful and obedient of the human race "— an allusion which is either Luciferian, meaningless sentimentality, or more probably a remnant of the Christianity which formerly pervaded the Craft in its earlier and operative days. Masons to-day tend to equate it with the " Blazing Star " of the first degree, or the " Sacred Symbol " of the second.

Catholic on the other hand would be supremely uncomfortable, to say the least of it, if the Rosary meditated the life of Christ accompanied by the repetition of an invocation to Baal or Osiris, however his priest tried to justify it on the grounds that it was the context of the meditations that mattered, not the words.

A play can be understood, and understood with accuracy, by reading it and following the stage directions. Even though it may come to life only by being performed, the meaning and significance of it remain fundamentally unchanged however much different nuances of interpretation are acted into it.

It must be admitted that lines which appear silly and trivial in cold print may in their right context almost achieve dignity when spoken on the stage. Sensitiveness to ridicule is a strong secondary motive in maintaining Masonic secrecy ; certain aspects of the workings, the forms of preparation of the candidate in particular, are when read on paper wide open to that form of attack. So to a lesser degree are the rites of the Church though the latter does not attempt to conceal her mysteries for such a reason. Educated Freemasons have always been aware that there are patent absurdities, anomalies, and turgid pomposities in their ritual which can but be smiled at by the cultured, sensitive and logical, however reverently they are performed and accompanied by solemn music from Bro. Organist. In this context they may lose something of their apparent absurdity, but " how *can* grown men be so silly ? " is not a valid theological argument unless it is felt that trivial silliness performed to the greater glory of God is so silly as to dishonour His supreme majesty. Silliness is relative, not absolute, and the greatest saints and doctors of the Church have not always been immune. Nor are the drawers-up of special services for firemen or animal-lovers nor some of the self-styled reformers of the Prayer-Book or other innovators in the Church of England to-day. Let us keep a sense of proportion.

This argument from context, then, is primarily emotional, not intellectual. There may be an atmosphere in some Lodges where the officers have attended Lodges of Instruction and work the ritual with a precision, reverence, and beauty, which is lacking in others where the working is careless and slipshod

—and this applies equally to the Churches. As too with the Church liturgy, this atmosphere may bring meaning and life to what on paper are dry forms, directions, and ceremonial rubrics. But it is difficult to understand how that meaning or life can be completely different from that lying dormant in the words and forms.

If it is alleged to be different, then Masons themselves are guilty of the offence of reading into the ritual something that is not there. Or what is more likely, of ignoring something that is.

What a Freemason really means when he says that "Masonry cannot be understood outside the Lodge" is that the atmosphere inside the Lodge is so charged with high moral principles, warm fellowship, benevolence and genuine friendliness that the anti-Christian implications of a ritual which is usually not taken very seriously sink into insignificance, if they are noticed at all. It is an argument which might equally justify a Christian (remaining a Christian at heart) in taking life vows as a Buddhist monk. Buddhists, as a rule, are extremely friendly and generous, even if they are not inclined to boast about it.

IX

MUCH ADO ABOUT NOTHING

Her listeners were perfectly quiet until she got to the part about her repeating, You are old, Father William, *to the Caterpillar, and the words all coming different, and then the Mock Turtle drew a long breath, and said, " That's very curious."*

" It's all about as curious as it can be," said the Gryphon.

* * * *

" Curiouser and curiouser ! " cried Alice.

Lewis Carroll, Alice in Wonderland.

THE religious interpretation which I have placed on the Masonic workings will of course be repudiated and dis-owned by Christian Masons. As there is no official interpretation they are perfectly at liberty to do this, but such a repudiation will only be convincing if they can produce an alternative. Expressions such as " preposterous ", " utterly wide of the mark ", " no Mason would think of reading into the ritual what you read into it " are inadequate answers without more factual refutation.

Speculative and mystical Masonic writers such as Wilms-hurst, Ward, Fort Newton, Castells, Sir John Cockburn, and a host of others have interpreted Freemasonry explicitly or implicitly as a mystery-cult and a separate religion. They are equally entitled to do so, and an impartial reading of the rituals and especially the Tracing Board Lectures would seem to justify the contention that this interpretation does indeed correspond not only with the ritual as we have it to-day, but with everything that we know of the tendencies of the period which gave it birth, and the Rosicrucianism that so strongly influenced it. Many such authors, some of high Masonic rank, have been re-printed and appear to be in fairly constant demand. Such books provoke no storm of indignation from Christian Masons. Yet when an outsider ventures to say almost exactly what these Masonic writers say, or to suggest that their religious interpretation of Freemasonry may after all have a certain validity from the Masonic point of view, the indignation of Christian Masons is thoroughly aroused. Is not this indignation mis-directed ? The analogy of heterodox opinions within the Church of England is almost groundless. Bishop Barnes's views, for instance, have been publicly disclaimed by the present Archbishop of Canterbury in the name of the Church. I am not aware, however, that the same Archbishop in his capacity as Past Grand Chaplain of the Craft has ever seen fit to disclaim the views of those who write books on Masonry as a religion. Wilmshurst, the most pagan and anti-Christian of them all, was even rewarded with Provincial Grand Lodge rank by the late Earl of Harewood for his services to Masonry—these services consisting mainly of lecturing to Lodges on this very subject. An organization known as the Dormer Study Circle exists to perpetuate his ideals.

The answer to the question as to whether Masonry is, or is not, a religion, then, must (in theological jargon) be regarded as ' pious opinion,' not as *de fide*. "*I* say Masonry is not a religion " is as as far as any Mason has the authority to go. And Grand Lodge itself could not make an official pronouncement to this effect with any sincerity until the ritual, particularly of the Holy Royal Arch, has been drastically overhauled. The very fact that the ritual is even capable of such an interpretation shows that Masonry has in itself at least the germs of a separate religion, a fact which justifies an investigation by the Church.

As far as I am aware, there is not one single Masonic commentary addressed primarily to Christians which seriously attempts to reconcile Masonry with the doctrines of the faith as held by the Church. Christianity is mentioned often enough ; analogies are drawn for instance between Baptism and Initiation, but always suggesting that the latter adds something of objective sacramental reality to a man's spiritual experience which cannot be obtained in the Church, or which at least can be equally obtained in the Lodge. This conception is repugnant to the convinced Christian who believes that the Holy Ghost guides the Church into *all* truth, and that in the Church alone is the fulness of spiritual experience.

How, then, can Christians interpret the Masonic ritual ? Realising that the *ipsissima verba* of the ritual (particularly in the Holy Royal Arch) are conclusively against them, they can only fall back on the assertion that they simply do not take their ritual seriously. It is a sort of morality play or

Christmas pantomime. If the morality is sound, why worry about the play ?

As this answer is not only widespread but indeed the only possible one, it deserves consideration.

No one except the extreme puritan could conceivably object that it is immoral for the Christian to witness or even act in plays such as those of the great dramatists of Greece and Rome, even though they were written under the religious inspiration of a paganism utterly rejected by the Church. It would be quite fantastic for ecclesiastics solemnly to ban a Punch-and-Judy show because some one managed to prove an Egyptian origin of the legend. And if indeed the spectators feel morally uplifted and improved by witnessing such spectacles it is all to the good, for that is a function of dramatic art.

But at this point the analogy significantly fails. If Lodges had public galleries whose entrances were uncontrolled by the ministrations of the Tyler with his drawn sword, or if the death and resurrection rite of Hiram Abiff were re-constructed and presented publicly on the stage of a London theatre, no one could reasonably object to the Christian attending or begrudge him an atom of moral profit which he might thereby acquire. But Masonic participation in these rites is surely a very different affair, even if they are not taken seriously *au pied de la lettre*. For the Freemason identifies himself with the mysteries, not in the sense that a good actor identifies himself with his part, but by a solemn oath and in the name of God he participates in the paganism of the play, and associates himself spiritually with it.

Secondly, to treat the ritual or even parts of the ritual as something not to be taken too seriously involves a trifling with holy things which seem impious. For everything is done in God's name, and the Bible is present and open throughout. Prayer is offered at every Initiation that " assisted by our Masonic art " the Candidate may " the better be enabled to unfold the beauties of true Godliness "—if the Masonic art is not to be taken seriously it would almost seem to follow that the true Godliness which it is supposed to promote is not to be taken too seriously either. If the Christian is to participate at all in such a ritual he should surely do so with the very utmost seriousness.

Thirdly, as every clergyman knows to his grief, there are a great many nominal Christians who do not take the ritual of the Church seriously either. They attend services two or three times a year at Christmas or a harvest festival because they enjoy it and feel that it is morally uplifting, and yet they have little use for creed or sacrament, and value the Church only in so far as it helps people to lead decent lives. Repentance, grace, and the atoning sacrifice of Christ play no part in their lives. They have been initiated by Baptism into the mystical body of Christ—but they do not take it too seriously.

No one would consider such people good Christians or Churchmen. Their conception of the faith, rejecting what is distasteful to them or what they only imperfectly understand, is too incomplete. No one, therefore, would regard them as ideal or even reputable defenders of the Church. What right, then, have Freemasons who refuse to take the teaching of their ritual seriously other than its moral uplift, to regard themselves as good Masons, or authoritative defenders of the Lodge ?

The Prophet Ezekiel was deeply perturbed when he saw in a vision women weeping in the Temple for Tammuz. He may have been singularly lacking in humour, and he may even have got the whole thing out of proportion, but he considered it nothing less than an abomination. It may be pointed out in passing that the Masonic writer J. S. M. Ward in one of his more fanciful moods declared that Hiram Abiff was the earthly counterpart of Tammuz, so it is quite possible that these misguided females might have been able to symbolize their tears into perfectly orthodox co-Masonic channels. Nevertheless, it is open to grave doubts whether Ezekiel would have been mollified or the anger of Jehovah mitigated had they pleaded that they didn't really mean it to be taken seriously. It was all part of a play, and everybody meant well.

X

ECCLESIASTICAL CONDEMNATIONS OF FREEMASONRY

" Let the jury consider their verdict," the King said, for about the twentieth time.

Lewis Carroll, Alice in Wonderland.

IT IS well known that Freemasonry has been condemned by the Roman Catholic Church, and that any Roman Catholic on initiation become *ipso facto* excommunicate. Contrary to popular rumour, she does not give dispensations for convert Masons to continue in Masonry.

This condemnation is resented by Grand Lodge Masons of the English-speaking world. It is popularly felt to be unjust, and the belief is widespread that the Papal condemnations, in so far as they include *all* Masonic systems, are based on a complete misunderstanding of what Grand Lodge Masonry really stands for, and on a regrettable confusion between Grand Lodges and Grand Orients.[1] " Rome " said a recent apologist for the Craft[2] " knows very little about Regular Masonry."

Actually Rome is remarkably well-informed about Regular Masonry. She has a mass of information to draw on, quite apart from the fact that both in this country and in America her converts have included Freemasons, and sometimes (like the Grand Master the Marquess of Ripon in the last century) very distinguished ones. In many cases they retain a loyalty

1. Masons who properly understand the Roman outlook, however, take a more realistic line. A. E. Waite, anti-Catholic but on the whole extremely fair, says in his *New Encyclopaedia of Freemasonry* (1925) " It is impossible that the Latin Church should tolerate an institution like Masonry. That Church has not only an elaborate and systematic literature of *theologia et philosophia moralis* but a doctrinal ruling thereon and....by its own hypothesis it is the sole and Divinely ordained custodian of faith and morals. Masonry sets out to be regarded as another and independent system of ethics, another guide to life. As such it is, implicitly and explicitly under judgment from the beginning, a competitor and a rival." (Vol. II, p. 264-5.)

2. The Rev. J. L. C. Dart, *Christianity and Freemasonry*, (*Theology*, April, 1951).

to their former Brethren in the Craft, and have testified to the appropriate authorities in terms stressing the political harmlessness, constitutional loyalty, and essential belief in the Great Architect which are Masonic landmarks. Rome knows all that, accepts it, and takes it into full consideration.

It must be admitted that many clauses in some of her censures are not only inapplicable to Regular Masonry, but also strike the honest God-fearing Protestant Mason as extremely offensive. When he thinks of the respectable pillars of society and commerce, including perhaps the vicar, who congregate quarterly in his Lodge, their breasts resplendent with the Charity Jewel, he considers himself entitled to feel that Clement XII was a little wide of the mark when he said that such assemblies " have become to the faithful such objects of suspicion that every good man now regards affiliation to them as a certain indication of wickedness and perversion."[1]

But " now " in this Encyclical means 1738; clearly Clement XII had in mind when he wrote this (among other factors) the bad reputation which French Masonry had acquired through the influence of the notorious Duc D'Orleans; later condemnations also took into account such movements as the degrading Illuminism of Weishaupt and the frankly seditious Alta Vendita in Italy, by which the Holy See was more nearly surrounded and threatened. It may then be frankly admitted even by the most rigid of Ultramontanists that not every clause of every condemnation could reasonably be expected to apply to every Masonic or quasi-Masonic secret society. Accusations of religious indifferentism, for instance, are quite as irrelevant to the militantly atheist organization as imputations of consciously " perverting the minds of the incautious, and shooting down innocent people from their hiding places "[2] would seem to a Lodge composed of respectable Anglican professional men. But to admit this is very far from admitting that Papal condemnations should not apply at all to Anglo-Saxon Masonry, or that they are wide of the mark in outlawing it.

A study of the whole series of Roman Catholic condemnations of Freemasonry from *In Eminente* (1738) to the Clauses in the *Codex Iuris Canonici* issued by Benedict XV in 1917 will show that the main reasons for which world Masonry

1. *In Eminente*, 1738.   2. ibid.

has been denounced, apart from political seditiousness and open atheism, are the fact that Masonry teaches a purely ' natural ' religion, the character of the Masonic rituals which are often blasphemous, the oaths and promises (with their extravagant penalties) which disregard the conditions required by the moral law for a just and reverent oath, and Masonic indifferentism in matters of religion which (however it may be explained away) in practice teaches that all Gods are equal. Here are ample grounds for Catholic condemnation—indeed any one of these points would justify such a course. And Anglo-Saxon Masonry is as guilty in these matters as the Grand Orients, who at least do not swear the ridiculous Masonic oaths on the Bible or in the name of God.

It is commonly thought by Masons that the Roman Catholic objections to Freemasonry are in some way bound up with the confessional—that there must be no secrets which could be withheld from the confessor. This is not so. A Catholic is as entitled to his secrets, provided they are not sinful, as anyone else.

The plea that Rome has condemned English Masonry on false and mistaken grounds, then, is based either on ignorance or on muddled thinking.

The suggestion has often been made that it was the hostility of the Holy See which drove the Grand Orients into atheism; and that were the Church of England to pronounce adversely on the theological implications of Freemasonry, Grand Lodge might likewise become the bitter enemy of God and society. The first point is, however, historically untenable. Continental Masonry almost from the very start was a manifestation of free thought, of liberalism, political and religious, anti-clericalism, and the neo-paganism which was infecting contemporary society, even before the ' Great Architect ' was rejected at the close of the nineteenth century. The second point, therefore, represents ' Anglican comprehensiveness ' at its most ludicrous and Laodicean. It is equivalent to suggesting that Irenaeus was wasting his time in denouncing the Gnostic mystery-religions and thereby risking their hostility instead of urging Christians to join them in order to prevent their becoming even more Gnostic and more mysterious. And is it worse for the Church to be openly attacked from without, rather than insidiously undermined from within ?

The well-known Papal attitude to Freemasonry will be found in the following documents; as all are readily obtainable no further summary is needed here.

In Eminente	Clement XII, 1738.
Ecclesiam	Pius VII, 1821.
Etsi Multa	Pius IX, 1873.
Humanum Genus	Leo XIII, 1884.

The Greek Orthodox Church, too, has set its face against Freemasonry. Although surrounded by Grand Orients rather than by Grand Lodges, the terms of the condemnation are directed mainly against the latter, particularly, it seems, in their American form. Much of it indeed is wholly inapplicable to any Masonic system that has abandoned the Great Architect. As this condemnation does not appear to have been translated or published in Great Britain before, despite its importance, and as it obviously has a vital bearing on any Anglo-Orthodox *rapprochement*, I reproduce it in full.[1] It will be noticed from the reference to the earlier condemnation of Freemasonry as a " false and anti-Christian system " by the Inter-Orthodox Commission which met on Mt. Athos that not only the Greek, but indeed all the autocephalous Orthodox Churches are committed to outlawing the Craft.

The Bishops of the Church of Greece in their session of October 12, 1933, concerned themselves with the study and examination of the secret international organization, Freemasonry. They heard with attention the introductory exposition of the Commission of four Bishops appointed by the Holy Synod at its last session ; also the opinion of the Theological Faculty of the University of Athens, and the particular opinion of Prof. Panag Bratsiotis which was appended thereto. They also took into consideration publications on this question in Greece and abroad. After a discussion they arrived at the following conclusions, accepted unanimously by all the Bishops.

" Freemasonry is not simply a philanthropic union or a philosophical school, but constitutes a mystagogical system which reminds us of the ancient heathen mystery-religions

1. *Ekklesia*, no. 48, Dec. 4, 1933, Athens. I am indebted to Fr. Krivoshein, Orthodox priest at Oxford, for obtaining this statement for me, and for the translation.

and cults—from which it descends and is their continuation and regeneration. This is not only admitted by prominent teachers in the lodges, but they declare it with pride, affirming literally :—' Freemasonry is the only survival of the ancient mysteries and can be called the guardian of them '; Freemasonry is a direct offspring of the Egyptian mysteries ; ' the humble workshop of the Masonic Lodge is nothing else than the caves and the darkness of the cedars of India and the unknown depths of the Pyramids and the crypts of the magnificent temples of Isis '; ' the Greek mysteries of Freemasonry, having passed along the luminous roads of knowledge under the mysteriarchs Prometheus, Dionysus and Orpheus, formulated the eternal laws of the Universe '.

" Such a link between Freemasonry and the ancient idolatrous mysteries is also manifested by all that is enacted and performed at the initiations. As in the rites of the ancient idolatrous mysteries the drama of the labours and death of the mystery god was repeated, and in the imitative repetition of this drama the initiate dies together with the patron of the mystery religion, who was always a mythical person symbolising the Sun of nature which dies in winter and is regenerated in spring, so it is also, in the initiation of the third degree, of the patron of Freemasonry Hiram and a kind of repetition of his death, in which the initiate suffers with him, struck by the same instruments and on the same parts of the body as Hiram. According to the confession of a prominent teacher of Freemasonry Hiram is ' as Osiris, as Mithra and as Bacchus, one of the personifications of the Sun '.

" Thus Freemasonry is, as granted, a mystery-religion, quite different, separate, and alien to the Christian faith. This is shown without any doubt by the fact that it possesses its own temples with altars, which are characterised by prominent teachers as ' workshops which cannot have less history and holiness than the Church ' and as temples of virtue and wisdom where the Supreme Being is worshipped and the truth is taught. It possesses its own religious ceremonies, such as the ceremony of adoption or the masonic baptism, the ceremony of conjugal acknowledgement or the masonic marriage, the masonic memorial service, the consecration of the masonic temple, and so on. It possesses its own initiations, its own ceremonial ritual, its own hierarchical order and a definite discipline. As may be concluded from the masonic *agapes* and from the feasting of the winter and summer solstices with religious meals and general rejoicings,[1] it is a physiolatric religion.

" It is true that it may seem at first that Freemasonry can be reconciled with every other religion, because it is not interested directly in the religion to which its initiates belong. This is, however, explained by its syncretistic character and proves that in this point also it is an offspring and a continuation of ancient idolatrous mysteries which accepted for initiation worshippers of all gods. But as the mystery religions, in spite of the apparent spirit of tolerance and acceptance of foreign gods, lead to a syncretism which undermined and gradually shook confidence in other religions, thus Freemasonry to-day, which seeks to embrace in itself gradually all mankind and which promises to give moral perfection and knowledge of truth, is lifting itself to the position of a kind of super-religion, looking on all religions (without excepting Christianity) as inferior to itself. Thus it develops in its initiates the idea that only in masonic lodges is performed the shaping and the smoothing of the unsmoothed and unhewn stone. And the fact alone that Freemasonry creates a brotherhood excluding all other brotherhoods outside it (which are considered by Freemasonry as ' uninstructed ' even when they are Christian) proves clearly its pretentions to be a super-religion. This means that by masonic initiation a Christian becomes a brother of the Muslim, the Buddhist, or any kind of rationalist, while the Christian not initiated in Freemasonry becomes to him an outsider.

" On the other hand, Freemasonry in prominently exalting knowledge and in helping free research as ' putting no limit in the search of truth ' (according to its rituals and constitution), and more than this by adopting the so-called natural ethic, shows itself in this sense to be in sharp contradiction with the

1. These ceremonies are quite unknown in Great Britain, except for the occasional Masonic funeral and of course the consecration ceremonies. The others, however, are occasionally found in the United States, particularly in the higher degrees. W.H.

Christian religion. For the Christian religion exalts faith above all, confining human reason to the limits traced by Divine Revelation and leading to holiness through the supernatural action of grace. In other words, while Christianity, as a religion of Revelation, possessing its rational and superrational dogmas and truths, asks for faith first, and grounds its moral structure on the supernatural Divine Grace, Freemasonry has only natural truth and brings to the knowledge of its initiates free thinking and investigation through reason only. It bases its moral structure only on the natural forces of man, and has only natural aims.

" Thus, the incompatible contradiction between Christianity and Freemasonry is quite clear. It is natural that various Churches of other denominations have taken a stand against Freemasonry. Not only has the Western Church branded for its own reasons the masonic movement by numerous Papal encyclicals, but Lutheran, Methodist and Presbyterian communities have also declared it to be incompatible with Christianity. Much more has the Orthodox Catholic Church, maintaining in its integrity the treasure of Christian faith, proclaimed against it every time that the question of Freemasonry has been raised. Recently, the Interorthodox Commission which met on Mount Athos and in which the representatives of all the Autocephalous Orthodox Churches took part, has characterised Freemasonry as a ' false and anti-Christian system ' ".

The Assembly of the Bishops of the Church of Greece in the above mentioned session heard with relief and accepted the following conclusions which were drawn from the investigations and discussions by its President, His Grace Archbishop Chrysostom of Athens :—

" Freemasonry cannot be at all compatible with Christianity as far as it is a secret organization, acting and teaching in mystery and secret and deifying rationalism. Freemasonry accepts as its members not only Christians, but also Jews and Muslims. Consequently clergymen cannot be permitted to take part in this association. I consider as worthy of degradation every clergyman who does so. It is necessary to urge upon all who entered it without due thought and without examining what Freemasonry is, to sever all connection with it, for

Christianity alone is the religion which teaches absolute truth and fulfils the religious and moral needs of men. Unanimously and with one voice all the Bishops of the Church of Greece have approved what was said, and we declare that all the faithful children of the Church must stand apart from Freemasonry. With unshaken faith in Our Lord Jesus Christ ' in whom we have our redemption through His blood, the forgiveness of our sins, according to the riches of His Grace, whereby He abounds to us in all wisdom and prudence ' (Ephes. 1, 7-9), possessing the truth revealed by Him and preached by the Apostles, ' not in persuasive words of wisdom, but in the manifestation of the Spirit of power ' (1 Cor. 2, 4): partaking in the Divine Sacraments through which we are sanctified and saved to eternal life, we must not fall from the grace of Christ by becoming partakers of other mysteries. It is not lawful to belong at the same time to Christ and to search for redemption and moral perfection outside Him. For these reasons true Christianity is incompatible with Freemasonry.

" Therefore, all who have become involved in the initiations of masonic mysteries must from this moment sever all relations with masonic lodges and activities, being sure that they are thereby of a certainty renewing their links with our one Lord and Saviour which were weakened by ignorance and by a wrong sense of values. The Assembly of the Bishops of the Church of Greece expects this particularly and with love from the initiates of the lodges, being convinced that most of them have received masonic initiation not realising that by it they were passing into another religion, but on the contrary from ignorance, thinking that they had done nothing contrary to the faith of their fathers. Recommending them to the sympathy, and in no wise to the hostility or hatred of the faithful children of the Church, the Assembly of the Bishops calls them to pray with her from the heart in Christian love, that the one Lord Jesus Christ ' the way, the truth and the life ' may illumine and return to the truth those who in ignorance have gone astray."

It is less well known that certain Protestant Churches have also condemned Freemasonry, and in each case it is Grand Lodge, and not Grand Orient Masonry that has been censured.

Four groups of Presbyterians have pronounced against it :—

1. The 'Original Secession' in Scotland repudiated Free-masonry as early as 1757, mainly on the grounds that it was against the moral law to bind oneself by oath to secrets which were not revealed till afterwards.[1]

2. The Reformed Presbyterian Church of Ireland makes abstention from Freemasonry a condition of member-ship.[2]

3. The Free Presbyterian Church of Scotland imposed a similar condition of membership in 1927.[3]

4. The Orthodox Presbyterian Church of America set up a Committee on Secret Societies which reported to the General Assembly at Rochester, N.Y. in 1942 condemn-ing Masonry mainly on the grounds of religious indifferentism.[4]

The English Methodists passed a resolution on Freemasonry (largely due to the stir made by the Rev. C. Penney Hunt's book *The Menace of Freemasonry to the Christian Faith*) at the Bradford Conference in 1927, which contained the following clause :—" Freemasonry, in its ritual and official language, is of purely Theistic nature......the distinctive faith of Christian-ity can find no expression in its formulae, and that the Christian message of salvation, through faith in Christ, as the basis alike for home and foreign evangelization, is wholly incompatible with the claims which have often been put for-ward by Freemasons."[5] Contrary to popular Masonic rumour, this resolution has never been rescinded.

Masonry has been outlawed by the Salvation Army. The late General Booth addressed a letter to every officer with these clauses :—

" No language of mine could be too strong in condemning any Officer's affiliation with any Society which shuts Him outside its Temples; and which in its religious ceremonies gives

1. This Act was published in full in the *Scots Magazine* (Vol. XIX, p. 432).
2. Rev. C. Penney Hunt, *The Menace of Freemasonry to the Christian Faith* (eighth edition) p. 92.
3. ibid. This is the body known colloquially as the " Wee Free's."
4. This Report has been published as a pamphlet *Christ or the Lodge ?* (published for the Committee on Christian Education, Orthodox Presbyterian Church, Philadelphia).
5. Minutes of the Methodist Conference, 1927.

neither Him nor His Name any place......As for the future, the Army's views upon this matter will be made known to all who wish to become Officers, and acceptance of these views will be necessary before Candidates can be received for training, and further from this time it will be contrary to our regulations for any Officer to join such a Society."[1]

American Lutherans have strongly condemned Freemasonry.[2]

The Missouri Synod, for instance, holds that "These organizations, which our Church terms 'lodges', demand belief in God, but not in the God and Father of our Lord Jesus Christ. Their rituals often provide for an oath which a Christian cannot but regard as unnecessary or even frivolous and blasphemous. These rituals oftentimes promote salvation by the Law and by good works, not by faith in Jesus Christ. They often provide for prayers not directed to the Triune God and not spoken in the name of Jesus......These organizations most frequently claim to be non-sectarian and to allow for complete religious freedom. Nevertheless, their rituals disregard, level out, or even deny the most precious truths of the Christian faith in order to make their moral and religious principles acceptable to anyone joining the organization regardless of his religious convictions.

"For more than a hundred years our Church has testified against doctrinal errors in many churches and cults. But it has also testified against the false religious views and principles expressed in the rituals and other literature of many secret oath-bound societies. It has done so because it believed that the worship of a 'god' other than the Triune God is idol worship ; because it was mindful of the Saviour's directive "All men should honor the Son even as they honor the Father; he that honoreth not the Son honoreth not the Father, which hath sent Him" (John 5 : 23). It has done so moved by its

1. The Rev. C. Penney Hunt, *The Menace of Freemasonry to the Christian Faith*, p. 67.

2. A complete account of the American Lutheran attitude, and of the resolutions passed by the various constituent Lutheran bodies on the subject of Freemasonry will be found in a series of two articles *To Join Or Not To Join* which appeared in *The Lutheran Witness* (Concordia Publishing House, St. Louis, Missouri) on July 10 and 24, 1951, by Dr. Paul M. Bretscher, Chairman of the Commission on Fraternal Organizations.

unflinching loyalty to the Word of God and to the saving truths of the Holy Scriptures. The most recent statement issued by our Church *re* secret oath-bound organizations appears as follows in the *Proceedings* of its triennial convention held in Milwaukee in June, 1950 :

" *Resolved*......that we urge all pastors and congregations to exercise great vigilance in this matter :

" That such pastors and congregations as neglect their duty in this respect be properly admonished according to Matthew 18 by fellow Christians, fellow Pastors, and District officials ; and

" That where all such evangelical dealing with offending pastors or congregations fails, the matter be taken to the *Praesidium* of Synod and finally to Synod itself, if necessary, for proper action."[1]

The American Lutheran Conference is committed to what is known as the Minneapolis Theses, of which the following is a pertinent paragraph :—

" These Synods agree that all such organizations or societies, secret or open, as are either avowedly religious or practice the forms of religion without confessing as a matter of principle the Triune God or Jesus Christ as the Son of God, come into the flesh, and our Savior from sin, or teach, instead of the Gospel, salvation by human works or morality, are anti-Christian and destructive of the best interests of the Church and the individual soul, and that, therefore, the Church of Christ and its congregation can have no fellowship with them.

" They agree that a Lutheran Synod should not tolerate pastors who have affiliated themselves with any anti-Christian society. And they admonish their pastors and congregations to testify against the sin of lodgery."[2]

The Dutch Reformed Church of South Africa (Cape Synod) appointed a commission to investigate Freemasonry which reported conclusively against the Craft in November, 1940. This report is admittedly rather inaccurate when it delves into Masonic history and organization. It quotes from a ritual which certainly appears to have been faulty. Yet none of these

1. See note 2 on p. 76.
2. ibid. The Lutheran attitude is stated in greater detail in the excellent book of Dr. Theodore Graebner, *Is Masonry a Religion ?* (Concordia Publishing House, 1946.)

limitations invalidate the condemnation on religious grounds
—salvation through works, the *religio naturae*, the improper
oaths, a false idea of God, and the underlying syncretism
upheld by the Craft. Accordingly the commission recommended that all Masonic members of the Dutch Reformed Church
should be urged to leave their Lodges, and that no Freemason
should in future be permitted to hold office.[1]

It may be felt that these Protestant bodies represent minori-
ties and are therefore unimportant. Take them together with
the vast Roman Catholic and Eastern Orthodox communions,
however, and it will be discovered that the majority of
Christians throughout the world have condemned Freemasonry
as incompatible with the claims of Our Lord and Saviour.
But numbers are not the final criteria ; what matters is, are the
reasons for such censures sound ?

One startling fact emerges, which should make the Christian
Mason more than a little thoughtful. *No Church that has
seriously investigated the religious teachings and implications of
Freemasonry has ever yet failed to condemn it.*

Is the Church of England too mortally involved to speak her
mind ?[2]

1. *A Review of the Report of the Synodic Commission of the Dutch
   Reformed Church (Cape) on Freemasonry.* (Cape Town, 1942).
   This pamphlet contains the condemnation in full and a Masonic
   reply to it ; the answer to the religious charges, as might be
   expected, is not only evasive and wide of the mark, but in places
   extremely disingenuous. For instance, Jah-Bul-On is misquoted in
   the Report as *Joabulon*, and the conclusion is drawn that " God
   is not addressed by the name by which He revealed Himself." This
   say the Masons who answer, is " entirely incorrect....the conclusion to which the Commissioners come on this subject, being
   based on wrong data, falls away." To the Commissioners' conclusion that the oath is " improper " for the Christian, the reply
   is made with incredible naivety " The fact that it is ratified on the
   Bible should be sufficient answer."
     Comment is superfluous, but will any who intend to reply to
   Darkness Visible please take note ?
2. The official formularies of the Church of England appear to condemn Freemasonry already. *Articles of Religion*, No. XVIII, states
   " They are also to be had accursed that presume to say, That every
   man shall be saved by the Law or Sect which he professeth, so that
   he be diligent to frame his life according to that Law, and the Light
   of Nature. For Holy Scripture doth set out unto us only the Name of
   Jesus Christ, whereby men must be saved."

PART II

THE FURNISHINGS OF A LODGE

Ideally the Lodge room should be in the form of a double cube, though this of course is not essential; any room, oblong for preference, can be used. Lodges, like Churches, are supposed to face East and West ; where they do not do so geographically the dais[1] end is referred to as the East, and the other sides to their relative compass points.

The door, leading from an anteroom, is in the North-West corner. The Brethren are seated in rows along the North, South, and West. The Past Masters sit in the East. The floor should be of a black and white checker-board pattern with an indented border; this is usually represented by a carpet. An emblem with the letter G irradiated is suspended from or depicted on the ceiling in the centre.

The Worshipful Master has his chair and pedestal in the East. These should be of the Ionic order, and his emblem, the square, may be carved or painted on the front of the pedestal. On the pedestal are the Volume of the Sacred Law resting on a cushion, with the square and compasses in silver or gilt resting on them when the Lodge is open, a gavel and sounding-board, sometimes the box of working-tools, and an Ionic column which is always upright.

The Senior Warden faces him in the West. His chair and pedestal are Doric. His emblem is the level. By his pedestal is the perfect ashlar, a cubic block usually suspended from a tripod. The Junior Warden who has the plumb rule for his emblem, has his chair and pedestal (Corinthian) in the middle of the South. By it is the rough ashlar, an unsmoothed block resting on a column. Both Wardens have gavels, sounding-boards, and columns ; the Senior Warden's column is erect when the Lodge is open and horizontal when it is closed, and the Junior Warden's *vice versa*. By each of the three pedestals is a candlestick.[2] The Master's must always be lighted when the Lodge is open. The Wardens' are normally lighted also, but are extinguished for the ceremony of raising to the Third Degree.

The Immediate Past Master sits on the dais to the left of the Worshipful Master. The Senior Deacon is at or near the right of the Worshipful Master, the Junior Deacon is on the right of the Senior Warden. The Inner Guard's position is by the door, and the Tyler's is outside it in the ante-room.

The First Degree apron is of plain white lambskin; that of the Second Degree is the same with the addition of two blue

1. The actual presence of a raised dais is tending to become obsolete, at least in London.
2. Many Lodge rooms, including those of the Masonic Temple in Great Queen Street, have electric candles.

rosettes in the lower corners. The Master Masons' is bordered with blue, has two falls from beneath the flap ending in metal tassels, and has a third rosette in the point of the flap. Those in or past the Chair (Installed Masters) substitute an inverted T in metal for the three rosettes. Office-bearers wear their jewels or emblems of office suspended from collars of blue silk. The Worshipful Master and the Wardens may in addition wear blue gauntlets and white gloves.[1]

There are three tracing boards, one for each Degree, which may be displayed in various ways. Only one is exposed at a time, according to the degree in which the Lodge is open.

A note may be added here on the Masonic system of dating which is *Anno Lucis*. This is based on Archbishop Ussher's chronology which placed the Creation in B.C. 4004, but the Masonic calendar usually takes this as 4000. B.C. 1000, then become A.L. 3000 ; A.D. 1954 is A.L. 5954.

SIGNS, GRIPS, WORDS
ENTERED APPRENTICE or FIRST DEGREE

Sign (penal) The right arm is held horizontal with the shoulder, elbow bent, hand held horizontally with the thumb to the left of the windpipe. The sign is ' cut ' (i.e., completed and dismissed) by drawing the hand across the throat and dropping it to the side.

Grip The thumb presses into the first joint of the forefinger, where it meets the hand.[2]

Word BOAZ.

1. The rule that all Masons should wear white gloves in the Lodge has been relaxed. But in 1951 the practice was again urged upon the Lodges.

2. Although this First Degree grip is in a sense *the* Masons' grip in that it is recognised by all Masons of whatever degree, it is not to be supposed that it is the only, or even the usual method of mutual recognition outside the Lodge. Recognition can be achieved in a hundred ways. Any little catch-phrase from the ritual worked innocently into ordinary conversation will serve ; " taught to be cautious " is one of the most popular. " How old " (or " who's) your Mother ? " is a familiar way of asking what Lodge one belongs to. Reference to knife and fork at table as " working tools " ; or even modified gestures in a bar or public house based on the toasting ceremonies at the Masonic banquet (indicating a triangle with the fingers of the right hand as in the point-left-right rigmarole, or drawing one's glass across the throat before drinking) will identify a Brother. It is interesting to notice that such phrases as " on the square," and " on the level " and " third degree methods " have been permanently given to the English language by Freemasonry, and although the first is still extensively used in a Masonic context, they are no longer distinctive.

PASS *from* FIRST *to* SECOND DEGREE

Pass-grip   The thumb presses between the first and second fingers.

Pass-word   SHIBBOLETH.

FELLOW-CRAFT *or* SECOND DEGREE

Signs   (i)   The sign of Fidelity. Right hand on left breast, with thumb squared upwards.

         (ii) The Hailing sign or sign of Perseverance. Arm horizontal from shoulder to elbow, vertical from elbow to wrist, thumb squared. The arm may be out at the front at right angles to the body, the palm facing right with the thumb pointing backwards, or it may be out at the side in line with the body.

        (iii) The Penal sign. Draw the right hand across the breast and drop it to the side.

Grip   The thumb presses on the first joint of the second finger.

Word   JACHIN. (Pronounced Yahkin).

PASS *from* SECOND *to* THIRD DEGREE

Pass-grip   The thumb presses between the second and third fingers.

Pass-word   TUBAL-CAIN.

MASTER MASON *or* THIRD DEGREE

Signs   (i)   The sign of Horror. Given from the Second Degree Hailing sign by dropping the left hand, a little out from the body, palm facing outwards. There is some variation in the position of the left hand, depending on whether the " dreadful and afflicting sight " is supposed to be in front or to the left. The right hand is raised with its back to the face, and the head is turned over the right shoulder.

        (ii) The sign of Sympathy. The head is bent slightly forward, and the forehead is struck gently with the right hand (in some workings thrice forming a triangle). These two signs are known as the casual signs.

        (iii) The Penal sign. The right hand is held horizontally, palm downwards, with the thumb at right angles to the left of navel. It is 'cut' by drawing the hand smartly across the body (sometimes this is done by moving it to the left, then across to the right) and dropping the hand to the side. The sign is ' recovered ' by returning the hand with the thumb to the navel. These are the three Third Degree signs given in succession to prove oneself a Master Mason.

(iv) The sign of Grief and Death, also known as the sign of Grief and Distress. This, in its three forms, is described in the Ceremony of Raising, and occurs nowhere else (see p. 147-8).

(v) The Grand or Royal sign, also known as the sign of Joy and Exultation, is given by raising both arms above the head, with the palms facing each other.

Grip (Only given on the Five Points of Fellowship). The fingertips dig into the wrist as if clutching it.

Words MACHABEN and MACHBINNA (never spelt, but rendered phonetically. Early disclosures give MAHABONE and MACBENACH, but the pronunciation through verbal transmission has tended to become corrupt in the past century).[1]

The so-called sign of Reverence is the same as the Second Degree sign of Fidelity, except that the thumb is closed. It is given during the prayers in each degree, but strictly speaking is not a sign at all.

The step, taken before giving a sign, is given by advancing a short pace (about six inches) with the left foot, bringing the right heel into the instep, with the feet at right-angles in a tau cross. This is the ' regular ' step, not to be confused with the ' proper ' steps by which the Candidate approaches the East in each degree, described in the ritual.

The knocks of the First Degree are three, evenly spaced. In the Second Degree, one, followed by two. (rat....tat-tat). In the Third Degree, two followed by one (rat-tat....tat).

CRAFT RITUALS

As has been already explained, there is no absolute uniformity in Masonic workings. As long as the general structure is the same, and the landmarks are preserved, verbal and ceremonial differences do not matter, and many local uses have evolved. Some have never been printed at all, but are recorded

1. See notes, pp. 142 and 145, for a fuller account of the pronunciation, history, and meaning of these words.

on manuscript or duplicated sheets which belong to the Lodges.[1]

Two workings claim to represent the Masonic ritual practised by the Lodge of Reconciliation, when the ' Ancients ' and the ' Moderns ' who had long been separated from each other, came together in 1813. These are Stability and Strict Emulation. It is not the function of this book to assess the validity of these rival claims. But Emulation workers have been more vigorous in establishing their position, and have succeeded to a great extent in getting themselves recognised as the norm (at least in London).

Among other workings may be mentioned Bristol (probably the oldest, as it includes several pre-union features not found elsewhere), Logic, Unanimity originating in North Walsham, Oxford, which is among the least guilty of grammatical errors; York, Humber, Plymouth Common-Sense; Exeter and Bury (which have the fuller workings in the Installation ceremony), Britannia (a Sheffield ritual); several London uses such as Domatic, Metropolitan, West London and South London, which are derived from Stability; the Revised Ritual, which makes a rather pedantic effort to eliminate certain anomalies but in the main follows Oxford, and the English Ritual, probably the most grammatical of them all but full of pedantries, and not very widely used.

Scottish, Irish and American deviations are dealt with in Appendix A, p. 187.

OPENING AND CLOSING THE LODGE
IN THE THREE DEGREES

OPENING THE LODGE IN THE FIRST DEGREE

    (*When the Brethren are assembled an opening hymn may be sung.[2] Then the Worshipful Master gives a single knock with his gavel, which is repeated in turn by the Senior and Junior Wardens*).

W.M.   Brethren, assist me to open the Lodge. (*All rise, if they are not already standing after the hymn*).

W.M.   (*Calling the Junior Warden by name*) Bro..........., what is the first care of every Mason ?

J.W.   To see that the Lodge is properly tyled.

W.M.   Direct that duty to be done.

1. I have seen and compared some of these local workings, but it would only get certain Lodges into difficulties were I to specify or describe them further.
2. The usual opening hymn is reproduced in Appendix C. on page 218.

J.W.	(*To Inner Guard, by name*) Bro. . . . ., see that the Lodge is properly tyled.
	(*The Inner Guard goes to the door, and without opening it, gives the knocks of the First Degree, which are answered from outside by the Tyler. The Inner Guard then reports to the Junior Warden by name*).
I.G.	Bro. . . . ., the Lodge is properly tyled.
J.W.	(*Giving First Degree knocks*) The Lodge is properly tyled.
W.M.	(*To Senior Warden, by name*) Bro. . . . ., the next care ?
S.W.	To see that none but Masons are present.
W.M.	To order, Brethren, in the First Degree.
	(*The Worshipful Master and the Brethren take the step and give the sign of the First Degree*).
W.M.	Bro. Junior Warden, how many principal officers are there in the Lodge ?
J.W.	Three: the Worshipful Master, and the Senior and Junior Wardens.
W.M.	Bro. Senior Warden, how many assistant officers are there ?
S.W.	Three, besides the Tyler or Outer Guard; namely the Senior and Junior Deacons and the Inner Guard.
W.M.	(*To Junior Warden*) The situation of the Tyler ?
J.W.	Outside the door of the Lodge.
W.M.	(*To Junior Warden*) His duty ?
J.W.	Being armed with a drawn sword, to keep off all intruders and Cowans to Masonry, and to see that the Candidates are properly prepared.
W.M.	(*To Senior Warden*) The situation of the Inner Guard ?
S.W.	Within the entrance of the Lodge.
W.M.	His duty ?
S.W.	To admit Masons on proof, receive the Candidates in due form, and obey the commands of the Junior Warden.
W.M.	(*To Junior Warden*) The situation of the Junior Deacon ?
J.W.	At the right of the Senior Warden.
W.M.	His duty ?
J.W.	To carry all messages and communications of the Worshipful Master from the Senior to the Junior Warden, and to see that the same are punctually obeyed.
W.M.	(*To Senior Warden*) The situation of the Senior Deacon ?
S.W.	At or near to the right of the Worshipful Master.
W.M.	His duty ?

S.W.	To bear all messages and commands from the Worshipful Master to the Senior Warden, and await the return of the Junior Deacon.
W.M.	Bro. Junior Warden, your place in the Lodge ?
J.W.	In the South.
W.M.	Why are you placed there ?
J.W.	To mark the sun at its meridian, to call the Brethren from labour to refreshment, and from refreshment to labour, that profit and pleasure may be the result.
W.M.	Bro. Senior Warden, your place in the Lodge ?
S.W.	In the West.
W.M.	Why are you placed there ?
S.W.	To mark the setting sun, to close the Lodge by command of the Worshipful Master, after having seen that every brother has had his due.
W.M.	(*To Senior Warden or Immediate Past Master*) The Master's place ?
S.W. or I.P.M.	In the East.
W.M.	Why is he placed there ?
S.W. or I.P.M.	As the sun rises in the East to open and enliven the day, so the Worshipful Master is placed in the East to open the Lodge, and employ and instruct the Brethren in Freemasonry.
W.M.	The Lodge being duly formed, before I declare it open, let us invoke the assistance of the Great Architect of the Universe in all our undertakings, may our labours, thus begun in order, be ~~continued~~ in peace, and closed in harmony. *Conducted*
I.P.M.	So mote it be. (*Where there is an organist, this may throughout the ceremonies be sung by all the Brethren*).
W.M.	Brethren, in the name of the Great Architect of the Universe, I declare the Lodge duly open (*Brethren here cut the sign*) for the purposes of Freemasonry in the First Degree. *(The Worshipful Master gives the First Degree knocks which are repeated by the Senior Warden who raises his column, and by the Junior Warden who lowers his. The Inner Guard goes to the door and gives the same knocks, which are answered outside by the Tyler. The Immediate Past Master opens the Volume of the Sacred Law and arranges the Square and Compasses on it so that both points of the Compasses are beneath the Square. The Junior Deacon displays the First Degree tracing board. The Brethren seat themselves when the Worshipful Master does so).*

Chaplain

The Minutes are read, and Candidates balloted for and initiated, in the First Degree. Sometimes the custom is to open the Lodge in all three Degrees successively, and then resume working in the appropriate Degree. At the end the Lodge should be resumed in the Third Degree, and closed fully in all three degrees. In the interests of brevity, however, this is often curtailed.

OPENING THE LODGE IN THE SECOND DEGREE

(All Entered Apprentices or First Degree Masons are requested to retire. The Worshipful Master gives a single knock, repeated by the Senior and Junior Wardens).

W.M.   Brethren, assist me to open the Lodge in the Second Degree *(All rise)*.

W.M.   Bro. Junior Warden, what is the first care of every Fellow-Craft Freemason ?

J.W.   To see that the Lodge is properly tyled.

W.M.   Direct that duty to be done.

J.W.   Bro. Inner Guard, see that the Lodge is properly tyled.

(The Inner Guard goes to the door and gives the knocks of the First Degree which are answered by the Tyler. He then returns to his position, takes the step and gives the First Degree sign).

I.G.   Bro. Junior Warden, the Lodge is properly tyled.

J.W.   *(Gives First Degree knocks, takes the step and gives the First Degree sign)* Worshipful Master, the Lodge is properly tyled. *(Cuts sign).*

W.M.   Brother Senior Warden, the next care ?

S.W.   To see the Brethren appear to order as Masons.

W.M.   To order, Brethren, in the First Degree.

(The Worshipful Master and the Brethren take the step and give the sign of the First Degree).

W.M.   Bro. Junior Warden, are you a Fellow-Craft Freemason ?

J.W.   I am, Worshipful Master; try me, and prove me.

W.M.   By what instrument in Architecture will you be proved ?

J.W.   The Square.

W.M.   What is a Square ?

J.W.   An angle of ninety degrees, or the fourth part of a circle.

W.M.   Being yourself acquainted with the proper method, you will prove the Brethren Craftsmen, and demonstrate that proof to me by copying their example.

J.W.   Brethren, it is the Worshipful Master's command that you prove yourselves Craftsmen.

(Junior Warden keeps up First Degree sign while the Brethren cut it, take the step and give the Second Degree signs).

J.W. Worshipful Master, the Brethren have proved themselves Craftsmen, and in obedience to your command I thus copy their example. *(Cuts First Degree sign, takes step and gives Second Degree signs).*

W.M. Brother Junior Warden, I acknowledge the correctness of the sign *(Worshipful Master stands to order in the Second Degree)* Before we open the Lodge in the Second Degree, let us supplicate the Grand Geometrician of the Universe, that the rays of Heaven may shed their influence, to enlighten us in the paths of virtue and science.

I.P.M. So mote it be.

W.M. Brethren, in the name of the Grand Geometrician of the Universe, I declare the Lodge duly open *(all dismiss Hailing sign)* on the Square *(all give Penal sign by cutting sign of Fidelity)* for the instruction and improvement of Craftsmen.

(Worshipful Master gives Second Degree knocks, repeated by the Senior and Junior Wardens. The Inner Guard gives the knocks on the door, and is answered by the Tyler. The Immediate Past Master exposes one point of the Compasses above the Square, and the Junior Deacon displays the Second Degree tracing board. All seat themselves when the Worshipful Master does so).

OPENING THE LODGE IN THE THIRD DEGREE

(All Fellow-Craft or Second Degree Masons are requested to retire. The Worshipful Master gives a single knock which is repeated by the Senior and Junior Wardens).

W.M. Brethren, assist me to open the Lodge in the Third Degree. *(All rise).*

W.M. Bro. Junior Warden, what is the first care of every Master Mason ?

J.W. To see that the Lodge is properly tyled.

W.M. Direct that duty to be done.

J.W. Bro. Inner Guard, see that the Lodge is properly tyled. *(The Inner Guard goes to the door and gives Second Degree knocks, which are answered by the Tyler. He takes the step and Second Degree sign).*

I.G. Bro. Junior Warden, the Lodge is properly tyled.

J.W. *(Gives the Second Degree knocks, takes step and gives Second Degree sign)* Worshipful Master, the Lodge is properly tyled.

W.M. Bro. Senior Warden, the next care ?

S.W.	To see that the Brethren appear to order as Craftsmen.
W.M.	To order, Brethren, in the Second Degree. (*The Worshipful Master and Brethren, take step and give sign of Second Degree*).
W.M.	Bro. Junior Warden, are you a Master Mason ?
J.W.	I am, Worshipful Master; try me and prove me.
W.M.	By what instruments in Architecture will you be proved ?
J.W.	The Square and Compasses.
W.M.	Being yourself acquainted with the proper method, you will prove the Brethren Master Mason by signs, and demonstrate that proof to me by copying their example.
J.W.	Brethren, it is the Worshipful Master's command that you prove yourselves Master Masons by signs. (*The Junior Warden maintains Second Degree signs while the Brethren prove themselves by taking the step and giving the full signs of a Master Mason, i.e., the sign of Horror, the sign of Sympathy, and the Penal sign, in succession*).
J.W.	Worshipful Master, the Brethren have proved themselves Master Masons by signs, and in obedience to your command, I thus copy their example. (*Takes step, and gives full signs of the Third Degree*).
W.M.	Bro. Junior Warden, I acknowledge the correctness of the signs. (*Takes step and gives full signs*).
W.M.	Bro. Junior Warden, whence come you ?
J.W.	The East.
W.M.	Bro. Senior Warden, whither directing your course ?
S.W.	The West.
W.M.	(*To J.W.*) What inducement have you to leave the East and go to the West ?
J.W.	To seek for that which was lost, which, by your instructions and our own industry, we hope to find.
W.M.	(*To S.W.*) What is that which was lost ?
S.W.	The genuine secrets of a Master Mason.
W.M.	(*To J.W.*) How came they lost ?
J.W.	By the untimely death of our Master, Hiram Abiff.
W.M.	(*To S.W.*) Where do you hope to find them ?
S.W.	With the Centre.
W.M.	(*To J.W.*) What is a Centre ?
J.W.	A point within a circle, from which every part of the circumference is equidistant.
W.M.	(*To J.W.*) Why with the Centre.
S.W.	That being a point from which a Master Mason cannot err.
W.M.	We will assist you to repair that loss, and may Heaven aid our united endeavours.

I.P.M.	So mote it be.
W.M.	Brethren, in the name of the Most High, I declare the Lodge duly open (*all cut Penal sign, no recovery*) on the Centre, for the purpose of Freemasonry in the Third Degree.
	(*The Worshipful Master gives Third Degree knocks, which are repeated by the Senior and Junior Wardens. The Inner Guard gives them on the door, and is answered by the Tyler, The Immediate Past Master exposes both points of the Compasses above the Square, and the Junior Deacon exposes Third Degree tracing board*).
W.M.	All Glory to the Most High.
	(*All give the Grand or Royal Sign, and the Brethren take their seats when the W.M. does so*).

CLOSING THE LODGE IN THE THIRD DEGREE

	(*Worshipful Master gives a single knock, which is repeated by the Senior and Junior Wardens*).
W.M.	Brethren, assist me to close the Lodge in the Third Degree. (*All rise*).
W.M.	Bro. Junior Warden, what is the constant care of every Master Mason ?
J.W.	To prove the Lodge close tyled.
W.M.	Direct that duty to be done.
J.W.	Bro. Inner Guard, prove the Lodge close tyled.
	(*The Inner Guard goes to the door and gives the Third Degree knocks, which are answered by the Tyler He takes step and gives Third Degree Penal sign*).
I.G.	Bro. Junior Warden, the Lodge is close tyled. (*Cuts sign, recovers, then drops his right hand*).
J.W.	(*Gives Third Degree knocks, takes step and gives Third Degree Penal sign*). Worshipful Master, the Lodge is close tyled. (*Cuts sign, recovers and drops his right hand*).
W.M.	Bro. Senior Warden, the next care ?
S.W.	To see that the Brethren appear to order as Master Masons.
W.M.	To order, Brethren, in the Third Degree. (*The Worshipful Master and Brethren take step and stand to order with Third Degree Penal sign*).
W.M.	Bro. Junior Warden, whence come you ?
J.W.	The West, whither we have been in search of the genuine secrets of a Master Mason.
W.M.	Bro. Senior Warden, have you found them ?
S.W.	We have not, Worshipful Master, but we bring with us certain substituted secrets, which we are anxious to impart for your approbation.

W.M.   Let those substituted secrets be regularly communicated to me.

*(The two Wardens keeping up the Penal sign leave
their pedestals and come into the centre of the Lodge
facing each other about three feet apart, the Senior
Warden facing South and the Junior Warden North.
The Junior Warden takes the step, and gives the
Senior Warden the pass-grip leading from the Second
to the Third Degree; with their hands raised he whispers the pass-word TUBAL-CAIN. They then loose
hands, and both return to the Third Degree Penal
sign. The Junior Warden then takes another step,
and goes through the full signs of the Third Degree.
Then on the Five Points of Fellowship (hand to hand
in the Master Masons' grip, right foot alongside right
foot, knee to knee, breast to breast, and left hand
over back) he whispers the words of the Third Degree,
MACHABEN and MACHBINNA. The Junior War-
den salutes the Senior Warden with the Third Degree
Penal sign, recovers, and returns to his pedestal, still
keeping up the sign. The Senior Warden goes to the
centre of the Lodge, faces East, and keeps the Penal
sign).*

S.W.   Worshipful Master, condescend to receive from me
the substituted secrets of a Master Mason.

W.M.   Bro. Senior Warden, I will receive them with pleasure,
and for the information of the Brethren you will speak
the words aloud.

*The Worshipful Master leaves his pedestal by the
left, advances to within a yard of the Senior Warden,
takes the step, and receives the substituted secrets
from the Senior Warden in the same way as the
Junior Warden communicated them, only speaking
the words aloud. The Senior Warden salutes with the
Penal sign, recovers, and both return to their pedestals
keeping the sign).*

W.M.   Brethren, the substituted secrets of a Master Mason
thus regularly communicated to me, I, as Master
of this Lodge, and thereby the humble representative
of King Solomon, sanction and confirm with my
approbation; and declare that they shall designate
you and all Master Masons throughout the universe,
until time or circumstances shall restore the genuine.
(The Brethren, bending a little forward all exclaim)
With gratitude to our Master we bend.

W.M.   All gratitude to the Most High. *(The Worshipful
Master and Brethren give the Grand or Royal sign
and recover to the Third Degree Penal sign).*

91

W.M.	Bro. Senior Warden, the labours of this Degree being ended, you have my command to close the Lodge. (*Gives Third Degree knocks with his left hand*).
S.W.	Brethren, in the name of the Most High, and by command of the Worshipful Master, I close (*all cut sign*) this Master Mason's Lodge (*all recover, and then drop the hand. The Senior Warden gives the Third Degree knocks*).
J.W.	And it is closed accordingly. (*Repeats knocks. The Inner Guard repeats them at the door, and is answered by the Tyler. The Immediate Past Master conceals one point of the Compasses beneath the Square. The Junior Deacon attends to the tracing board. The Brethren sit when the Master does. Fellow-Craftsmen are admitted*).

CLOSING THE LODGE IN THE SECOND DEGREE
(The Worshipful Master gives single knock, which is repeated by the Senior and Junior Wardens).

W.M.	Brethren, assist me to close the Lodge in the Second Degree. (*All rise*).
W.M.	Bro. Junior Warden, what is the constant care of every Fellow-Craft Freemason ?
J.W.	To prove the Lodge close tyled.
W.M.	Direct that duty to be done.
J.W.	Bro. Inner Guard, prove the Lodge close tyled. (*The Inner Guard goes to the door and gives the knocks of the Second Degree, which are answered by the Tyler. He returns, gives step and sign of the Second Degree*).
I.G.	Bro. Junior Warden, the Lodge is close tyled. (*Cuts sign*).
J.W.	(*Knocks, step, and sign of the Second Degree*) Worshipful Master, the Lodge is close tyled. (*Cuts sign*).
W.M.	Bro. Senior Warden, the next care ?
S.W.	To see that the Brethren appear to order as Craftsmen.
W.M.	To order, Brethren, in the Second Degree. (*Worshipful Master and the Brethren take step and show sign of the Second Degree, which they hold until the Lodge is declared closed*).
W.M.	Bro. Junior Warden, in this position, what have you discovered ?
J.W.	A sacred symbol.
W.M.	Bro. Senior Warden, where is it situated ?
S.W.	In the centre of the building.
W.M.	(*To J.W.*) To whom does it allude ?
J.W.	The Grand Geometrician of the Universe.
W.M.	Then, Brethren, let us remember that wherever we are, and whatever we do, He is with us, and His

all-seeing eye observes us, and whilst we continue to act in conformity with the principles of the Craft, let us not fail to discharge our duty to Him with fervency and zeal.

I.P.M.   So mote it be.

W.M.   Bro. Senior Warden, the labours of this Degree being ended, you have my command to close the Lodge. (*Gives Second Degree knocks with his left hand, keeping up the sign with his right*).

S.W.   Brethren, in the name of the Grand Geometrician of the Universe, and by the command of the Worshipful Master, I close (*all drop Hailing sign with the left hand*) this Fellow-Crafts Lodge. (*All cut sign of Fidelity with the right hand. The Senior Warden gives Second Degree knocks*).

J.W.   Happy have we met.
Happy may we part.
And happy meet again.[1] (*Gives Second Degree knocks. The Inner Guard repeats them on the door, and is answered by the Tyler. The Immediate Past Master conceals both points of the Compasses under the Square. The Junior Deacon attends to the tracing boards. The Entered Apprentices are admitted*).

CLOSING THE LODGE

(*The Worshipful Master gives single knock, followed by the Senior and Junior Wardens*).

W.M.   Brethren, assist me to close the Lodge. (*All stand*).

W.M.   Bro. Junior Warden, what is the constant care of every Mason ?

J.W.   To prove the Lodge close tyled.

W.M.   Direct that duty to be done.

J.W.   Bro. Inner Guard, prove the Lodge close tyled.
(*The Inner Guard goes to the door and gives First Degree knocks, which are answered by the Tyler, and reports with step and sign of the First Degree*).

I.G.   Bro. Junior Warden, the Lodge is close tyled. (*Cuts sign*).

J.W.   (*With knocks, step and sign of the First Degree*) Worshipful Master, the Lodge is close tyled (*Cuts sign*).

W.M.   Bro. Senior Warden, the next care ?

S.W.   To see that the Brethren appear to order as Masons.

W.M.   To order, Brethren, in the First Degree. (*All take step and sign of First Degree*).

1. Other workings have what was probably the complete version of this jingle :

> Happy have we met,
> Happy have we been,
> Happy may we part,
> And happy meet again.

W.M.	Bro. Senior Warden, your constant place in the Lodge?
S.W.	In the West.
W.M.	Why are you placed there ?
S.W.	As the sun sets in the West to close the day, so the Senior Warden is placed in the West to close the Lodge by command of the Worshipful Master, after having seen that every Brother has had his due.
W.M.	Brethren, before we close the Lodge, let us with all reverence and humility express our gratitude to the Great Architect of the Universe for favours already received; may He continue to preserve the Order by cementing and adorning it with every moral and social virtue.
I.P.M.	So mote it be.
W.M.	Bro. Senior Warden, the labours of the evening being ended, you have my command to close the Lodge. (*Holding the sign, he gives First Degree knocks with his left hand*).
S.W.	Brethren, in the name of the Great Architect of the Universe and by command of the Worshipful Master, I close the Lodge. (*All cut sign. The Senior Warden gives First Degree knocks and lowers his column*).
J.W.	And it is closed accordingly, until the......day of ....emergencies excepted, of which every Brother will have due notice. (*Gives First Degree knocks, and raises his column. The knocks are repeated by the Inner Guard and Tyler. The Junior Deacon attends to the tracing board*).
I.P.M.	(*Removes Square and Compasses, and closes the Volume of the Sacred Law*) Brethren, nothing now remains, but, according to ancient custom, to lock up our secrets in a safe repository, uniting in the act of Fidelity, Fidelity, Fidelity.[1] *The Immediate Past Master and the Brethren strike their left breasts with the right hand, thumb closed as in so-called sign of Reverence, at each repetition of the word Fidelity*).

CEREMONY OF INITIATION

The Candidate is prepared for initiation by the Tyler in an anteroom outside the Lodge. He is divested of his coat, waistcoat, collar, and tie, and all articles of metal—money, keys, rings, studs and cuff-links, watch etc. His shirt is unbuttoned and opened to expose the left breast, and the right sleeve is rolled up above the elbow. His left trouser leg is rolled up above the knee, though it is the practice in some

---

1. The words " and may God preserve the Craft " are frequently added in conclusion. The closing hymn which may follow is given in Appendix C, p. 220.

Lodges to provide pyjama trousers to save spoiling the creases and to avoid difficulties over metal attachments to the braces or belt. The right shoe is taken off and replaced by a slipper (slipshod) of the " mule " type. A rope noose (cable-tow) usually of craft-blue silk is placed about his neck, the end hanging down his back. The Candidate is blindfolded with a ' hoodwink ' which may be of black velvet or of craft-blue.

In the meantime, the Lodge is opened in the First Degree, the minutes are read and confirmed, the Candidate is balloted for (if this has not been done before) and other business may be attended to. The Candidate signs the declaration book.

When all is ready, the Tyler gives the First Degree knocks on the door.

I.G.	*(Taking step and giving First Degree sign)* Keeps up sign Bro. Junior Warden, there is a report.
J.W.	*(Gives First Degree knocks, then rises with step and sign)* Worshipful Master, there is a report.
W.M.	Bro. Junior Warden, inquire who wants admission.
J.W.	*(Cuts sign and takes his seat)* Bro. Inner Guard see who wants admission.
I.G.	*(Cuts sign, opens the door, and addresses the Tyler outside)* Whom have you there ?
Ty.	Mr. A.B., a poor Candidate in a state of darkness who has been well and worthily recommended, regularly proposed and approved in open Lodge, and now comes of his own free will and accord, properly prepared, humbly soliciting to be admitted to the mysteries and privileges of Freemasonry.
I.G.	How does he hope to obtain those privileges ?
Can.	*(Prompted by Tyler)* By the help of God, being free and of good report.
I.G.	Halt while I report to the Worshipful Master. *(Closes the door, takes step and sign)* Worshipful Master, Mr. A.B., a poor Candidate in a state of darkness. etc. *(Same report as given by the Tyler).*
W.M.	How does he hope to obtain those privileges ?
I.G.	By the help of God, being free and of good report.
W.M.	The tongue of good report has already been heard in his favour; do you, Bro. Inner Guard, vouch that he is properly prepared ?
I.G.	I do, Worshipful Master.
W.M.	Then let him be admitted in due form. *(Inner Guard cuts sign)* Bro. Deacons. *(The Senior Deacon places the kneeling-stool in the North-East corner. The Candidate is met at the door by the Inner Guard who applies the point of a poniard to his bared left breast, and asks ;* Do you feel

anything ? On receiving an affirmative answer, the Inner Guard raises the poniard aloft to show the Worshipful Master that this duty has been done. The Junior Deacon then takes the Candidate's right hand with his left and leads him to the kneeling-stool).

W.M. Mr. A.B., as no person can be made a Mason unless he is free and of mature age, I demand of you, are you a free man and of the full age of twenty-one years?

Can. I am.

W.M. Thus assured, I will thank you to kneel, while the blessing of Heaven is invoked on our proceedings. *(Gives single knock, which is answered by the Wardens. The Brethren stand to order with the sign of Reverence, and the Deacons cross their wands over the Candidate's head. The Worshipful Master or Chaplain if there is one offers the following prayer).* Vouchsafe Thine aid, Almighty Father and Supreme Governor of the Universe, to our present convention, and grant that this Candidate for Freemasonry may so dedicate and devote his life to Thy service as to become a ~~pure~~ and faithful Brother among us. Endue him with a competency of Thy Divine Wisdom, that, assisted by the secrets of our Masonic art, he may the better be enabled to unfold the beauties of true Godliness, to the honour and glory of Thy Holy Name.

I.P.M. So mote it be. *(All dismiss the sign of Reverence and the Deacons lower their wands).*

W.M. In all cases of difficulty and danger, in whom do you put your trust ?

Can. In God.

W.M. Right glad am I to find your faith so well founded : relying on such sure support you may safely rise and follow your leader with a firm but humble confidence, for where the name of God is invoked we trust no danger can ensue.
(The Junior Deacon assists the Candidate to rise, and the Senior Deacon draws aside the kneeling-stool. The Worshipful Master and the Brethren seat themselves).

W.M. *(Give single knock, repeated in turn by the Wardens)* The Brethren from the North, East, South and West will take notice that Mr. A. B. is about to pass in view before them, to show that he is the Candidate properly prepared, and a fit and proper person to be made a Mason.
(The Senior Deacon places the kneeling-stool in

position before the Worshipful Master's pedestal in the East, and gives the poniard to him. The Junior Deacon takes the Candidate firmly by the right hand, leads him up the North, across the East, and down the South, carefully ' squaring' the Lodge at the corners by coming to a halt, turning, and leading off again with the left foot. Arriving at the Junior Warden, he taps that officer's right shoulder three times with the Candidate's right hand).

J.W. Whom have you there ?

J.D. Mr. A.B., a poor candidate in a state of darkness, etc., *(Same report as before).*

J.W. How does he hope to obtain those privileges ?

J.D. By the help of God, being free and of good report.

J.W. *(Taking Candidate's right hand)* Enter, free and of good report.

(The Junior Deacon conducts the Candidate to the Senior Warden, squaring the Lodge at the South-West corner. The same examination is gone through again. They then pass to the left of the Senior Warden, and face East). Hand over Can.

S.W. *(Taking step and sign)* Worshipful Master, I present to you Mr. A.B., a Candidate properly prepared to be made a Mason.

W.M. Bro. Senior Warden, your presentation shall be attended to, for which purpose I shall address a few questions to the Candidate, which I trust he will answer with candour.
Do you seriously declare on your honour that, unbiased by the improper solicitation of friends against your own inclination, and uninfluenced by mercenary or other unworthy motive, you freely and voluntarily offer yourself a Candidate for the mysteries and privileges of Freemasonry ?

Can. I do.

W.M. Do you likewise pledge yourself that you are prompted to solicit those privileges by a favourable opinion preconceived of the Institution, a general desire of knowledge, and a sincere wish to render yourself more extensively serviceable to your fellow-creatures ?

Can. I do.

W.M. Do you further seriously declare on your honour, that, avoiding fear on the one hand, and rashness on the other, you will steadily persevere through the ceremony of your initiation, and if once admitted, you will afterwards act and abide by the ancient usages and established customs of the order ?

Can. I do.

W.M. Brother Senior Warden, you will direct the Junior Deacon to instruct the Candidate to advance to the pedestal in due form.

S.W. Bro. Junior Deacon, it is the Worshipful Master's command that you instruct the Candidate to advance to the pedestal in due form.
(*The Junior Deacon leads the Candidate to within about a yard of the pedestal. He then directs him to stand with his heels together and his feet at right angles, the left foot facing East and the right foot facing South*).

J.D. Take a short pace with your left foot, bringing the heels together in the form of a square. Take another, a little longer, heel to heel as before. Another still longer, heels together as before.
(*The Candidate should now be in a position to kneel before the pedestal. Meanwhile the Senior Deacon has come up, and stands to the left of the Candidate, the Junior Deacon on the right, all three facing East*).

W.M. It is my duty to inform you that Masonry is free, and requires a perfect freedom of inclination in every Candidate for its mysteries. It is founded on the purest principles of piety and virtue ; it possesses great and invaluable privileges ; and in order to secure those privileges to worthy men, and we trust to worthy men alone, vows of fidelity are required ; but let me assure you that in those vows there is nothing incompatible with your civil, moral, or religious duties ; are you therefore willing to take a Solemn Obligation, founded on the principles I have stated, to keep inviolate the secrets and mysteries of the Order ?

Can. I am.

W.M. Then you will kneel on your left knee, your right foot formed in a square, give me your right hand which I place on the Volume of the Sacred Law, while your left will be employed in supporting these compasses, one point presented to your naked left breast.
(*The Senior Deacon helps to make this adjustment. The Compasses are open at right angles, the upper point held to the Candidate's bare breast. The Master gives a single knock, repeated by the Wardens. The Brethren rise and stand to order with the sign of the Degree. The Deacons cross their wands over the Candidate's head, holding them in their left hands, keeping up the sign with the right*).

W.M. Repeat your name at length, and say after me :—

OBLIGATION

Can. I, A. B. in the presence of the Great Architect of
the Universe, and of this worthy, worshipful, and
warranted Lodge of Free and Accepted Masons, regularly assembled and properly dedicated, of my own
free will and accord, do hereby (*W.M. touches Candidate's right hand with his left hand*) and hereon
(*W.M. touches the Bible with his left hand*) sincerely
and solemnly promise and swear, that I will always
hele, conceal, and never reveal any part or parts,
point or points of the secrets or mysteries of or
belonging to Free and Accepted Masons in Masonry,
which may heretofore have been known by me, or
shall now or at any future period be communicated
to me, unless it be to a true and lawful Brother or
Brothers, and not even to him or them, until after
due trial, strict examination, or sure information from
a well-known Brother, that he or they are worthy
of that confidence, or in the body of a just, perfect,
and regular Lodge of Ancient Freemasons. I further
solemnly promise that I will not write those secrets,
indite, carve, mark, engrave or otherwise them
delineate, or cause or suffer it to be so done by others,
if in my power to prevent it, on anything movable or
immovable, under the canopy of Heaven, whereby
or whereon any letter, character or figure, or the least
trace of a letter, character or figure, may become
legible, or intelligible to myself or anyone in the
world, so that our secret arts and hidden mysteries
may improperly become known through my unworthi-
ness.   These several points I solemnly swear to
observe, without evasion, equivocation, or mental
reservation of any kind, ~~under no less a~~ penalty, on
the violation of any of them, ~~than that~~ of having ~~my~~ *the*
throat cut across, ~~my~~ tongue torn out by the root,
and buried in the sand of the sea at low water mark,
or a cable's length from the shore, where the tide
regularly ebbs and flows twice in twenty-four hours,
or the more effective punishment of being branded
as a wilfully perjured individual, void of all moral
worth, and totally unfit to be received into this
worshipful Lodge, or any other warranted Lodge or
society of men, who prize honour and virtue above
the external advantages of rank and fortune.[1] So
help me, God, and keep me steadfast in this my Great

1. Bristol workings have " or until this horrible punishment shall be
inflicted, the less dreadful (but to an honest mind) of being further
branded as etc." For the Irish version, see p. 192.

99

OBLIGATION

and Solemn Obligation of an Entered Apprentice Freemason.

(*All cut sign, the Deacons lower their wands, and the Worshipful Master removes the compasses from the Candidate's hand*).

W.M. What you have repeated may be considered but a serious promise ; as a pledge of your fidelity, and to render it a Solemn Obligation, you will seal it with your lips on the Volume of the Sacred Law. (*Candidate does so*).

W.M. Having been kept for a considerable time in a state of darkness, what in your present situation is the predominant wish of your heart ?

Can. Light.

W.M. Bro. Junior Deacon, let that blessing be restored to the Candidate.

(*The Worshipful Master waves his gavel left, right, then down on the pedestal. The Brethren simultaneously clap their hands, the Junior Deacon removes the hoodwink, and shields the Candidate's eyes so that they are directed to the Bible in front of him. He then removes the cable-tow*).

W.M. Having been restored to the blessing of material light, let me point out to your attention what we consider the three great, though emblematical lights in Freemasonry ; they are, the Volume of the Sacred Law, the Square, and Compasses ; the Sacred Writings are to govern our faith, the Square to regulate our actions, and the Compasses to keep us in due bounds with all mankind, particularly our brethren in Freemasonry. (*He takes the Candidate's right hand in his*). Rise, newly obligated Brother among Masons. You are now enabled to discover the three lesser lights ; they are situated East, South, and West, and are meant to represent the Sun, Moon, and Master of the Lodge ; the Sun to rule the day, the Moon to govern the night, and the Master to rule and direct his Lodge. Bro. A. B., by your meek and candid behaviour this evening, you have escaped two great dangers, but there is a third which will await you until the latest period of your existence. The dangers you have escaped are those of stabbing and strangling, for on your entrance into the Lodge this poniard (*unsheathes it and shows it to the Candidate*) was presented to your naked left breast, so that had you rashly attempted to rush forward you would have been accessory to your own death by stabbing, whilst the Brother who held it would have remained firm

The W.M. SD & Brethren resume their seats. Can is placed by SD at R. of W.M.

ENTRUST

would ~~would~~ traditionally ~~would~~
have awaited

referred to in

W.M. and done his duty. There was likewise this cable-
tow (*shows it*) with a running noose about your neck,
which would have rendered any attempt at retreat
equally fatal ; but the danger which ~~will await~~ you
until your latest hour ~~is~~ the penalty ~~of~~ your Obligation,
of having ~~your~~ throat cut across should you improperly
disclose the secrets of Masonry.

Having taken the Great and Solemn Obligation of a
Mason, I am now permitted to inform you that there
are several degrees in Freemasonry, and peculiar
secrets restricted to each ; these, however, are not
communicated indiscriminately, but are conferred on
Candidates according to merit and abilities. I shall,
therefore, proceed to entrust you with the secrets of
this degree, or those marks by which we are known
to each other, and distinguished from the rest of the
world ; but must premise for your general information that all s——, l——, and p—————— are
true and proper signs, to know a Mason by. You
are therefore expected to stand perfectly erect, your
feet formed in a square, your body being thus
considered an emblem of your mind, and your feet
of the rectitude of your actions.

You will now take a short pace towards me with your
left foot, bringing the right heel into its hollow.
That is the first regular step in Freemasonry, and it
is in this position that the secrets of the degree are
communicated. They consist of a s——, t——, and
w——.

Place your ——— in this position with the ———
extended in the form of a square to the ———
————. The sign is given by ——————————
——— ——— ——— ——— ——— ——— ———.
(*He illustrates the sign, which the Candidate copies*).
This is in allusion to the penalty of your Obligation,
implying that as a man of honour ~~and~~ a Mason
~~——~~ would rather have ~~your throat cut across~~ (*again
illustrates sign*) than improperly disclose the secrets
entrusted to ~~you~~ *him*.

The grip or token is given by a distinct ~~pressure~~ of
the ~~thumb~~ on the ~~first joint of the hand~~ ; (*demonstrates
with Candidate*) this, when regularly given and received, serves to distinguish a Brother by night as well
as by day. This grip or token demands a word, a
word highly prized amongst Masons as a guard to
their privileges. Too much caution, therefore, cannot
be observed in communicating it ; it should never be
given at length, but always by letters or syllables ; to

ENTRUSTING (handwritten in left margin)

W.M.	enable you to do which, I must first tell you what that word is : it is ▓▓▓▓.
	(*The Candidate repeats the word. The Worshipful Master then spells it, which the Candidate also repeats*).
W.M.	As in the course of the ceremony you will be called on for this word, the Junior Deacon will now dictate the answers you are to give.
W.M.	(*Giving the grip*) What is this ?
Can.	(*Who is prompted by the Junior Deacon in giving these answers*) The grip or token of an Entered Apprentice Freemason.
W.M.	What does it demand ?
Can.	A word.
W.M.	Give me that word.
Can.	At my initiation I was taught to be cautious ; I will letter or halve it with you.
W.M.	Which you please, and begin.
Can.	(*Still prompted by Junior Deacon*) ▓▓.
W.M.	▓▓.
Can.	▓▓▓▓▓.
W.M.	This word is derived from the ▓▓▓ h▓▓▓ p▓▓▓ at the p▓▓▓▓▓▓ or e▓▓▓▓▓ of K▓▓ S▓▓▓▓▓▓ T▓▓▓▓▓, so named after ▓▓▓▓, the g▓▓▓ g▓▓▓▓▓▓▓▓ of D▓▓▓▓, a P▓▓▓▓ and R▓▓▓ in I▓▓▓▓. The import of the word is ' in ▓▓▓▓▓▓.' Pass, ▓▓▓▓.
	(*The Junior Deacon leads the Candidate to the Junior Warden's Pedestal, instructing him how to ' square the Lodge ' at the South-East corner*).
J.D.	(*With step and sign*) Bro. Junior Warden, I present to you Bro. A. B. on his Initiation.
J.W.	I will thank Bro. A. B. to advance to me as a Mason. (*Candidate takes step and gives sign*). Have you anything to communicate ?
Can.	I have. (*Gives the grip, assisted by Junior Deacon*).
J.W.	What is this ?
Can.	The grip or token of an Entered Apprentice Freemason.
J.W.	What does it demand ?
Can.	A word.
J.W.	Give me that word.
Can.	At my initiation I was taught to be cautious ; I will letter or halve it with you.
J.W.	Which you please, and begin.
Can.	B.
J.W.	O.
Can.	A.
J.W.	Z.

Can.	BO.
J.W.	AZ.
Can.	BOAZ.
J.W.	Pass, Boaz.
	(The Junior Deacon conducts the Candidate, squaring the Lodge at the corner, to the Senior Warden's pedestal, where he takes step and gives sign).
J.D.	Bro. Senior Warden, I present to you Bro. A. B. on his Initiation *(cuts sign)*.
S.W.	I will thank Bro. A. B. to advance to me as a Mason *(Candidate takes step)*. What is that ?
Can.	The first regular step in Freemasonry.
S.W.	Do you bring anything else ?
Can.	I do. *(Gives sign)*.
S.W.	What is that ?
Can.	The sign of an Entered Apprentice Freemason.
S.W.	To what does it allude ?
Can.	The penalty of my Obligation, implying that as a man of honour, and a Mason, I would rather have my throat cut across *(gives sign again)* than improperly disclose the secrets entrusted to me.
S.W.	Have you anything to communicate ?
Can.	I have. *(Gives grip)*.
S.W.	What is this ?
Can.	The grip or token of an Entered Apprentice Freemason.
S.W.	What does it demand ?
Can.	A word.
S.W.	Give me that word.
Can.	At my initiation I was taught to be cautious ; I will letter or halve it with you.
S.W.	Which you please, and begin. *(The word is halved exactly as in the first place with the Worshipful Master).*
S.W.	Whence is this word derived ?
Can.	From the left hand pillar at the porchway or entrance to King Solomon's Temple, so named after Boaz, the great-grandfather of David, a Prince and Ruler in Israel.
S.W.	The import of the word ?
Can.	In strength.
S.W.	Pass, Boaz.
	(The Junior Deacon conducts the Candidate to the Worshipful Master in the East).
S.W.	*(With step and sign)* Worshipful Master, I present to you Bro. A. B. on his Initiation, for some mark of your favour.
W.M.	Brother Senior Warden, I delegate you to invest him

W.M.   with the distinguishing badge of a Mason.

(The Senior Warden, assisted by the Junior Deacon, invests the Candidate with the Entered Apprentice badge or apron. This is of pure white lambskin, with no adornment of any kind. The Senior Warden holds the lower right hand corner of the apron in his right hand while he is speaking).

S.W.   Bro. A. B., by the Worshipful Master's command, I invest you with the distinguishing badge of a Mason. It is more ancient than the Golden Fleece or Roman Eagle, more honourable than the Garter or any other Order in existence, being the badge of innocence and the bond of friendship. I strongly exhort you ever to wear and consider it as such ; and further inform you, that if you never disgrace that badge *(Senior Warden here strikes the Candidate's apron with his right hand ; the Brethren simultaneously strike theirs)* it will never disgrace you.

W.M.   Let me add to the observations of the Senior Warden, that you are never to put on that badge should you be about to visit a Lodge in which there is a Brother with whom you are at variance, or against whom you entertain animosity. In such cases it is expected that you will invite him to withdraw, in order amicably to settle your differences, which being happily effected, you may then clothe yourselves, enter the Lodge, and work with that love and harmony which should at all times characterise Freemasons. But if, unfortunately, your difficulties be of such a nature as not to be so easily adjusted, it were better that one or both of you retire than that the harmony of the Lodge should be disturbed by your presence.

Brother Junior Deacon, you will place our new-made Brother at the North East part of the Lodge. *(This is done. Both face South).*

J.D.   Left foot across the Lodge, right foot down the Lodge, pay attention to the Worshipful Master.

W.M.   It is customary, at the erection of all stately and superb edifices, to lay the first foundation stone at the North East corner of the building. You, being newly admitted into Masonry, are placed at the North-East part of the Lodge, figuratively to represent that stone, and from the foundation, laid this evening, may you raise a superstructure perfect in its parts and honourable to the builder.

You now stand, to all external appearances, a just and upright Mason, and I give it you in strong terms of recommendation ever to continue and act as such.

W.M. Indeed, I shall immediately proceed to put your
principles, in some measure, to the test, by calling
upon you to exercise that virtue which may justly
be denominated the distinguishing characteristic of
a Freemason's heart—I mean charity. I need not
here dilate on its excellences; no doubt it has often
been felt and practised by you. Suffice it to say,
it has the approbation of Heaven and earth, and, like
its sister, mercy, blesses him who gives as well as
him who receives.
In a society so widely extended as Freemasonry, the
branches of which are spread over the four quarters
of the globe, it cannot be denied that we have many
members of rank and opulence; neither can it be concealed that, among the thousands who range under its
banners, there are some who, perhaps from circumstances of unavoidable calamity and misfortune, are
reduced to the lowest ebb of poverty and distress. On
their behalf it is our usual custom to awaken the
feelings of every new-made Brother by such a claim
on his charity as his circumstances in life may fairly
warrant. Whatever therefore you feel disposed to
give you will deposit with the Junior Deacon; it will
be thankfully received and faithfully applied.

J.D. (*Presenting the alms dish*) Have you anything to give
in the cause of charity ?
(*The Candidate is left in some embarrassment to
form his own answer, which will probably indicate
in his own words that his money has been left behind
in the ante-room, and he has nothing on him*).

J.D. Were you deprived of everything valuable previously
to entering the Lodge ? (*Candidate is left to answer
affirmatively*). If you had not been so deprived,
would you give freely ? (*Again an affirmative answer
is expected. But he should not be prompted*).

J.D. (*With step and sign*) Worshipful Master, our new-
made Brother affirms that he was deprived of everything valuable previously to entering the Lodge, or he
would give freely. (*Cuts sign*).

W.M. I congratulate you on the honourable sentiments by
which you are actuated, likewise on the inability
which in the present instance precludes you from
gratifying them; believe me, this trial was not made
with a view to sport with your feelings; far be from
us any such intention; it was done for three especial
reasons—first, as I have already premised, to put
your principles to the test; secondly, to evince to the
Brethren that you had neither money nor metallic

W.M.   substance about you, for if you had, the ceremony of your initiation, thus far, must have been repeated; and thirdly, as a warning to your own heart, that should you at any future period meet a Brother in distressed circumstances, who might solicit your assistance, you will remember the peculiar moment you were received into Masonry, poor and penniless, and cheerfully embrace the opportunity of practising that virtue you have professed to admire.

(The Junior Deacon places the Candidate in front of the Worshipful Master. The Immediate Past Master places the box of working tools on the pedestal if they are not already there).

W.M.   I now present to you the working tools of an Entered Apprentice Freemason: they are the 24 inch Gauge, the common Gavel and Chisel. The 24 inch Gauge is to measure our work; the common Gavel to knock off all superfluous knobs and excrescences, and the Chisel to further smooth and prepare the stone and render it fit for the hands of the more expert workman. But, as we are not all operative Masons, but rather free and accepted or speculative, we apply these tools to our morals. In this sense, the 24 inch Gauge represents the twenty-four hours of the day, part to be spent in prayer to Almighty God ; part in labour and refreshment ; and part in serving a friend or Brother in time of need, without detriment to ourselves or connections. The common Gavel represents the force of conscience, which should keep down all vain and unbecoming thoughts which might obtrude during any of the aforementioned periods, so that our words and actions may ascend unpolluted to the Throne of Grace. The Chisel points out to us the advantages of education, by which means alone we are rendered fit members of regularly organised society.

As in the course of the evening you will be called on for certain fees for your initiation, it is proper you should know by what authority we act. This is our Charter or Warrant from the Grand Lodge of England (*opens and shows the Charter*) which is for your inspection on this or any future evening. This is the Book of Constitutions (*presents a copy to the Candidate*) and these are our by-laws (*presents copy*), both of which I recommend to your serious perusal, as by one you will be instructed in the duties you owe to the Craft in general, and by the other in those you owe to this Lodge in particular.

W.M.   You are now at liberty to retire, in order to restore yourself to your personal comforts, and on your return to the Lodge I shall call your attention to a Charge, founded on the excellence of the Institution and the qualifications of its members.

(The Junior Deacon conducts the Candidate to the left of the Senior Warden, and instructs him to salute the Worshipful Master as a Mason, with step and sign. The Candidate then retires and resumes his ordinary clothing, including his apron. When he is ready, the Tyler gives the First Degree knocks).

I.G.   *(With step and sign)* Brother Junior Warden, there is a report.
        (Junior Warden gives one knock, Inner Guard opens the door).
Ty.   The Candidate on his return.
I.G.   *(With step and sign)* Worshipful Master, the Candidate on his return.
W.M.   Admit him. *(Inner Guard cuts sign. Junior Deacon goes to the door and takes the Candidate by the hand on his entry. He again orders him to salute the Worshipful Master as a Mason, and conducts him to the North of the Senior Warden's pedestal while the Charge is given. This is delivered by the Worshipful Master, by a Past Master, or by a Warden).*

CHARGE AFTER INITIATION

Bro. A. B. as you have passed through the ceremony of your initiation, let me congratulate you on being admitted a member of our ancient and honourable institution. Ancient, no doubt it is, as having subsisted from time immemorial, and honourable it must be acknowledged to be, as by a natural tendency it conduces to make those so who are obedient to its precepts. Indeed no institution can boast a more solid foundation than that on which Freemasonry rests, the practice of every moral and social virtue. And to so high an eminence has its credit been advanced that in every age monarchs themselves have been promoters of the art ; have not thought it derogatory to their dignity to exchange the sceptre for the trowel ; have patronised our mysteries and joined in our assemblies.

As a Freemason, let me recommend to your most serious contemplation the Volume of the Sacred Law, charging you to consider it as the unerring standard of truth and justice, and to regulate your actions by the divine precepts it contains. Therein you will be taught the important duties you owe to God, to your neighbour, and to yourself. To God, by never mentioning His name but with that awe and reverence which are due from the creature to his Creator, by imploring His aid in all your lawful undertakings, and by looking up to Him in every emergency for comfort and support. To your neighbour, by acting with him on the square, by rendering him every kind office which justice or mercy may require, by relieving his necessities and soothing his afflictions, and by doing to him as in similar cases you would wish he would do to you. And to yourself, by such a prudent and well-regulated course of discipline as may best conduce to the preservation of your corporeal and mental faculties in their fullest energy, thereby enabling you to exert those talents wherewith God has blessed you, as well to His glory as the welfare of your fellow-creatures.

As a citizen of the world, I am to enjoin you to be exemplary in the discharge of your civil duties by never proposing or at all countenancing any act that may have a tendency to subvert the peace and good order of society ; by paying due obedience to the laws of any State which may for a time become the place of your residence or afford you its protection and above all, by never losing sight of the allegiance due to the Sovereign of your native land, ever remembering that nature has implanted in your breast a sacred and indissoluble attachment towards that country whence you derived your birth and infant nurture.

As an individual, let me recommend the practice of every domestic as well as public virtue : let Prudence direct you, Temperance chasten you, Fortitude support you, and Justice be the guide of all your actions. Be especially careful to maintain in their fullest splendour those truly Masonic ornaments which have already been amply illustrated, Benevolence and Charity.

Still as a Freemason there are other excellences of character to which your attention may be peculiarly and forcibly directed. Amongst the foremost of these are secrecy, fidelity, and obedience. Secrecy consists in an inviolable adherence to the Obligation you have entered into, never improperly to disclose any of those Masonic secrets which have now been, or may, at any future period, be entrusted to your keeping, and cautiously to avoid all occasions which may inadvertently lead you so to do. Your fidelity must be exemplified by a strict observance of the Constitutions of the Fraternity, by adhering to the ancient landmarks of the Order, by never attempting to extort or otherwise unduly obtain the secrets of a superior degree, and by refraining from recommending anyone to a participation of our secrets unless you have strong grounds to believe that by a similar fidelity he will ultimately reflect honour on your choice. Your obedience must be proved by a strict observance of our laws and regulations, by prompt attention to all signs and summonses, by modest and correct demeanour in the Lodge, by abstaining from every topic of political or religious discussion, by a ready acquiescence in all votes and resolutions duly passed by a majority of the brethren, and by perfect submission to the Master and his Wardens whilst acting in the discharge of their respective offices.

And as a last general recommendation, let me exhort you to dedicate yourself to such pursuits as may at once enable you to be respectable in life, useful to mankind, and an ornament to the society of which you have this day become a member. To study more especially such of the liberal arts and sciences as may lie within the compass of your attainment, and without neglecting the ordinary duties of your station, to endeavour to make a daily advancement in Masonic knowledge.

From the very commendable attention you appear to have given to this charge, I am led to hope you will duly appreciate the value of Freemasonry, and indelibly imprint on your heart the sacred dictates of Truth, of Honour, and of Virtue.

EXPLANATION OF THE
FIRST DEGREE TRACING-BOARD

The usages and customs among Freemasons have ever borne a near affinity to those of the ancient Egyptians. Their philosophers, unwilling to expose their mysteries to vulgar eyes, couched their systems of learning and polity under signs and hieroglyphical figures, which were communicated to their chief priests or Magi alone, who were bound by solemn oath to conceal them. The system of Pythagoras was founded on a similar principle, as well as many others of more recent date. Masonry, however, is not only the most ancient but the most honourable Society that ever existed, as there is not a character or emblem here depicted but serves to inculcate the principles of piety and virtue among all its genuine professors. Let me first call your attention to the form of the Lodge, which is a parallelopipedon, in length from East to West, in breadth between North and South, in depth from the surface of the earth to the centre, even as high as the heavens. The reason a Freemasons' Lodge is described of this vast extent is to show the universality of the science ; likewise a Mason's charity should know no bounds save those of prudence.

Our Lodges stand on holy ground, because the first Lodge was consecrated on account of three grand offerings thereon made, which met with Divine approbation. First, the ready

First Degree Tracing Board

compliance of Abraham with the will of God in not refusing to offer up his son Isaac as a burnt sacrifice, when it pleased the Almighty to substitute a more agreeable victim in his stead. Secondly, the many pious prayers and ejaculations of King David, which actually appeased the wrath of God and stayed a pestilence which then raged among his people, owing to his inadvertently having them numbered. Thirdly, the many thanksgivings, oblations, burnt sacrifices, and costly offerings, which Solomon, King of Israel, made at the completion, dedication, and consecration of the Temple of Jerusalem to God's service. Those three did then, do now, and I trust ever will, render the ground of Freemasonry holy.

Our Lodges are situated due East and West, because all places of Divine Worship as well as Masons' regular, well-formed, constituted Lodges are, or ought to be, so situated : for which we assign three Masonic reasons : first, the Sun the Glory of the Lord, rises in the East and sets in the West ; second, learning originated in the East and thence spread its benign influence to the West ; the third, last and grand reason, which is too long to be entered upon now, is explained in the course of our Lectures, which I hope you will have many opportunities of hearing.[1]

Our Lodges are supported by three great pillars. They are called Wisdom, Strength, and Beauty ; Wisdom to contrive, Strength to support, and Beauty to adorn : Wisdom to conduct us in all our undertakings, Strength to support us under all our difficulties, and Beauty to adorn the inward man. The Universe is the Temple of the Deity whom we serve ; Wisdom, Strength and Beauty are about His throne as pillars of His works, for His Wisdom is infinite, His Strength omnipotent, and Beauty shines through the whole of the creation in symmetry and order. The Heavens He has stretched forth as a canopy ; the earth He has planted as a footstool ; He crowns His Temple with Stars as with a Diadem, and with His hand He extends the Power and Glory. The Sun and Moon are messengers of His will, and all His Law is concord. The three great pillars supporting a Freemasons' Lodge are emblematic of those Divine attributes, and further represent Solomon King of Israel, Hiram King of Tyre, and Hiram Abiff. Solomon King of Israel for his Wisdom in building, completing, and dedicating the Temple at Jerusalem to God's service ; Hiram King of Tyre for his Strength in supporting him with men and materials ; and Hiram Abiff for his curious and masterly workmanship in beautifying and adorning the same.

1. The three reasons are explained at length in the fourth section of the first lecture. The third reason is that Moses pitched his tent or tabernacle on Mount Sinai East and West, and this provided the ground plan for King Solomon's Temple.

But as we have no noble orders of Architecture known by the names of Wisdom, Strength, and Beauty, we refer them to the three most celebrated, which are the Ionic, Doric, and Corinthian.

The covering of a Freemasons' Lodge is a celestial canopy of divers colours, even the Heavens. The way by which we, as Masons, hope to arrive there is by the assistance of a ladder, in Scripture called Jacob's ladder. It is composed of many staves or rounds, which point out as many moral virtues, but three principal ones, which are Faith, Hope, and Charity : Faith in the Great Architect of the Universe, Hope in salvation, and to be in Charity with all men. It reaches to the Heavens, and rests on the Volume of the Sacred Law, because, by the doctrines contained in that Holy Book, we are taught to believe in the dispensations of Divine Providence, which belief strengthens our faith, and enables us to ascend the first step ; this Faith naturally creates in us a Hope of becoming partakers of the blessed promises therein recorded, which Hope enables us to ascend the second step ; but the third and last, being Charity, comprehends the whole, and the Mason who is possessed of this virtue in its most ample sense may justly be deemed to have attained the summit of his profession ; figuratively speaking, an Ethereal Mansion, veiled from mortal eyes by the starry firmament, emblematically depicted here by seven stars, which have an allusion to as many regularly made Masons, without which number no Lodge is perfect, neither can any Candidate be legally initiated into the Order.

The interior of a Freemasons' Lodge is composed of Ornaments, Furniture, and Jewels. The Ornaments of the Lodge are the Mosaic pavement, the Blazing Star, and the Indented or Tesselated border ; the Mosaic pavement is that beautiful flooring of the Lodge, the Blazing Star the Glory in the centre, and the indented or Tesselated Border the skirtwork round the same. The Mosaic pavement may justly be deemed the beautiful flooring of a Freemasons' Lodge, by reason of its being variegated and chequered. This points out the diversity of objects which decorate and adorn the creation, the animate as well as the inanimate parts thereof. The Blazing Star, or Glory in the centre, refers us to the Sun, which enlightens the earth, and by its benign influence dispenses its blessings to mankind in general. The indented or Tesselated Border refers us to the Planets, which in their various revolutions form a beautiful border or skirtwork round that Grand Luminary, the Sun, as the other does round that of a Freemasons' Lodge. The Furniture of the Lodge consists of the Volume of the Sacred Law, the Compasses and Square ; the Sacred Writings are to rule and govern our faith, on them we obligate our Candidates for Freemasonry ; so are the Compasses and Square, when united to regulate our lives and actions. The Sacred Volume is derived from God to man in general, the Compasses belong to the Grand Master in particular, and the Square to the whole Craft.

The jewels of the Lodge are three movable and three immovable, the movable Jewels are the Square, Level, and Plumb Rule. Among operative Masons the Square is to try and adjust rectangular corners of buildings, and assist in bringing rude matter into due form ; the Level to lay levels and prove horizontals ; and the Plumb Rule to try and adjust uprights, while fixing them on their proper bases. Among Free and Accepted Masons, the Square teaches morality, the Level equality, and the Plumb Rule justness and uprightness of life and actions. They are called Movable Jewels, because they are worn by the Master and his Wardens, and are transferable to their successors on nights of Installation. The Master is distinguished by the Square, the Senior Warden by the Level, and the Junior Warden by the Plumb Rule. The Immovable Jewels are the Tracing Board, and the Rough and Perfect Ashlars. The Tracing Board is for the Master to lay lines and draw designs on ; the rough Ashlar for the Entered Apprentice to work, mark, and indent on ; and the Perfect Ashlar for the experienced Craftsman to try and adjust his jewels on. They are called Immovable Jewels, because they lie open and immovable in the Lodge for the Brethren to moralise on.

As the Tracing Board is for the Master to lay lines and draw designs on, the better to enable the Brethren to carry on the intended structure with regularity and propriety, so the Volume of the Sacred Law may justly be deemed the Spiritual Tracing Board of the Great Architect of the Universe, in which are laid down such Divine Laws and Moral Plans, that were we conversant therein, and adherent thereto, would bring us to an Ethereal Mansion not made with hands, eternal in the Heavens. The Rough Ashlar is a stone, rough and unhewn as taken from the quarry, until by the industry and ingenuity of the workman it is modelled, wrought into due form and rendered fit for the intended structure ; this represents man in his infant or primitive state, rough and unpolished as that stone, until by the kind care and attention of his parents or guardians, in giving him a liberal and virtuous education, his mind becomes cultivated, and he is thereby rendered a fit member of civilised society. The Perfect Ashlar is a stone of true die or square fit only to be tried by the Square and Compasses ; this represents man in the decline of years, after a regular well-spent life in acts of piety and virtue, which can no otherwise be tried and approved than by the Square of God's Word and the Compass of his own self-convincing conscience.

In all regu...
point within...
circle is bou...
parallel lines...
Solomon ; o...
of the Sacred...
reaches to th...
Holy Book, a...
as those para...
not deceive...
round this c...
parallel lines...
Mason keeps...

The word...
certain piece...
cramp, and...
powers, such...
Mason to r...
encumbrance...
likewise den...
is to bear t...
reason of th...
in time of...
happy and...
being made...
dignified.

Pendant t...
to remind u...
Fortitude, F...
informs us,...
our ancient...
good Freem...
ever be four...

Analysis of F.C.

1. Questions
2. Entrusting P.W
3. Entrance
4. Prayer
5. Perambulation 1 — S.W. ...
6. Perambulation — 2 — S.W. P...
7. Advance to E
8. Obligation
9. Entrusting
10. Perambulation 3 — S.W
    ditto.   S.W.
11. Badge
12. Charge
13. Tools
14. Exit
15. Tracing Board.

CEREMONY OF PASSING TO THE ...

(*The Lodge is opened in the First Degree, and the Candidate is examined with the following catechism, which he should have committed to memory after his Initiation*).[1]

W.M.   Brethren, Bro. A. B. is this evening a Candidate to be passed to the Second Degree, but it is first requisite

1. There is a minimum interstice of four weeks between taking the Craft degrees. It is taken for granted that every initiate will almost automatically reach the Third Degree ; the first two correspond, in a way, to minor orders in the Church which are but a necessary preliminary to the priesthood.

W.M.	that he give proofs of proficiency in the former ; I shall therefore proceed to put the necessary questions :—
	Where were you first prepared to be made a Mason ?
Can.	In my heart.
W.M.	Where next ?
Can.	In a convenient room adjoining the Lodge.
W.M.	Describe the mode of your preparation.
Can.	I was divested of metal and hoodwinked, my right arm, left breast, and knee were made bare, my right heel was slipshod, and a cable-tow placed about my neck.
W.M.	Where were you made a Mason ?
Can.	In the body of a Lodge, just, perfect, and regular.
W.M.	And when ?
Can.	When the Sun was at its meridian.
W.M.	In this country Freemasons' Lodges are usually held in the evening ; how do you account for that which at first view appears a paradox ?
Can.	The Earth constantly revolving on its axis in its orbit round the Sun, and Freemasonry being universally spread over its surface, it necessarily follows that the Sun must always be at its meridian with respect to Freemasonry.
W.M.	What is Freemasonry ?
Can.	A peculiar system of Morality, veiled in Allegory, and illustrated by Symbols.
W.M.	Name the grand principles on which the Order is founded.
Can.	Brotherly Love, Relief, and Truth.
W.M.	Who are fit and proper persons to be made Masons ?
Can.	Just, upright, and free men, of mature age, sound judgment, and strict morals.
W.M.	How do you know yourself to be a Mason ?
Can.	By the regularity of my initiation, repeated trials and approbations, and a willingness at all times to undergo an examination when properly called on.
W.M.	How do you demonstrate the proof of your being a Mason to others ?
Can.	By signs, tokens, and the perfect points of my entrance.[1]
W.M.	These are the usual questions. I will put others if any Brother wishes me to do so. (*But this right is seldom exercised*).

1. This phrase is not usually explained to the initiate and often puzzles him. One of the lectures, however, defines the points of entrance as " Of, At, and On ; Of my own free will, At the door of the Lodge, and On the point of a sharp instrument presented to my naked left breast."

E
N
T
R
U
S
T
I
N
G

W.M.	Do you pledge your honour as a man, and your fidelity as a Mason, that you will steadily persevere through the ceremony of being passed to the Degree of a Fellow-Craft ?
Can.	I do.
W.M.	Do you likewise pledge yourself, ~~under the penalty of your Obligation,~~ that you will conceal what I shall now impart to you with the same strict caution as the other secrets in Masonry ?
Can.	I do.
W.M.	Then I will entrust you with a test of merit, which is a pass grip and a pass word leading to the Degree to which you seek to be admitted. The pass grip is given by a distinct pressure of the thumb between the first and second joints of the hand. This pass grip demands a pass word which is SHIBBOLETH.
Can.	(*Prompted by Junior Deacon, repeats*) Shibboleth.
W.M.	Shibboleth denotes plenty, and is usually depicted in our Lodges by an ear of corn near to a fall of water. You must be particularly careful to remember this word, as without it you cannot gain admission into a Lodge in a superior degree. Pass, Shibboleth.

(*The Junior Deacon escorts the Candidate to the door, instructing him to salute the Worshipful Master as a Mason. He retires to be prepared, and meanwhile the Lodge is opened or resumed in the Second Degree. The Candidate is not again deprived of metals, blindfolded, or haltered. His left breast is bared as before,[1] but the other members are reversed; the left arm, right knee are bared, and left foot slipshod. He wears the First Degree apron with the triangular flap turned up. When the Candidate is ready, the Tyler gives the First Degree knocks on the door*).

E
N
T
R
A
N
C
E

1

I.G.	(*With step and Second Degree sign*) Bro. Junior Warden, there is a report.
J.W.	(*With step and sign*) Worshipful Master, there is a report.
W.M.	Bro. Junior Warden, inquire who wants admission.
J.W.	(*Cuts sign*) Brother Inner Guard, see who wants admission.
I.G.	(*Cuts sign, opens the door*) Whom have you there ?
Ty.	Bro. A. B., who has been regularly initiated into Freemasonry, and has made such progress as he hopes will recommend him to be passed to the Degree of a

1. A few workings bare the right breast for the Second Degree.

Ty.	Fellow-Craft, for which ceremony he is properly prepared.	
I.G.	How does he hope to obtain the privileges of the Second Degree ?	
Ty.	By the help of God, the assistance of the Square, and the benefit of a pass word.	
I.G.	Is he in possession of the pass word ?	
Ty.	Will you prove him ?	

(Inner Guard extends his right hand, and the Candidate gives him the pass grip and pass word).

I.G. Halt, while I report to the Worshipful Master. *(Closes the door, takes step and sign)* Worshipful Master, Bro. A. B. who has been regularly initiated into Freemasonry, and has made such progress as he hopes will recommend him to be passed to the Degree of a Fellow-Craft, for which ceremony he is properly prepared.

W.M. We acknowledge the propriety of the aid by which he seeks admission ; do you, Bro. Inner Guard, vouch that he is in possession of the pass word ?

I.G. I do, Worshipful Master.

W.M. Then let him be admitted in due form. *(I.G. cuts sign)* Bro. Deacons.

(The Candidate is received at the door by the Deacons and Inner Guard; the latter applies the Square to the Candidate's breast, and holds it aloft to show that he has done so. The Senior Deacon conducts the Candidate to the kneeling-stool at the left of the Senior Warden, and directs him to advance as a Mason, at which he takes step and First Degree sign).

W.M. Let the Candidate kneel, while the blessing of Heaven is invoked on what we are about to do.

(One knock, followed by Wardens. The Brethren stand to order with sign of Reverence. The Deacons cross their wands over the Candidate's head).

W.M. or Chaplain We supplicate the continuance of thine aid, O merciful Lord, on behalf of ourselves, and him who kneels before Thee ; may the work, begun in Thy Name, be continued to Thy glory, and evermore established in us by obedience to Thy precepts.

I.P.M. So mote it be. *(Deacons lower their wands, and all dismiss sign).*

W.M. Let the Candidate rise.

(The Junior Deacon draws aside the kneeling-stool and places it in position before the Master's pedestal. The Senior Deacon conducts the Candidate round the Lodge, ' squaring ' it at the corners, ordering him to salute the Worshipful Master as a Mason as he

	passes across the East. He then leads him to the Junior Warden's pedestal).
S.D.	Advance to the Junior Warden as such, showing the sign and communicating the token and word. (*Candidate takes step and gives sign*).
J.W.	Have you anything to communicate ?
Can.	I have. (*Gives the First Degree grip*).
J.W.	What is this ?
Can.	The grip or token of an Entered Apprentice Freemason.
J.W.	What does it demand ?
Can.	A word.
J.W.	Give me that word, freely and at length.
Can.	BOAZ.
J.W.	Pass, Boaz.
	(*The Senior Deacon continues round the Lodge with the Candidate, and halts before the Senior Warden, directing him to salute as a Mason as before*).
W.M.	(*Gives single knock, repeated by the Wardens*) The Brethren will take notice that Bro. A. B., who has been regularly initiated into Freemasonry, is about to pass in view before them to show that he is the Candidate properly prepared to be passed to the degree of a Fellow-Craft.
	(*The Senior Deacon again conducts the Candidate round the Lodge, directing him to salute the Worshipful Master and the Junior Warden in turn as he passes them. He then leads him down to the right of the Senior Warden*).
S.D.	Advance to the Senior Warden as such, showing the sign and communicating the pass grip and pass word you received from the Worshipful Master previously to leaving the Lodge. (*Candidate gives step and First Degree sign and cuts it*).
S.W.	Have you anything to communicate ?
Can.	I have. (*Gives the pass grip*).
S.W.	What is this ?
Can.	The pass grip leading from the First to the Second Degree.
S.W.	What does this pass grip demand ?
Can.	A pass word.
S.W.	Give me that pass word.
Can.	SHIBBOLETH.
S.W.	What does Shibboleth denote ?
Can.	Plenty.
S.W.	How is it usually depicted in our Lodges ?
Can.	By an ear of corn near to a fall of water.
S.W.	Pass, Shibboleth.

(The Senior Deacon conducts Candidate to the Senior Warden's left, where they face East).

S.W. *(With sign of Fidelity)* Worshipful Master, I present to you Bro. A. B., a Candidate properly prepared to be passed to the Second Degree.

W.M. Bro. Senior Warden, you will direct the Senior Deacon to instruct the Candidate to advance to the East in due form.

S.W. *(Cuts sign)* Bro. Senior Deacon, it is the Worshipful Master's command that you instruct the Candidate to advance to the East in due form.

S.D. *(Placing Candidate in the North)* The method of advancing from West to East in this degree is by five steps, as if ascending a winding staircase. For your information I will go through them, and you will afterwards copy me.

(The Senior Deacon demonstrates the steps, which start with the right foot pointing to the Senior Warden, and the left foot pointing to the Junior Warden. He steps off with the left foot, lifting the feet at each step as if going up a stair. A quarter circle wheel of five steps takes him to before the Worshipful Master's pedestal). JD arrives at same

W.M. As in every case the Degrees in Freemasonry are to tim at be kept separate and distinct, another Obligation will pedestal. now be required of you, in many respects similar to the former ; are you willing to take it ?

Can. I am.

W.M. Then you will kneel on your right knee, your left foot formed in a square, place your right hand on the Volume of the Sacred Law, while your left arm will be supported in the angle of the Square.

(Gives single knock, answered by the Deacons. The Brethren stand to order with the sign of Fidelity and the Deacons cross their wands over the Candidate's head).

W.M. Repeat your name at length, and say after me :—

OBLIGATION

Can. I., A. B., in the presence of the Grand Geometrician of the Universe, and of this worthy and worshipful Lodge of Fellow-Craft Freemasons, regularly held, assembled, and properly dedicated, of my own free will and accord do hereby *(the Worshipful Master touches Candidate's right hand with his left)* and hereon *(Worshipful Master touches the Bible with his left hand)* solemnly promise and swear that I will

119

Can. always hele, conceal and never improperly reveal, any or either of the secrets or mysteries of or belonging to the Second Degree in Freemasonry, denominated the Fellow-Crafts, to him who is but an Entered Apprentice, any more than I would either of them to the uninstructed and popular world who are not Masons. I further solemnly pledge myself to act as a true and faithful Craftsman, answer signs, obey summonses, and maintain the principles inculcated in the former Degree. These several points I solemnly swear to observe, without evasion, equivocation, or mental reservation of any kind, under no less a penalty, on the violation of any of them, than that of having my left breast laid open, my heart torn therefrom, and given to the ravenous birds of the air, or devouring beasts of the field as a prey. So help me Almighty God, and keep me steadfast in this my Solemn Obligation of a Fellow-Craft Freemason.

W.M. As a pledge of your fidelity, and to render this a Solemn Obligation which might otherwise be considered but a serious promise, you will seal it with your lips twice on the Volume of the Sacred Law. (*Candidate does so*). Your progress in Masonry is marked by the position of the Square and Compasses. When you were made an Entered Apprentice, both points were hid ; in this degree one is disclosed, implying that you are now in the midway of Freemasonry, superior to an Entered Apprentice, but inferior to that to which I trust you will hereafter attain. Rise, newly obligated Fellow-Craft Freemason.

W.M. Having taken the Solemn Obligation of a Fellow-Craft, I shall proceed to entrust you with the secrets of the Degree. You will therefore advance to me as at your initiation. (*Candidate takes step and sign of First Degree*). You will now take another short pace towards me with your left foot, bringing the right heel into its hollow as before. That is the second regular step in Freemasonry, and it is in this position that the secrets of the Degree are communicated. They consist, as in the former instance, of a sign, token, and word, with this difference, that in this Degree the sign is of a three fold nature. The first part of the three fold sign is called the sign of Fidelity, and is given by placing the right hand on the left breast with the thumb extended in the form of a square, (*Worshipful Master demonstrates these signs and the Candidate copies him*), emblematically to

W.M.   shield the repository of your secrets from the attacks of the insidious. The second part is called the Hailing sign, or sign of Perseverance, and is given by throwing up the left hand (*horizontal from the shoulder to the elbow, and perpendicular from the elbow to the fingertips*) with the thumb level extended in the form of a square. This took its rise at the time that Joshua fought the battles of the Lord, when it was in this position he prayed fervently to the Almighty to continue the light of day, that he might complete the overthrow of his enemies. The third part is the Penal sign, and is given by dropping the left hand, drawing the right smartly across the breast and dropping it to the side. This is in allusion to the penalty of your Obligation, implying, that as a man of honour and a Fellow Craft Freemason you would rather have your heart torn from your breast than improperly disclose the secrets entrusted to you. The grip or token is given by a distinct pressure of the thumb on the second joint of the hand. (*Demonstrates it*). This grip or token demands a word, a word to be given with the same strict caution as that in the former Degree ; that is to say, never at length, but always by letters or syllables, to enable you to do which, I must tell you that the word is JACHIN. (*Senior Deacon repeats the word, followed by the Candidate. The Worshipful Master then spells it, followed by the Junior Deacon and the Candidate*). As in the course of this ceremony you will be called on for this word, the Senior Deacon will now dictate the answers you are to give. What is this ?

Can.   (*Prompted in his answers by the Senior Deacon*) The grip or token of a Fellow Craft Freemason.

W.M.   What does it demand ?

Can.   A word.

W.M.   Give me that word.

Can.   I was taught to be cautious in this Degree as well as in the former. I will letter or halve it with you.

W.M.   Which you please, and begin.
(*The word is halved in exactly the same way as in the First Degree*).

W.M.   This word is derived from the right hand pillar at the porchway or entrance of King Solomon's Temple, so named after Jachin, the Assistant High Priest who officiated at its dedication. The import of the word is to establish, and when conjoined with that in the former degree, stability, for God said : " In strength will establish this Mine house to stand firm for ever."

W.M. Pass, Jachin.[1]
(The Senior Deacon conducts the Candidate to the right of the Junior Warden, squaring the Lodge at the corner).

S.D. *(With step and sign)* Bro. Junior Warden, I present to you Bro. A. B. on his being passed to the Second Degree. *(Cuts sign).*

J.W. I will thank Bro. A. B. to advance to me as a Fellow-Craft. *(Candidate takes step and shows Second Degree signs)* Have you anything to communicate?

Can. I have. *(Gives grip).*

J.W. What is this?

Can. The grip or token of a Fellow-Craft Freemason.

J.W. What does it demand?

Can. A word.

J.W. Give me that word.

Can. I was taught to be cautious in this Degree as well as in the former. I will letter or halve it with you.

J.W. Which you please, and begin.
(Here the word is both lettered and halved, as in the First Degree).

J.W. Pass, Jachin.
(The Senior Deacon, squaring the Lodge, conducts the Candidate to the Senior Warden).

S.D. *(With step and sign)* Bro. Senior Warden, I present to you Bro. A. B. on his being passed to the Second Degree. *(Cuts sign).*

S.W. I will thank Bro. A. B. to advance to me as a Fellow-Craft, first as an Entered Apprentice. *(Candidate takes step and gives sign of the First Degree, then takes second step).* What is that?

Can. The second regular step in Freemasonry.

S.W. Do you bring anything else?

Can. I do. *(Gives sign of Fidelity).*

S.W. What is that?

Can. The sign of Fidelity, emblematically to shield the repository of my secrets from the attacks of the insidious.

S.W. Do you bring anything else?

Can. I do. *(Gives Hailing sign).*

S.W. What is that?

Can. The Hailing Sign, or sign of Perseverance.

S.W. When did it take its rise?

Can. At the time when Joshua fought the battles of the

1. This text is not to be found in the Bible, nor is there any mention of an Assistant High Priest called Jachin. The two pillars Boaz and Jachin are of course named in I Kings VII, 21 and II Chron. III, 17.

Can.	Lord, when it was in this position he prayed fervently to the Almighty to continue the light of day, so that he might complete the overthrow of his enemies.
S.W.	Do you bring anything else ?
Can.	I do. (*Gives Penal sign*).
S.W.	What is that ?
Can.	The Penal sign.
S.W.	To what does it allude ?
Can.	The penalty of my Obligation, implying that as a man of honour and a Fellow-Craft Freemason I would rather have my heart torn from my breast than improperly disclose the secrets entrusted to me.
S.W.	Have you anything to communicate ?
Can.	I have. (*Gives grip*).
S.W.	What is this ?
Can.	The grip or token of a Fellow-Craft Freemason.
S.W.	What does it demand ?
Can.	A word.
S.W.	Give me that word.
Can.	I was taught to be cautious in this Degree as well as in the former. I will letter or halve it with you.
S.W.	Which you please, and begin. (*Here the word is halved as in the First Degree*). Whence is this word derived ?
Can.	From the right hand pillar at the porchway or entrance of King Solomon's Temple, so named after Jachin, the Assistant High Priest who officiated at its dedication.
S.W.	The import of the word ?
Can.	To establish.
S.W.	And when conjoined with that in the former degree ?
Can.	Stability, for God said : " In strength will I establish this Mine house to stand firm for ever."
S.W.	Pass, Jachin. (*Gives sign of Fidelity*). Worshipful Master, I present to you Bro. A. B. on his being passed to the Second Degree, for some further mark of your favour.
W.M.	Bro. Senior Warden, I delegate you to invest him with the distinguishing badge of a Fellow-Craft Freemason.
S.W.	(*Cuts sign, and invests Candidate with the Fellow-Craft apron, which is the same as that of the First Degree with the addition of two blue rosettes in the bottom corners*). Bro. A. B., by the Worshipful Master's command, I invest you with the distinguishing badge of a Fellow-Craft Freemason, to mark the progress you have made in the science.

123

BADGE

W.M. Let me add to what has been stated by the Senior Warden that the badge with which you have now been invested points out that, as a Craftsman, you are expected to make the liberal arts and sciences your future study, that you may the better be enabled to discharge your duties as a Mason, and estimate the wonderful works of the Almighty. Bro. Senior Deacon, you will place our Brother at the South East part of the Lodge. (*Senior Deacon does so*).

S.D. Right foot across the Lodge, left foot down the Lodge; pay attention to the Worshipful Master

CHARGE

W.M. Masonry being a progressive science, when you were made an Entered Apprentice you were placed at the North East part of the Lodge, to show that you were newly admitted ; you are now placed at the South East part to mark the progress you have made in the science. You now stand to all external appearance a just and upright Fellow-Craft Freemason, and I give it you in strong terms of recommendation ever to continue and act as such ; and, as I trust, the import of the former charge neither is, nor ever will be, effaced from your memory, I shall content myself with observing that, as in the previous Degree you made yourself acquainted with the principles of moral Truth and Virtue, you are now permitted to extend your researches into the hidden mysteries of Nature and Science.

(*The Senior Deacon conducts the Candidate to the Worshipful Master's Pedestal*).

TOOLS

W.M. I now present to you the working tools of a Fellow-Craft Freemason ; they are the Square, Level, and Plumb-Rule. The Square is to try and adjust rectangular corners of buildings, and assist in bringing rude matter into due form ; the Level to lay levels and prove horizontals ; the Plumb-Rule to try and adjust uprights, while fixing them on their proper bases. But as we are not all operative Masons, but rather free and accepted or speculative, we apply these tools to our morals. In this sense, the Square teaches morality, the Level equality, and the Plumb-Rule justness and uprightness of life and actions. Thus by square conduct, level steps and upright intentions we hope to ascend to those immortal mansions whence all goodness emanates.

You are now at liberty to retire in order to restore yourself to your personal comforts, and on your return to the Lodge I shall call your attention to an explanation of the Tracing-Board.

S.D.	Salute the Worshipful Master as a Fellow-Craftsman, first as an Entered Apprentice.
	(*The Candidate takes step, gives sign of First Degree, cuts it, takes the second step, and gives sign of the Second Degree. The Senior Deacon leads him to the door, where the Candidate retires to dress himself, not forgetting his apron. When he is ready, the Tyler gives the knocks of the Second Degree*).
I.G.	(*With step and sign*) Bro. Junior Warden, there is a report. (*Junior Warden gives one knock, and the Inner Guard opens the door*).
Ty.	The Candidate on his return.
I.G.	(*Closes the door, gives step and sign*) Worshipful Master, the Candidate on his return.
W.M.	Admit him.
	(*The Inner Guard cuts sign and opens the door. The Senior Deacon leads the Candidate to the North of the Senior Warden's pedestal, and both face East. He orders the Candidate to salute in full, the Worshipful Master leaves his pedestal and goes to the tracing board, borrowing the Junior Deacon's wand to point out the details as he explains it*).

E
X
I
T

TRACING BOARD LECTURE, SECOND DEGREE

When the Temple at Jerusalem was completed by King Solomon its costliness and splendour became objects of admiration to the surrounding nations, and its fame spread to the remotest parts of the then known world. There was nothing, however, in connection with this magnificent structure more remarkable, or that more particularly struck the attention, than the two great pillars which were placed at the porchway or entrance. That on the left was called BOAZ, which denotes in strength ; that on the right, JACHIN, which denotes to establish ; and when conjoined, stability, for God said : In strength will I establish this Mine house to stand firm for ever. The height of those pillars was seventeen cubits and a half each, their circumference twelve, their diameter four ; they were formed hollow, the better to serve as archives to Masonry, for therein were deposited the constitutional rolls. Being formed hollow, the outer rim or shell was four inches or a hand's breadth in thickness. They were made of molten brass, and were cast in the plains of Jordan, in the clay ground between Succoth and Zeredathah, where King Solomon ordered those and all his holy vessels to be cast. The superintendent of the casting was Hiram Abiff. Those pillars were adorned with two chapiters, each five cubits high ; the chapiters were enriched with network, lily-work, and pomegranates. Network,

Second Degree Tracing Board

from the connection of its meshes, denotes unity ; lily-work, from its whiteness, peace ; and pomegranates, from the exuberance of their seed, denote plenty. There were two rows of pomegranates on each chapiter, one hundred in a row. Those pillars were further adorned with two spherical balls, on which were delineated maps of the celestial and terrestrial globes, pointing out ' Masonry universal.' They were considered finished when the network or canopy was thrown over them.

They were set up as a memorial to the children of Israel of that miraculous pillar of fire and cloud, which had two wonderful effects : the fire gave light to the Israelites during their escape from their Egyptian bondage, and the cloud proved darkness to Pharaoh and his followers when they attempted to overtake them. King Solomon ordered them to be placed at the entrance of the Temple as the most proper and conspicuous situation for the children of Israel to have the happy deliverance of their forefathers continually before their eyes, in going to and returning from Divine worship.

At the building of King Solomon's Temple an immense number of Masons were employed ; they consisted of Entered Apprentices and Fellow-Crafts ; the Entered Apprentices received a weekly allowance of corn, wine, and oil ; the Fellow-Crafts were paid their wages in specie, which they went to receive in the middle chamber of the Temple. They got there by the porchway or entrance on the south side. After our ancient Brethren had entered the porch they arrived at the foot of the winding staircase, which led to the middle chamber. Their ascent was opposed by the Junior Warden, who demanded of them the pass grip and the pass word leading from the first to the second degree.

The pass grip you are all in possession of, and the pass word I dare say you recollect, is Shibboleth ; Shibboleth denotes plenty, and is here depicted by an ear of corn near to a fall of water.[1] The word Shibboleth dates its origin from the time that an army of Ephraimites crossed the river Jordan in a hostile manner against Jephtha, the renowned Gileaditish general ; the reason they assigned for this unfriendly visit was that they had not been called out to partake of the honours of the Ammonitish war ; but their true aim was to partake of the rich spoils with which, in consequence of that war, Jephtha and his army were then laden. The Ephraimites had always been considered a clamorous and turbulent people, but then broke out into open violence, and after many severe taunts to

1. Some workings insert here a lengthy historical account of Jephtha and of his warfare with the Ammonites which apart from being a great strain on the memory is irrelevant to the explanation of the word.

the Gileadites in general threatened to destroy their victorious commander and his house with fire. Jephtha, on his part, tried all lenient means to appease them, but finding these ineffectual had recourse to rigorous ones ; he therefore drew out his army, gave the Ephraimites battle, defeated and put them to flight ; and to render his victory decisive and to secure himself from like molestation in future, he sent detachments of his army to secure the passages of the river Jordan, over which he knew the insurgents must of necessity attempt to go, in order to regain their own country, giving strict orders to his guards that if a fugitive came that way, owning himself an Ephraimite, he should immediately be slain ; but if he prevaricated, or said nay, a test word was to be put to him to pronounce, the word Shibboleth. They, from a defect in aspiration peculiar to their dialect, could not pronounce it properly, but called it Sibboleth, which small variation discovered their country and cost them their lives. And Scripture informs us that there fell on that day, on the field of battle and on the banks of the Jordan, forty and two thousand Ephraimites. And as Shibboleth was then a test word to distinguish friend from foe, King Solomon afterwards caused it to be adopted as a pass word in a Fellow-Crafts' Lodge to prevent any unqualified person ascending the winding staircase which led to the middle chamber of the Temple.

After our ancient Brethren had given those conclusive proofs to the Junior Warden he said " Pass, Shibboleth ". Then they passed up the winding staircase, consisting of three, five, seven, or more steps. Three rule a Lodge, five hold a Lodge, seven or more make it perfect. The three who rule a Lodge are the Master and his two Wardens ; the five who hold a Lodge are the Master, two Wardens, and two Fellow-Crafts ; the seven who make it perfect are two Entered Apprentices added to the former five. Three rule a Lodge because there were but three Grand Masters who bore sway at the building of the first Temple at Jerusalem, namely, Solomon King of Israel, Hiram King of Tyre, and Hiram Abiff. Five hold a Lodge, in allusion to the five noble orders of Architecture, namely, The Tuscan, Doric, Ionic, Corinthian, and Composite. Seven or more make a perfect Lodge, because King Solomon was seven years and upwards in building, completing, and dedicating the Temple at Jerusalem to God's service. They have likewise a further allusion to the seven liberal Arts and Sciences, namely, Grammar, Rhetoric, Logic, Arithmetic, Geometry, Music and Astronomy.

After our ancient Brethren had gained the summit of the winding staircase, they arrived at the door of the middle chamber, which they found open, but properly tyled against all under the Degree of a Fellow-Craft by the Senior Warden, who demanded of them the sign, token, and word of a Fellow-Craft. After they had given him those convincing proofs he said ' Pass, JACHIN '. They then passed into the middle chamber of the Temple where they went to receive their wages, which they did without scruple or diffidence ; without scruple, well knowing that they were justly entitled to them, and without diffidence, from the great reliance they placed on the integrity of their employers in those days.

When our ancient Brethren were in the middle chamber of the Temple their attention was peculiarly drawn to certain Hebrew characters[1] which are here depicted by the letter G, (*the Immediate Past Master gives a single knock, followed by the Wardens*) denoting God (*all stand to order with the sign of Reverence*) the Grand Geometrician of the Universe, to whom we must all submit, and whom we ought humbly to adore.

CEREMONY OF RAISING TO THE THIRD DEGREE

> (*The Lodge is opened in the Second Degree, and the Candidate is examined in the following catechism which he should have committed to memory*).

W.M. Brethren, Bro. A. B. is this evening a Candidate to be raised to the Third Degree, but it is first requisite that he give proofs of proficiency in the Second. I shall therefore proceed to put the necessary questions. How were you prepared to be passed to the Second Degree ?

Can. In a manner somewhat similar to the former, save that in this Degree I was not hoodwinked.[2] My left arm, breast, and right knee were made bare, and my left heel was slipshod.

W.M. On what were you admitted ?

Can. The Square.

W.M. What is a Square ?

Can. An angle of 90 degrees, or the fourth part of a circle.

W.M. What are the peculiar objects of research in this Degree ?

Can. The hidden mysteries of Nature and Science.

W.M. As it is the hope of reward that sweetens labour, where did our ancient Brethren go to receive their wages ?

Can. Into the middle chamber of King Solomon s Temple.

W.M. How did they receive them ?

---

1. The Hebrew letters referred to are those spelling Jahweh or Jehovah, for which the letter G is now substituted.

2. Other workings have " I was not deprived of metals nor hoodwinked."

Can.	Without scruple or diffidence.
W.M.	Why in this peculiar manner ?
Can.	Without scruple, well knowing they were justly entitled to them ; and without diffidence, from the great reliance they placed on the integrity of their employers in those days.
W.M.	What were the names of the two great pillars which were placed at the porchway or entrance of King Solomon's Temple ?
Can.	That on the left was called Boaz, and that on the right, Jachin.
W.M.	What are their separate and conjoint significations ?
Can.	The former denotes in strength, the latter, to establish ; and when conjoined, stability, for God said, " In strength will I establish this Mine house to stand firm for ever."[1]
W.M.	These are the usual questions. I will put others if any Brother wishes me to do so. (*But this right is seldom exercised*).
W.M.	Do you pledge your honour as a man and your fidelity as a Craftsman that you will steadily persevere through the ceremony of being raised to the sublime Degree of a Master Mason ?
Can.	I do.
W.M.	Do you likewise pledge yourself, ~~under the penalty of both your Obligation~~s, that you will conceal what I shall now impart to you with the same strict caution as the other secrets in Masonry ?
Can.	I do.
W.M.	Then I will entrust you with a test of merit, which is a pass grip and a pass word, leading to the degree to which you seek to be admitted. The pass grip is given by a distinct pressure of the thumb between the second and third joints of the hand. This pass grip demands a pass word, which is TUBAL CAIN. Tubal Cain was the first artificer in metals. The import of the word is worldly possessions. You must be particularly careful to remember this word, as without it you cannot gain admission into a Lodge in a superior Degree. Pass, Tubal Cain.
	(*The Senior Deacon conducts the Candidate to the door, instructing him to salute the Worshipful Master with the signs of the first two Degrees. He retires to be prepared for the Third Degree : both arms, both breasts, and both knees are made bare, and both heels are slippered, He wears the Fellow Crafts apron. In the meantime the Lodge is opened in the Third*)

1. See note p. 122.

Degree. The Deacons lay a sheet along the mid line of the Lodge some five feet west of the Worshipful Master's pedestal : on this sheet is depicted the 'open grave', surrounded by skulls and cross-bones. In a few Lodges there is an actual grave-trap in the floor. The practice of using a real coffin is almost but not quite extinct. Sometimes real or plastic ' emblems of mortality' are used.[1] When all is ready the Tyler gives the Second Degree knocks).

I.G.   (*With step and Penal sign of Third Degree*) Bro. Junior Warden, there is a report.

J.W.   (*With step and sign*) Worshipful Master, there is a report.

W.M.   Brother Junior Warden, inquire who wants admission.

J.W.   (*Cuts sign*) Bro. Inner Guard, see who wants admission.

I.G.   (*Cuts sign, opens the door*) Whom have you there ?

Ty.   Bro. A. B., who has been regularly initiated into Freemasonry, passed to the Degree of a Fellow-Craft, and has made such further progress as he hopes will entitle him to be raised to the sublime Degree of a Master Mason, for which ceremony he is properly prepared.

I.G.   How does he hope to obtain the privileges of the Third Degree ?

Ty.   By the help of God, the united aid of the Square and Compasses, and the benefit of a pass word.

I.G.   Is he in possession of the pass word ?

Ty.   Will you prove him ? (*The Inner Guard extends his right hand, and receives the pass grip and pass word from the Candidate*).

I.G.   Halt, while I report to the Worshipful Master. (*Closes door, takes step and sign*) Worshipful Master, Bro. A. B. who has been regularly initiated into Freemasonry, passed to the Degree of Fellow-Crafts, and has made such further progress as he hopes will entitle him to be raised to the sublime Degree of a Master Mason, for which ceremony he is properly prepared.

W.M.   How does he hope to obtain the privileges of the Third Degree ?

I.G.   By the help of God, the united aid of the Square and Compasses, and the benefit of a pass word.

ENTRANCE

---

1. At a well-known Masonic outfitters I saw a goodly array of realistic skulls and cross-bones in plastic. On my remarking to the attendant that I supposed these were for the higher degrees (particularly Knights Templar and Rose Croix) he assured me that they were also sold for use in the Third Degree ceremonies.

E
N
T
R
A
N
C
E

W.M.	We acknowledge the powerful aid by which he seeks admission ; do you, Bro. Inner Guard, vouch that he is in possession of the pass word ?
I.G.	I do, Worshipful Master.
W.M.	Then let him be admitted in due form. Brother Deacons.

(At this point all lights are extinguished in the Lodge except the candle by the Worshipful Master's pedestal. The Junior Deacon places the kneeling stool in position, and both Deacons proceed to the door. The Inner Guard opens it, presents the extended points of a pair of compasses to the Candidate's breasts, and holds the compasses above his head to show that he has done so. The Senior Deacon leads the Candidate to the kneeling stool).

S.D.	Advance as a Fellow-Craft, first as an Entered Apprentice.

(Candidate takes step and gives First Degree sign then another step and the sign of the Second Degree).

W.M.	Let the Candidate kneel while the blessing of Heaven is invoked on what we are about to do.

(Worshipful Master gives one knock, repeated by the Wardens. All stand with sign of Reverence, and the Deacons cross their wands over the Candidate's head).

P
R
A
Y
E
R

W.M. or Chaplain	Almighty and Eternal God, Architect and Ruler of the Universe, at whose creative fiat all things first were made, we, the frail creatures of Thy providence, humbly implore Thee to pour down on this convocation assembled in Thy Holy Name the continual dew of Thy blessing. Especially, we beseech Thee, to impart Thy grace to this Thy servant, who offers himself a Candidate to partake with us the mysterious secrets of a Master Mason. Endue him with such fortitude that in the hour of trial he fail not, but that, passing safely under Thy protection through the valley of the shadow of death, he may finally rise from the tomb of transgression, to shine as the stars for ever and ever.
I.P.M.	So mote it be. (*The Deacons lower their wands, and the Brethren dismiss sign*).
W.M.	Let the Candidate rise. (*He does so. The kneeling stool is removed and placed before the Worshipful Master's pedestal. The Senior Deacon takes the Candidate by the right hand, and begins the perambulations of the Lodge, carefully squaring it at the corners. A halt is made before the pedestal in the East, and the Senior Deacon instructs the Candidate to salute the Worshipful Master as a Mason. They*

then proceed to the Junior Warden's pedestal in the South).

S.D.   Advance to the Junior Warden as such, showing the sign and communicating the token and word. (*Candidate takes step and gives sign of First Degree*).

J.W.   Have you anything to communicate ?

Can.   I have. (*Gives First Degree grip*).

J.W.   What is this ?

Can.   The grip or token of an Entered Apprentice Free-mason.

J.W.   What does it demand ?

Can.   A word.

J.W.   Give me that word, freely and at length.

Can.   BOAZ.

J.W.   Pass, Boaz.

(The Senior Deacon continues round the Lodge with the Candidate, and halts in front of the Senior Warden, whom the Candidate is instructed to salute as a Mason with step and sign of the First Degree. The perambulation is continued, squaring the Lodge, and the Candidate is directed to salute the Worshipful Master as a Fellow-Craft, which he does with step and sign of the Second Degree. Continuing round the Lodge ; he next salutes the Junior Warden as a Fellow-Craft, and on to the Senior Warden again).

S.D.   Advance to the Senior Warden as such, showing the sign, and communicating the token and word of that Degree. (*Candidate takes step and gives sign*).

S.W.   Have you anything to communicate ?

Can.   I have. (*Gives grip*).

S.W.   What is this ?

Can.   The grip or token of a Fellow-Craft Freemason.

S.W.   What does it demand ?

Can.   A word.

S.W.   Give me that word freely and at length.

Can.   JACHIN.

S.W.   Pass, Jachin.

W.M.   (*Gives single knock, repeated by the Wardens*) The Brethren will take notice that Bro. A. B., who has been regularly initiated into Freemasonry, and passed to the Degree of a Fellow-Craft, is about to pass in view before them, to show that he is the Candidate properly prepared to be raised to the Sublime Degree of a Master Mason.

(The Senior Deacon conducts the Candidate round the Lodge the third time, followed by the Junior Deacon. They halt before the Worshipful Master's

P
R
A
M

3

pedestal, where the Senior Deacon instructs the Candidate to salute as a Fellow-Craft, then on to the Junior Warden, who is similarly saluted. They then proceed to the right of the Senior Warden).

S.D.   Advance to the Senior Warden as such, showing the sign and communicating the pass grip and pass word you received from the Worshipful Master previously to leaving the Lodge. *(Candidate takes step and gives Fellow-Craft sign).*

S.W.   Have you anything to communicate ?

Can.   I have. *(Gives pass grip to the Third Degree).*

S.W.   What is this ?

Can.   The pass grip leading from the Second to the Third Degree.

S.W.   What does this pass grip demand ?

Can.   A pass word.

S.W.   Give me that pass word.

Can.   TUBAL CAIN.

S.W.   What was Tubal Cain ?

Can.   The first artificer in metals.

S.W.   The import of the word ?

Can.   Worldly possessions.

S.W.   Pass, Tubal Cain. *(Senior Warden takes step and Penal Sign of the Third Degree).* Worshipful Master I present Bro. A. B., a Candidate properly prepared to be raised to the Third Degree.

W.M.   Bro. Senior Warden, you will direct the Deacons to instruct the Candidate to advance to the East by the proper steps.

S.W.   Bro. Deacons, it is the Worshipful Master's command that you instruct the Candidate to advance to the East by the proper steps.

S.D.   The method of advancing from West to East in this Degree is by seven steps, the first three as if stepping over a grave. For your information I will go through them, and you will afterwards copy me.

(The exact process of taking these steps, if followed to the letter, is extremely difficult to achieve gracefully. Suffice it to say that they are taken diagonally back and forth ; starting at the West or head of the grave as depicted on the sheet, the first step is taken in a North Easterly direction, the second South Easterly, and the third brings the Candidate to the foot of the grave, facing due East. After each separate step the heels are brought together with the feet squared. Four ordinary walking steps, described in some workings as " bold marching steps," taken due East, bring the Candidate into position before the

Worshipful Master's pedestal).

W.M. It is but fair to inform you that a most serious trial of your fortitude and fidelity and a more solemn Obligation await you. Are you prepared to meet them as you ought ?

Can. I am.

W.M. Then you will kneel on both knees, place both hands on the Volume of the Sacred Law. (*Candidate does so. The Worshipful Master gives one knock, followed by the Wardens, the Brethren stand to order with the Penal sign of the Third Degree, and the Deacons cross their wands over the Candidate's head*). Repeat your name at length, and say after me :—

OBLIGATION

Can. I, A. B., in the presence of the Most High, and of this worthy and worshipful Lodge of Master Masons, duly constituted, regularly assembled, and properly dedicated, of my own free will and accord, do hereby (*Worshipful Master touches Candidate's hands with his left hand*) and hereon (*Worshipful Master touches the Bible with his left hand*) most solemnly promise and swear that I will always hele, conceal, and never reveal any or either of the secrets or mysteries of or belonging to the Degree of a Master Mason to anyone in the world, unless it be to him or them to whom the same may justly and lawfully belong, and not even to him or them until after due trial, strict examination, or full conviction that he or they are worthy of that confidence, or in the body of a Master Masons' Lodge duly opened on the Centre. I further solemnly pledge myself to adhere to the principles of the Square and Compasses, answer and obey all lawful signs, and summonses sent to me from a Master Masons' Lodge, if within the length of my cable-tow, and plead no excuse except sickness or the pressing emergencies of my own public or private avocations.

I further solemnly engage myself to maintain and uphold the Five Points of Fellowship in act as well as in word ; that my hand, given to a Master Mason, shall be a sure pledge of brotherhood ; that my feet shall travel through dangers and difficulties to unite with his in forming a column of mutual defence and support ; that the posture of my daily supplications shall remind me of his wants and dispose my heart to succour his weakness and relieve his necessities, so far as may fairly be done without detriment to myself or connections ; that my breast shall be the

Can. sacred repository of his secrets when entrusted to my care—murder, treason, felony, and all other offences contrary to the laws of God and the ordinances of the realm being at all times most especially excepted.

And finally, that I will maintain a Master Mason's honour and carefully preserve it as my own ; I will not injure him myself, or knowingly suffer it to be done by others if in my power to prevent it ; but on the contrary, will boldly repel the slanderer of his good name, and most strictly respect the chastity of those nearest and dearest to him, in the persons of his wife, his sister, and his child.

All these points I solemnly swear to observe, without evasion, equivocation, or mental reservation of any kind, under no less a penalty, on the violation of any of them, than that of being severed in two, my bowels burned to ashes,[1] and those ashes scattered over the face of the earth and wafted by the four cardinal winds of heaven, that no trace or remembrance of so vile a wretch may longer be found among men, particularly Master Masons.

So help me the Most High, and keep me steadfast in this my solemn Obligation of a Master Mason.

W.M. As a pledge of your fidelity and to render this binding as a Solemn Obligation for so long as you shall live, you will seal it with your lips thrice on the Volume of the Sacred Law. (*Candidate does so*). Let me once more call your attention to the position of the Square and Compasses. When you were made an Entered Apprentice, both points were hid ; in the Second Degree one was disclosed, in this the whole is exhibited, implying that you are now at liberty to work with both those points in order to render the circle of your Masonic duties complete. Rise, newly obligated Master Mason. (*Deacons and Candidate step back to the foot of the grave*).

Having entered upon the Solemn Obligation of a Master Mason, you are now entitled to demand that last and greatest trial, by which alone you can be admitted to a participation of the secrets of this Degree. But it is first my duty to call your attention to a retrospect of those Degrees in Freemasonry through which you have already passed, that you may

1. Some workings commit the whole body to the flames and not merely the bowels. If only the bowels are consumed it makes nonsense of the following passage " no trace or remembrance ... may longer be found."

W.M. the better be enabled to distinguish and appreciate the connection of our whole system, and the relative dependency of its several parts.

Your admission among Masons in a state of helpless indigence was an emblematical representation of the entrance of all men on this, their mortal existence. It inculcated the useful lessons of natural equality and mutual dependence. It instructed you in the active principles of universal beneficence and charity, to seek the solace of your own distress by extending relief and consolation to your fellow-creatures in the hour of their affliction. Above all, it taught you to bend with humility and resignation to the will of the Great Architect of the Universe ; to dedicate your heart, thus purified from every baneful and malignant passion, fitted only for the reception of truth and wisdom, to His glory and the welfare of your fellow-mortals.

Proceeding onwards, still guiding your progress by the principles of moral truth, you were led in the Second Degree to contemplate the intellectual faculty, and to trace it from its development, through the paths of heavenly science, even to the Throne of God Himself. The secrets of Nature and the principles of intellectual truth were then unveiled to your view. To your mind, thus modelled by virtue and science, Nature, however, presents one great and useful lesson more. She prepares you, by contemplation, for the closing hour of existence ; and when by means of that contemplation she has conducted you through the intricate windings of this mortal life, she finally instructs you how to die.

Such, my Brother, are the peculiar objects of the Third Degree in Freemasonry ; they invite you to reflect on this awful subject and teach you to feel, that, to the just and virtuous man, death has no terrors equal to the stain of falsehood and dishonour. Of this great truth the annals of Masonry afford a glorious example in the unshaken fidelity and noble death of our Master, Hiram Abiff, who was slain just before the completion of King Solomon's Temple, at the construction of which he was, as no doubt you are well aware, the principal architect. The manner of his death was as follows. Brother Wardens.

(*The Wardens come up and stand on either side of the Candidate, who is instructed to cross his feet right over left*).

W.M. Fifteen Fellow Crafts of that superior class appointed

W.M. to preside over the rest, finding that the work was nearly completed and that they were not in possession of the secrets of the Third Degree, conspired to obtain them by any means, even to have recourse to violence. At the moment, however, of carrying their conspiracy into execution, twelve of the fifteen recanted, but three, of a more determined and atrocious character than the rest, persisted in their impious design, in the prosecution of which they planted themselves respectively at the East, North and South entrances of the Temple, whither our Master had retired to pay his adoration to the Most High, as was his wonted custom at the hour of high twelve. Having finished his devotions, he attempted to return by the South entrance, where he was opposed by the first of those ruffians, who, for want of other weapon, had armed himself with a heavy Plumb Rule, and in a threatening manner demanded the secrets of a Master Mason, warning him that death would be the consequence of a refusal. Our Master, true to his Obligation, answered that those secrets were known to but three in the world, and that without the consent and co-operation of the other two he neither could nor would divulge them, but intimated that he had no doubt patience and industry would, in due time, entitle the worthy Mason to a participation of them, but that, for his own part, he would rather suffer death than betray the sacred trust reposed in him.

This answer not proving satisfactory, the ruffian aimed a violent blow at the head of our Master, but, being startled at the firmness of his demeanour, it missed his forehead and only glanced on his right temple (*here the Junior Warden touches the Candidate's right temple with the Plumb Rule*) but with such force as to cause him to reel and sink on his left knee (*the Candidate goes down on his left knee*). Recovering from the shock (*Candidate rises*) he made for the North entrance, where he was accosted by the second of those ruffians, to whom he gave a similar answer with undiminished firmness, when the ruffian, who was armed with a Level, struck him a violent blow on the left temple (*the Senior Warden touches the Candidate's left temple with the Level*) which brought him to the ground on his right knee (*here the Candidate goes down on his right knee, and recovers*). Finding his retreat cut off at both these points, he staggered faint and bleeding to the East entrance, where the third ruffian was posted, who received a

138

W.M. similar answer to his insolent demand (for even at this trying moment our Master remained firm and unshaken), when the villain, who was armed with a heavy Maul, struck him a violent blow on the fore-head. (*Here, according to Emulation Workings, the Worshipful Master makes a gesture only from his seat of slaying the Candidate with the Maul; in some workings he leaves his place and touches the Candidate's forehead*) which laid him lifeless at his feet. (*The Wardens lower the Candidate backwards into the grave—if he has his feet crossed a slight push is all that is needed to make him lose his balance, and with care and practice they can support him from behind and lower him gently. Various refinements are sometimes employed to heighten the solemnity of the pause; a clock or gong may strike twelve, Bro. Organist may render the Dead March from Saul, while Ecclesiasticus XII, " Remember now thy Creator— " may be recited*).

W.M. The Brethren will take notice that in the recent cere-mony, as well as in his present situation, our Brother has been made to represent one of the brightest characters recorded in the annals of Masonry, namely, Hiram Abiff, who lost his life in consequence of his unshaken fidelity to the sacred trust reposed in him, and I hope this will make a lasting impression on his and your minds, should you ever be placed in a similar state of trial.
Brother Junior Warden, you will endeavour to raise the representative of our Master by the Entered Apprentice's grip.
(*The Junior Warden raises the Candidate's right arm with his left, gives the First Degree grip with his right hand and lets it slip, then lowers the Candidate's arm again*).

J.W. (*With step and sign*) Worshipful Master, it proves a slip. (*Cuts sign*).

W.M. Brother Senior Warden, you will try the Fellow-Crafts'. (*The Senior Warden attempts the Second Degree grip and lets it slip, in the same way as the Junior Warden did*).

S.W. (*With step and sign*) Worshipful Master, it proves a slip likewise. (*Cuts sign*).

W.M. Brother Wardens, having both failed in your attempts, there remains a third method, by taking a more firm hold of the sinews of the hand and raising him on the Five Points of Fellowship, which, with your assistance, I will make trial of.

(The Worshipful Master leaves his chair and advances to the Candidate's feet, which he uncrosses. He then takes the Candidate's right hand in the Third Degree grip, places his right foot to the Candidate's right foot, and then, as the Wardens lift the Candidate, places right knee to right knee, right breast to right breast, and left hand over the Candidate's back).[1]

W.M.   *(Still holding the Five Points of Fellowship)* It is thus all Master Masons are raised from a figurative death to a reunion with the former companions of their toils. Brother Wardens, resume your seats. Let me now beg you to observe that the light of a Master Mason is darkness visible, serving only to express that gloom which rests on the prospect of futurity. It is that mysterious veil which the eye of human reason cannot penetrate unless assisted by that light which is from above. Yet, even by this glimmering ray, you may perceive that you stand on the very brink of the grave into which you have just figuratively descended, and which, when this transitory life shall have passed away, will again receive you into its cold bosom. Let the emblems of mortality which lie before you lead you to contemplate on your inevitable destiny, and guide your reflections to that most interesting of all human studies, the knowledge of yourself. Be careful to perform your allotted task while it is yet day; continue to listen to the voice of Nature, which bears witness, that even in this perishable frame resides a vital and immortal principle, which inspires a holy confidence that the Lord of Life will enable us to trample the King of Terror beneath our feet, and lift our eyes to that bright Morning Star, whose rising brings peace and salvation to the faithful and obedient of the human race.

(The Worshipful Master changes places with the Candidate, the former is in the North facing South, the latter in the South facing North).

W.M.   I cannot better reward the attention you have paid to this exhortation and charge than by entrusting you with the secrets of the Degree. You will therefore advance to me as a Fellow-Craft, first as an Entered

---

1. Emulation Lodge of Improvement appears to have introduced an error which has become widespread, particularly in London, with regard to the position of the left hand in the Five Points of Fellowship, in which the hand is held aloft in the air with the wrist bent backwards rather than making actual contact with the back.

W.M.   Apprentice. (*Candidate takes step and gives First Degree sign, then another step and the sign of the Second Degree*). You will now take another short pace towards me with your left foot, bringing the right heel into its hollow as before. That is the third regular step in Freemasonry, and it is in this position that the secrets of the degree are communicated. They consist of signs, a token and word.

Of the signs, the first and second are Casual, the third Penal. The first Casual sign is called the sign of Horror, and is given from the Fellow-Crafts. Stand to order as a Fellow-Craft, by dropping the left hand into this position (*down, with palm outwards as if shielding the eyes from some object on the ground*), elevating the right (*with the back of the hand to the face, shielding the eyes*) with the head turned over the right shoulder, as if struck with horror at some dreadful and afflicting sight.

The second Casual sign is called the sign of Sympathy, and is given by bending the head forward, and smiting the forehead gently with the right hand.

Place your hand in this position (*that is, with the forearm parallel with the ground and in line with the navel, palm downwards*) with the thumb extended in the form of a square. (*The tip of the thumb touching the body*). The Penal sign is given by drawing the hand smartly across the body, dropping it to the side, and recovering with the thumb to the navel. This is in allusion to the penalty of your obligation, implying that as a man of honour and a Master Mason you would rather be severed in two than improperly disclose the secrets entrusted to you. (*In each case the Worshipful Master demonstrates the signs, and the Candidate copies him*).

The grip or token is the first of the Five Points of Fellowship. They are hand to hand, foot to foot, knee to knee, breast to breast, and hand over back. (*Worshipful Master illustrates with Candidate, and disengages*) and may be thus briefly explained. (*He again demonstrates each point with the Candidate as he explains it*).

Hand to hand, I greet you as a brother; foot to foot I will support you in all your laudable undertakings knee to knee, the posture of my daily supplications shall remind me of your wants ; breast to breast, your lawful secrets when entrusted to me as such I will keep as my own ; and hand over back, I will sup-

W.M. port your character in your absence as in your presence. It is in this position, and this only, and then only in a whisper, except in open Lodge, that the word is given ; it is MACHABEN or MACHBINNA.[1]

You are now at liberty to retire in order to restore yourself to your personal comforts, and on your return to the Lodge the sign, tokens, and word will be further explained.

(The Senior Deacon conducts the Candidate to the door, instructing him to salute the Worshipful Master in the three Degrees, but only with the Penal sign in the Third Degree. The Candidate dresses himself, not forgetting his Fellow-Craft apron, and in the Lodge meanwhile the lights are fully restored. When the Candidate is ready, the Tyler gives the Third Degree knocks).

I.G. *(With step and sign)* Bro. Junior Warden, there is a report. *(Junior Warden gives one knock, and the Inner Guard opens the door).*

Ty. The Candidate on his return. *(Inner Guard closes door).*

I.G. *(With step and sign)* Worshipful Master, the Candidate on his return.

W.M. Admit him. *(Inner Guard opens door, the Senior Deacon takes the Candidate and leads him to the*

---

1. This, at least, is a common pronunciation in English Lodges to-day, phonetically rendered, with the ' ch ' pronounced as in Scotland or Germany. But many local variations are almost inevitable, for these words, unlike other Masonic words, are neither English nor recognisable Hebrew, and have therefore no standard spelling or pronunciation. Generations of purely oral transmission have corrupted them from their unknown originals. The Sloane M.S. (C. 1700) gives *Mahabyn*, and the Trinity College, Dublin M.S. (1711) has *Matchpin*. The doggerel poem *Mason's Examination* written in 1723 gives *Maughbin*. Early disclosures such as Carlile (1825) give *Mahabone* and *Macbenach ;* the American disclosure by William Morgan gives *Mah-hah-bone*, and there is no reason to believe that these were not the pronunciations of their time, and indeed still are in many Lodges. Writing a century later the Rev. F. de P. Castells (*The Apocalypse of Freemasonry*) gives them Masonically as " M.......... ben or ....bena " thus showing a mutation in the vowel sounds, precedents for which will be familiar to the student of Anglo-Saxon in the days when the written language was the knowledge of the very few. On the other hand, there is evidence that the pronunciation *Mahaboné* (quadrisyllabic) is also found, particularly in the North and West, and purists are not wanting who urge the correctness of this rendering as corresponding with that in use at the time of the Union. According to E. H. Cartwright (*A Commentary on the Free-masonic Ritual*, p. 195) the printing of the word in illicit rituals, and the ignorant ascription in the 18th century of such meanings as " rotten to the bone " have helped to crystallize the trisyllabic pronunciation.

North of the Senior Warden).

S.D.   Salute the Worshipful Master in the three degrees. *(Which the Candidate does, with full signs).*

S.W.   *(With step and sign)* Worshipful Master, I present to you Bro. A. B., on his being raised to the Third Degree, for some further mark of your favour.

W.M.   Brother Senior Warden, I delegate you to invest him with the distinguishing badge of a Master Mason. *(The Senior Warden cuts the sign, and invests the Candidate with the apron, the right hand corner of which he holds with his left hand during his next speech).*

S.W.   Bro. A. B. by the Worshipful Master's command I invest you with the distinguishing badge of a Master Mason to mark the further progress you have made in the science.

W.M.   I must state that the badge with which you have now been invested not only points out your rank as a Master Mason, but is meant to remind you of those great duties you have just solemnly engaged yourself to observe, and whilst it marks your own superiority, it calls on you to afford assistance and instruction to the Brethren in the inferior degrees.

We left off at that part of our traditional history which mentions the death of our Master Hiram Abiff. A loss so important as that of the principal architect could not fail of being generally and severely felt. The want of those plans and designs which had hitherto been regularly supplied to the different classes of workmen was the first indication that some heavy calamity had befallen our Master. The Menatschin or prefects, or more familiarly speaking, the overseers, deputed some of the most eminent of their number to acquaint King Solomon with the utter confusion into which the absence of Hiram had plunged them, and to express their apprehension that to some fatal catastrophe must be attributed his sudden and mysterious disappearance. King Solomon immediately ordered a general muster of the workmen throughout the different departments, when three of the same class of overseers were not to be found. On the same day the twelve Craftsmen who had originally joined in the conspiracy came before the King and made a voluntary confession of all they knew, down to the time of withdrawing themselves from the number of conspirators. This naturally increased the fears of King Solomon for the safety of his chief artist. He therefore selected fifteen trusty

W.M.   Fellow-Crafts, and order them to make diligent search after the person of our Master, to ascertain if he were yet alive, or had suffered death in the attempt to extort from him the secrets of his exalted Degree.

Accordingly, a stated day having been appointed for their return to Jerusalem, they formed themselves into three Fellow-Craft Lodges, and departed from the three entrances of the Temple. Many days were spent in fruitless search ; indeed, one class returned without having made any discovery of importance. A second, however, were more fortunate, for on the evening of a certain day, after having suffered the greatest privations and personal fatigues, one of the Brethren, who had rested himself in a reclining posture, to assist his rising caught hold of a shrub that grew near, which to his surprise came easily out of the ground. On a closer examination he found that the earth had been recently disturbed. He therefore hailed his companions and with their united endeavours re-opened the ground, and there found the body of our Master very indecently interred. They covered it again with all respect and reverence, and to distinguish the spot, stuck a sprig of acacia at the head of the grave.

They then hastened to Jerusalem to impart the afflicting intelligence to King Solomon. He, when the first emotions of his grief had subsided, ordered them to return and raise our Master to such a sepulture, as became his rank and exalted talents, at the same time informing them that by his untimely death the secrets of a Master Mason were lost. He therefore charged them to be particularly careful in observing whatever casual sign, token, or word might occur whilst paying this last sad tribute of respect to departed merit.

They performed their task with the utmost fidelity, and on re-opening the ground one of the Brethren looking round observed some of his companions in this position (*Worshipful Master demonstrates sign of Horror*) struck with horror at the dreadful and afflicting sight, while others viewing the ghastly wound still visible on his forehead, smote their own in sympathy with his sufferings. (*Worshipful Master demonstrates sign of Sympathy*). Two of the Brethren then descended the grave and endeavoured to raise him by the Entered Apprentice's grip, which proved a slip. They then tried the Fellow-Crafts'

W.M. which proved a slip likewise. Having both failed in their attempts, a zealous and expert brother took a more firm hold on the sinews of the hand, and with their assistance raised him on the Five Points of Fellowship ; while others, more animated, exclaimed MACHABEN or MACHBINNA, both words having a nearly similar import, one signifying the death of the builder, the other the builder is smitten.[1]

King Solomon therefore ordered that those casual signs, and that token and word, should designate all Master Masons throughout the universe, until time or circumstances should restore the genuine.

It only remains to account for the third class, who had pursued their researches in the direction of Joppa, and were meditating their return to Jerusalem, when, accidentally passing the mouth of a cavern, they heard sounds of deep lamentation and regret. On entering the cave to ascertain the cause, they found three men answering the description of those missing, who, on being charged with the murder, and finding all chance of escape cut off, made a full confession of their guilt. They were then bound and led to Jerusalem, when King Solomon sentenced them to that death the heinousness of their crime so amply merited.

(*The remainder of the Traditional History is given from the tracing board*).

Our Master was ordered to be re-interred as near to the Sanctum Sanctorum as the Israelitish law would permit ; there in a grave, from the centre three feet East and three feet West, three feet between North and South, and five feet or more perpendicular. He was not buried in the Sanctum Sanctorum, because nothing common or unclean was allowed to enter there ; not even the High Priest, but once a year ; nor then until after many washings and purifications against the great day of expiation for sins ; for by Israelitish law, all flesh was deemed unclean. The same fifteen trusty Fellow-Crafts were ordered to attend the funeral, clothed in white aprons and gloves as emblems of their innocence.

---

1. Slight variations are found in the alleged meanings of these words. There is some early authority for *brother* instead of builder, and *master* is a not uncommon rendering. *Slain* occasionally re-places smitten (e.g., in Exeter workings) in the meaning of the second word. The true etymology and history of these words (or word, for they are two derivations from a single original) is obscure ; a corrupt exegesis from the Hebrew *moth* (death) and *benaim* (builders) is possible.

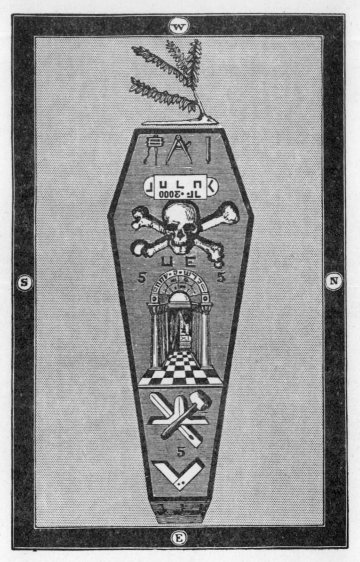

Third Degree Tracing Board

*The cypher is based on a simple noughts-and-crosses formula
and reads as follows :—on the plate, H.A.B. (for Hiram Abiff),
A(nno) L(ucis) 3000, flanked by T(ubal) C(ain).   Beneath the
skull is M.B. for the Third Degree word.*

W.M.   You have already been informed that the working tools with which our Master was slain were the Plumb Rule, Level, and heavy Maul. The ornaments of a Master Masons' Lodge are the Porch, Dormer, and Square Pavement. The Porch was the entrance to the Sanctum Sanctorum, the Dormer the window that gave light to the same, and the Square Pavement for the High Priest to walk on. The High Priest's office was to burn incense to the honour and glory of the Most High, and to pray fervently that the Almighty, of His unbounded wisdom and goodness, would be pleased to bestow peace and tranquility on the Israelitish nation during the ensuing year. The coffin, skull and cross-bones, being emblems of mortality, allude to the untimely death of our Master Hiram Abiff. He was slain three thousand years after the creation of the world.

(*This ends the tracing-board explanation*).

In the course of the ceremony you have been informed of three signs in this Degree. The whole of them are five, corresponding in number with the Five Points of Fellowship. They are the sign of Horror, the sign of Sympathy, the Penal sign, the sign of Grief and Distress, and the sign of Joy and Exultation, likewise called the Grand or Royal sign. For the sake of regularity I will go through them again, and you will copy me.

This is the sign of Horror ; this, of Sympathy ; this, the Penal sign. The sign of Grief and Distress is given by passing the right hand across the face, and dropping it over the left eyebrow in the form of a square. This took its rise at the time our Master was making his way from the North to the East entrance of the Temple, when his agony was so great that the perspiration stood in large drops on his forehead, and he made use of this sign (*demonstrates it again, and Candidate copies it*) as a temporary relief to his sufferings. This is the sign of Joy and Exultation. (*The hands are raised above the head, with the palms facing each other*). It took its rise at the time the Temple was completed, and King Solomon with the princes of his household went to view it, when they were so struck with its magnificence that with one simultaneous motion they exclaimed, O wonderful Masons.[1]

On the continent of Europe the sign of Grief and Dis-

1. *Worthy* instead of wonderful is found in some workings.

W.M. tress is given in a different manner, by clasping the hands and elevating them with their backs to the forehead, exclaiming " Come to my assistance, ye children of the widow " on the supposition that all Master Masons are Brothers to Hiram Abiff, who was a widow's son.[1] In Scotland, Ireland and the States of America the sign of Grief and Distress is given in a still different manner by throwing up the hands with the palms extended towards the heavens, and dropping them, with three distinct movements, to the sides, exclaiming, O Lord my God, O Lord my God, O Lord my God, is there no help for the widow's son ?

(The Candidate copies these signs as they are demonstrated).

I now present to you the working tools of a Master Mason. They are the Skirret, Pencil, and Compasses. The Skirret is an implement which acts on a centre pin, whence a line is drawn to mark out ground for the foundation of the intended structure. With the Pencil the skilful artist delineates the building in a draft or plan for the instruction and guidance of the workman. The Compasses enable him, with accuracy and precision, to ascertain and determine the limits and proportions of its several parts. But as we are not all operative, but rather free and accepted, or speculative, we apply these tools to our morals.
In this sense, the Skirret points out that straight and undeviating line of conduct laid down for our pursuit in the Volume of the Sacred Law. The Pencil teaches us that our words and actions are observed and recorded by the Almighty Architect, to whom we must give an account of our conduct through life. The Compasses remind us of His unerring and impartial justice, who, having defined for our instruction the limits of good and evil, will reward or punish, as we have obeyed or disregarded His Divine commands. Thus the working tools of a Master Mason teach us to bear in mind, and act according to, the laws of our Divine Creator, that when we shall be summoned from this sublunary abode, we may ascend to the Grand Lodge above, where the world's Great Architect lives and reigns for ever.

---

1. This is a Grand Orient sign ; its inclusion here indicates a certain ' economic inter-communion ' between the two Masonic systems.

THE INSTALLATION OF THE WORSHIPFUL MASTER

A DESCRIPTION OF THE CEREMONY

The Lodge is opened in the First Degree, then all Entered Apprentices are requested to retire. Then the Lodge is opened in the Second Degree. The Master Elect, who is usually the Senior Warden, as promotion is normally by seniority, is presented by a Past Master to the Installing Master ; as it is customary for each Master to instal his successor this will probably be the Worshipful Master whose year of office is concluded.

The Installing Master recites a list of qualities which are needful for the office, a Master must be of good report, well skilled in Masonry, exemplary in conduct, steady and firm in principle, and so on. Next the Ancient Charges are read to him, to each clause of which the Master Elect signifies assent by giving the sign of Fidelity. He then takes an Obligation on the Bible, swearing that he will faithfully discharge his duties, and abide by the landmarks of the order ; this Obligation, incidentally, carries no penalty.

The Fellow-Crafts are then dismissed and the Lodge is raised to the Third Degree, before which all who are not Installed Masters are requested to withdraw. The secrets of the Chair can, of course, be conferred only in the presence of Installed Masters, which makes the Chair almost the equivalent of a separate degree.

Prayer is then offered for the Master Elect, and it is explained to him that a second Obligation is required to preserve the secrets. This is taken kneeling on both knees, with both hands resting on the Bible, and the penalty is to have the right hand struck off and slung over the left shoulder, there to wither and decay.

The three emblematical lights in Freemasonry, the Bible, Square and Compasses, are brought to his notice, and he is raised from his knees with both hands by the Installing Master.

The secrets are conferred in the context of a further piece of traditional history—King Solomon (sometimes accompanied by the Queen of Sheba) visited the Temple when it was completed, and beckoned Adoniram, who succeeded Hiram Abiff as Temple Architect, to approach him. This, then is the sign ; a beckoning movement with the right hand thrice from the shoulder which is frequently (though illogically and probably incorrectly) given to the side instead of to the front. Adoniram was about to kneel before his royal master, when King Solomon prevented him and raised him up with the Installed Master's grip. This is the Third Degree or lion's grip, with each placing his left hand on the left shoulder of the other, the arms being kept straight. As King Solomon did this, he said, Rise, GIBLUM. This is the Installed Master's word, and signifies Excellent Mason. As the Royal party were about to retire, Adoniram gave a humble salute, bowing and saluting with the right hand from the forehead three times, stepping backwards with the right foot. This is the sign of Salutation.

The new Master is now invested with his collar and jewel (the Square), placed in the Chair with the Installed Masters' grip and word, and presented with the gavel. His first act as Master is to invest his predecessor with the Past Master's jewel, after which he is saluted three (or five) times as an Installed Master.

This concludes the Inner Workings of the Installation ceremony as it is usually performed. There is, however, a much lengthier version to be found in some Lodges, in which the Board of Installed Masters is opened and closed in full form, and the Master Elect is given a pass word to it (RABBONI) A further penalty may be added to the Obligation, in which the tongue cleaves to the roof of the mouth. The Traditional History is given in greater detail. In addition to the Beckoning sign and the sign of Salutation, three further signs are given, the sign of the Plumb Line (in which the right hand is extended as if holding that implement), the sign of Secrecy (given by placing the first finger on the lips, with the thumb pointing vertically from below the jaw), and the Penal sign (the left hand is placed across the right wrist, and then a second movement is made as if throwing the right hand over the left shoulder). In this extended ceremony there are Installed Masters' working tools, the trowel, the plumb line, and the plan of the work.

If this longer working is employed, it must be explained to the newly-installed Master that these extra signs and words are not obligatory, nor required from Installed Masters generally.

When the Board of Installed Masters is closed, the Master Masons are recalled. They perambulate the Lodge and salute their new Master who is duly proclaimed to them. The working-tools of the Third Degree are then presented. Then the Lodge is lowered to the Second Degree, when the ceremonies are repeated with the Fellow-Crafts, and the Second Degree working tools are presented. The procedure is finally repeated in the First Degree, when the Entered Apprentices are admitted. The ceremonies are concluded with the investiture, accompanied by suitable words, of the officers of the Lodge by the newly-installed Worshipful Master.

DARKNESS VISIBLE

THE FURNISHINGS OF THE ROYAL ARCH CHAPTER

The form of a Holy Royal Arch Chapter, as the Symbolical Lecture points out, is that of a catenarian arch, that is, an arch based on the curve, inverted, formed by a chain freely hanging between two supports. This arch is in the East, and the keystones, so to speak, are formed by the three Principals, Most Excellent Zerubbabel in the centre, Excellent Haggai on his right, and Excellent Joshua on his left. Unlike the officers in the Craft, they have no pedestals ; their knocks are given, not with gavel and sounding-board, but with the ends of their sceptres on the floor.

The Arch is further formed by five banners. The centre one is white, and bears the device of a triple tau within a triangle. The other four are the leading standards of the four divisions of the army of Israel ; the Ox (Ephraim) the Man (Reuben) on the left, the Eagle (Dan) and Lion (Judah) on the right.

The sides or columns supporting the Arch are made up of the Companions on the North and South ; above them are ranged twelve further banners or ensigns bearing the devices of the Twelve Tribes. The arrangements of these varies somewhat, but the usual order (followed by the Supreme Grand Chapter) is, from East to West on the North side, Judah, Naphtali, Asher, Dan, Benjamin, Manasseh ; on the South side, Issachar, Zabulon, Reuben, Simeon, Gad, and Ephraim. Scribe Ezra, the secretary, has his seat on the North side, Scribe Nehemiah, who has the duties of the Inner Guard in the Craft, either faces him in the South, or else (less correctly) takes his place in the North-West corner by the door. The Sojourners sit in the West. The Janitor corresponds to the Tyler, and remains in the anteroom outside the door.

In front of the Principals is the Altar. This is a double cube, the top being about fourteen or sixteen inches square. The West front of the Altar is inscribed with the initials S.K.I., H.K.T., and H.A.B., standing for Solomon King of Israel, Hiram King of Tyre, and Hiram Abiff, the " Three Grand Masters " at the building of the first Temple, and also has inscribed on it the triple tau. On top of the Altar is a brass plate with a raised triangle within a circle. Brass letters are arranged to spell out the sacred words, JE-HO-VAH on the circle, JAH-BUL-ON on the three sides of the triangle, with the Hebrew characters Aleph, Beth, and Lamed at the three points of the triangle.[1] At the end of the ceremonies

---

1. See frontispiece. But Oxford workings transpose the words, and place Jehovah on the triangle and Jah-Bul-On on the circle.

these letters and characters are stirred around and mixed. A white satin veil covers the Altar before the Chapter is declared open, and at certain points in the Ceremony of Exaltation. Six candlesticks flank the Altar in the form of an equilateral triangle, with the apex pointing to the East.

On the floor is spread the vault-cloth or floor-cloth, usually about eleven by five feet ; instances are known, however, of the vault itself being represented by an actual wooden arch with three removable keystones. On the floor-cloth to the West (in front of the Principal Sojourner) is the Volume of the Sacred Law on its cushion,[1] open so that it can be read from the West. On the North side of it are the Square and Compasses, on the South the Sword lying across the Trowel. At the extreme West of the floor-cloth are arranged the working-tools, the Shovel on the left, the Crow-bar in the Centre, and the Pickaxe on the right. In the North-West corner of the floor-cloth are arranged the life-lines, in the South-West the scroll. In a few workings (notably Aldersgate) the five regular platonic bodies explained in the Symbolical Lecture should actually be displayed in line on the floor-cloth, the tetrahedron, octahedron, cube, icosahedron, and the dodeca-hedron. The kneeling-stool is placed in the West, just outside the floor-cloth.

Royal Arch regalia for all Companions consists of apron, sash, and jewel. The apron is of white kid with a crimson and purple irradiated border, crimson falls with metallic tassels, and the triple tau in a triangle on the three-cornered flap. The sash is also of crimson and purple indented, worn over the left shoulder and joined under the right arm, with the triple tau and triangle in gold, and gold fringes at the end. The jewel is described in its appropriate lecture on p. 183.

Over this regalia the three Principals wear robes : Zerub-babel's is crimson, Haggai's purple and Joshua's blue. Other officers wear surplices. The Principals have sceptres with distinctive emblems, a crown for Zerubbabel, the all-seeing eye for Haggai, and a mitre for Joshua. Royal Arch officers, like those of the Craft, wear their distinctive jewels of office suspended from collars.

1. A smaller Bible should be available for ceremonial use in opening the Chapter and for the Candidate's Obligation.

DARKNESS VISIBLE
ROYAL ARCH SIGNS AND WORDS

There are five signs in the Royal Arch, a lack of uniformity even greater than that in the Craft, however, makes them difficult to describe with precision. Royal Arch Masons themselves freely admit this ; the Rev. F. de P. Castells, for instance, writes : " We feel strongly that even if the Supreme Grand Chapter does not restore the old Ceremonies, it should at least standardize the signs so that they might be given in the same way everywhere." (*Historical Analysis of the Holy Royal Arch Ritual*, p. 112).

1   The Penal sign. This is similar to the Penal sign of the Entered Apprentice, only given with the left hand to the throat. According to the usage of the Aldersgate Chapter of Improvement which declares that the thumb should never be visible in any Royal Arch sign, the thumb is not squared. In dismissing the sign the hand is not drawn across the throat, but dropped straight to the side. Sometimes, but less correctly, the left hand is placed to the back of the neck for this sign.

2   The Reverential or Hailing sign. The head is slightly bowed, and the left hand is raised to the forehead shielding the eyes like a vizor. Commonly (but perhaps again less correctly) the forehead is between the extended thumb and first finger. Then in a second movement the right hand is raised to the left breast as in the sign of Reverence, though sometimes again the thumb is squared. The sign is dismissed by dropping both hands simultaneously.
This is the sign used by Companions in addressing the Principals, or when entering or leaving the Chapter while it is open.

3   The Penitential or Supplicatory sign. The knees are bent, and the hands are either clasped as in prayer (Aldersgate) or extended above the head with the palms facing upwards. The right foot may be in advance.

4   The Monitorial sign. The hands are placed behind the hips, thumbs forward, the elbows extended to form two triangles.

5   The Fiducial sign. The arms are stretched forward with palms facing downwards, not unlike a diver about to take off. Usually the knees are slightly bent, and the head bent forward. Sometimes the body is thrown forward on the left foot.

Pass-Words :— AMMI RUHAMAH.[1]
Words :—   JE-HO-VAH, JAH-BUL-ON.[2]

There is no Royal Arch ' grip ' in the sense of a hand-clasp as in the Craft. What is sometimes known as the grip is the series of hand-over-hand movements used to raise the Candidate from his knees (in the vault) which is described on p. 164-5. Nor is there any ' regular step ' in Royal Arch workings.

The pass-words, words, and signs of the three Principals are given in the Installation ceremonies, pp. 184-186.

ROYAL ARCH RITUALS

Although probably of more recent origin than the three Craft Degrees, the Royal Arch has considerable diversity in its workings. Apart from Carlile's disclosure of 1825, the earliest recorded post-Union Ritual is a manuscript one bearing the date 1834, in Grand Lodge Library, which preserves the general outline of what is known of earlier Rituals, yet makes certain departures. In 1853 a ' Chapter of Promulgation ' was set up which made an attempt (quite unsuccessfully) to establish a greater degree of uniformity, by disseminating the ritual as revised by the Rev. Adam Brown in 1834.

Hence, as in the Craft, there are many workings, such as Domatic, which claims to be the oldest, Aldersgate, which follows it very closely indeed, Grenadiers, Hornsey, Oxford, Standard, Sussex, Midland, Complete, Perfect, Metropolitan and many local uses. Certain differences between the workings, however, are indicated in footnotes.

CEREMONY OF OPENING A ROYAL ARCH CHAPTER

(When the Companions are in their places,[3] and the Bible opened at Isaiah XII, the three Principals enter and stand in line in the West, and Zerubbabel says, " To Order, Companions." They take a step towards the East, with the Reverential or Hailing Sign, when

1. See Hosea II, 1. The use of this pass-word is of fairly recent origin, for when the Royal Arch was restricted to those past the Chair in the Craft the Installed Master's word GIBLUM was used. As this qualification is still demanded of the Principals, GIBLUM is now the pass-word to the Third Chair.
2. Carlile and other English disclosures give JAO-BUL-ON. But it seems that the earlier practice (still not altogether extinct) was to spell the words on the altar-top in Hebrew characters, hence there was no fixed English spelling. The Latin alphabet letters now in general use, however, give the first syllable more logically as JAH. The Aleph, Beth, and Lamed at the tips of the triangle are, of course, still represented by their Hebrew characters.
3. Until fairly recent times the opening ceremony was performed by and in the presence of Principals and Past Principals only, the Companions being admitted when the Chapter was open. The earlier custom still lingers in places.

Joshua says " Omnipotent." They advance a further step, and Haggai says " Omniscient." Then another step, and Zerubbabel says " Omnipresent."[1] Zerubbabel then offers the following prayer).[2]

Z.   Omnipotent God, unto whom all hearts are open, all desires known, and from whom no secrets are hid, cleanse the thoughts of our hearts by the inspiration of Thy Holy Spirit, that we may perfectly love Thee and worthily magnify Thy Holy Name.

All   So mote it be.

(A Bible, not the official one from the cushion, but a smaller one, is handed to the Principals by Scribe Nehemiah or by the Director of Ceremonies. This is supported on a triangle made by the left hands of the three Principals, palms upwards, the fingers in each case touching the wrist of the Principal to the right. The right hands, palms downwards, similarly form a triangle on the Bible, the fingers touching the wrist of the Principal to the left).

Z.H.&J. We three do meet and agree.... in love and unity.... the sacred word to keep.... and never to divulge the same.... unless when three.... such as we.... do meet and agree.... agree.... agree.... agree...... agree. *(This is said in turn, phrase by phrase, Zerubbabel leading).*

(The three Principals kiss the Bible in turn, Zerubbabel doing so twice, i.e., first and last. They resume the Reverential or Hailing Sign. Zerubbabel then advances East alone, by way of the North, with seven steps, halting and bowing to the Altar after the third, fifth, and seventh step. He turns and faces West, still holding the sign. Joshua and Haggai then advance East simultaneously, Joshua by the South and Haggai by the North, each by seven steps, halting and bowing at the third, fifth, and seventh. The Triple Triangle is formed, (i) with the right feet, (ii) with the left hands, each taking his right-hand companion by the left wrist, and (iii) with the right hands, each taking his left-hand companion by the right wrist. The right hands are raised, to form an arch.[3] In this

1. In Metropolitan and some other workings, three steps, followed by two and two, are taken at this point, and the words spoken by Joshua and Zerubbabel are transposed.

2. This prayer is of course a bowdlerized form of the Collect for Purity from the Book of Common Prayer, with the Christian ending omitted.

3. Aldersgate Chapter of Improvement refers to *four* triangles, an additional one being made by joining the right knees bent inwards

position the Sacred Words are recited syllable by syllable as follows, the J pronounced Y :—

Z.	H.	J.
JE—	HO—	VAH
—	JE—	HO—
VAH	—	JE—
HO—	VAH	—
JAH—	BUL—	ON
—	JAH—	BUL—
ON	—	JAH—
BUL—	ON	—

The Principals then take up their sceptres which are in readiness on their chairs, salute them with a kiss, and repeat mentally their words of office, Zerubbabel's is JAH, Haggai's EL SHADDAI, and Joshua's EL ELOHE ISRAEL.[1] Haggai and Joshua then remove the veil from the Altar. The three take their chairs. Four knocks are given, evenly spaced, with the sceptres ; Zerubbabel first, followed by the other two, then Zerubbabel last).

Z.   Companions, in the name of the True and Living God Most High, I declare this Holy Royal Arch Chapter duly opened.
(The knocks are repeated as before).

THE CEREMONY OF CLOSING A ROYAL ARCH CHAPTER

(Four knocks, given as in the Opening ceremony).
Z.   Companions, assist me to close the Chapter.
(The Principals leave their chairs and stand near the Altar, facing West, holding their sceptres under their left arms.[2] The Companions stand to order with the Reverential or Hailing Sign. The Bible is passed up, and held as in the Opening).
Z.   To order, Companions.
Z.H. & J. We all do meet and agree......in love and unity...... etc. *(As in the Opening. The Principals salute the Bible, which is then closed and handed round to the Companions to salute in turn.[3] The three Principals form a triangle with their sceptres).*

1. These words are given them at their installation, see pp. 184-186. Aldersgate workings, incidentally, omit ISRAEL from Joshua's words.
2. Or in some workings leaving their sceptres on their chairs.
3. The salutation of the Bible by the Companions is frequently omitted. This ceremony has been dropped in Grand Chapter as taking up too much time, but private Chapters are free to do so or not as they please.

Z. Companion Principal Sojourner, the labours of this convocation being ended, you have my command to close the Chapter.

P.S. Companions, in the name of the True and Living God Most High, and by command of the Most Excellent, I close this Chapter until................., emergencies excepted, of which every Companion will receive due notice.
(*Principals extend their hands in the Fiducial sign*).

Z. Glory to God on high.

H. On earth peace.

J. Goodwill towards men.
(*The Principals dismiss Fiducial sign, Past Zerubbabel steps up to the Altar and mixes the letters and characters*).

P.Z. Companions, nothing now remains but, according to ancient custom, to lock up our secrets in a safe repository, uniting in the act Fidelity, Fidelity, Fidelity, Fidelity.
(*The Companions strike their breasts with the right hand, fingers extended, thumb closed, at each repetition of the word Fidelity*).

CHARGE GIVEN WHEN THE CHAPTER IS CLOSED, BUT BEFORE THE COMPANIONS HAVE SEPARATED

Z. You are now about to quit this sacred retreat of friendship and virtue, to mix again with the world. Amidst its concerns and employments, forget not the duties you have heard forcibly and so frequently inculcated at our meetings. Be ye therefore diligent, prudent, temperate, and discreet ; remember also that around our Altar you have solemnly and repeatedly engaged yourself to befriend and relieve with unhesitating cordiality, so far as shall be in your power, every Brother who shall need your assistance, that you have promised to remind him, in the most tender manner, of his failings, and aid his reformation, to vindicate his character when wrongly traduced, and to suggest in his behalf the most candid, favourable, and palliating circumstances in extenuation of his conduct, even when it is justly reprehended ; that the world may observe and feel how truly Masons love one another. These generous principles ought to extend beyond the limited arena of our own society, for every human being has a claim upon your kind offices, so much we enjoin you to do good unto all, but

Z.   more especially to the household of the faithful.[1] By diligence in the duties of your respective callings, by liberal benevolence and diffusive charity, by constancy and fidelity in your friendship, by uniformly just, amiable, and virtuous deportment, we charge you to manifest the beneficial effects of our ancient and honourable institution ; and let it not be supposed, Brethren, that you will labour in vain, or spend your strength for nought, for your work will be with the Lord, and your recompense with God. Finally, Brethren, be ye all of one heart and one mind, love one another and live in peace ; and may the God of love and peace delight to dwell with you, and to bless you.

CEREMONY OF EXALTATION

(When the Chapter is opened and the minutes have been read and confirmed, the Candidate, who must have been a Master Mason for a period of at least four weeks, is balloted for if this has not been done previously. If the ballot is favourable, the ceremony proceeds. Joshua and Haggai re-veil the Altar).

Z.   Companion Principal Sojourner, you will retire and entrust the Candidate.[2]

(The Principal Sojourner retires, and examines the Candidate in the anteroom. Sometimes this examination takes the form of the test questions in the Third Degree, but commonly this shorter form is used).

P.S.   Bro. A. B., advance to me in the three Degrees of Craft Masonry, communicating the words of a Master Mason on the Five Points of Fellowship. *(Which is done).*

P.S.   Do you pledge your honour as a man, and your fidelity as a Mason, that you have been raised to the Sublime Degree of a Master Mason for four weeks and upwards ?

Can.   I do. *(And he must, of course, produce his Grand Lodge Certificate to that effect).*

P.S.   Do you likewise pledge yourself, under the penalties of all your Obligations, that you will conceal what I shall now impart to you with the same strict caution as the other secrets in Freemasonry ?

Can.   I do.

P.S.   Then I will entrust you with the pass words leading to this supreme Degree, they are AMMI RUHAMAH.

1. See Galatians, VI, 10. But " faithful " in this Masonic context does not mean what St. Paul meant by the household of faith !
2. Metropolitan workings add " and ascertain his proficiency in the former degrees."

P.S. The import of the words is, " My people have found mercy."

   (*The Candidate is prepared by the Janitor. All that is necessary is that he should be hoodwinked, but the practice still holds in some Chapters of preparing him as for the ceremony of raising to the Third Degree, i.e., both breasts, both arms, and both knees bare, and both feet slippered. He wears the Master Mason's apron. When all is ready the Janitor knocks*).[1]

N. Most Excellent, there is a report.

Z. Companion Scribe Nehemiah, see who seeks admission.

N. (*Opening door, to Janitor*) Whom have you there ?

Jan. Bro. A. B., who has been regularly initiated into Freemasonry, passed to the Degree of a Fellow-Craft, and in due time raised to the Sublime Degree of a Master Mason, in which capacity he has exercised himself for four weeks and upwards, and as a reward of merit has been entrusted with the pass words leading to the Supreme Degree to which he seeks to be admitted, and for which ceremony he is properly prepared.

N. How does he hope to obtain the privileges of this Supreme Degree ?

Jan. By the assistance of the True and Living God Most High, the united aid of the Circle and Triangle, and the benefit of the pass words.

N. Is he in possession of the pass words ?

Jan. Ask him.

N. (*To Candidate*) Will you give me the pass words ?

Can. AMMI RUHAMAH.

N. The import of the words ?

Can. " My people have found mercy."

N. Wait, while I report to the Most Excellent. (*Closes door*). Most Excellent, Bro. A. B., who has been regularly initiated, etc., etc. (*same as report Janitor's*) for which ceremony he is properly prepared.

Z. How does he hope to obtain the privileges of this Supreme Degree ?

N. By the assistance of, etc., etc., and the benefit of the

---

1. Custom varies in the forms which the Janitor's reports take. The usual report (e.g., to announce a Companion arriving late) is a single knock. A Candidate for Exaltation and the " Three Sojourners who were sent to prepare the ground " may be announced with four evenly-spaced knocks, but in some workings the former is announced with the Third Degree knocks (rat-tat ....tat), which are also used to announce the " three Master Masons from Babylon " later in the ceremony.

N.   pass words.

Z.   Is he in possession of the pass words ?

N.   He is, Most Excellent.

Z.   Admit him.

(Nehemiah opens the door. The Principal Sojourner takes the Candidate's right hand in his left and leads him to the kneeling stool in the West. The Assistant Sojourner is on the Candidate's left).

Z.   Bro. A. B., as you seek preferment in our Order, and have been entrusted with the pass words leading to this Supreme Degree, we must inquire if you freely and voluntarily offer yourself a Candidate for Royal Arch Masonry ?

Can.   I do.

Z.   Do you present yourself with a desire of improving in Freemasonry, and directing that improvement to the glory of God and the good of man ?

Can.   I do.

Z.   Are you willing to take the sacred and Solemn Obligation, restricted to this Supreme Degree, and if admitted, to keep inviolate our mystic rites ?

Can.   I am.

Z.   Then you will kneel and receive the benefit of Masonic prayer.

(The Principals give four knocks, the Candidate kneels, and the Companions stand to order with the sign of Reverence).

Z.   Almighty God, at whose command the world burst forth from chaos, and all created nature had its birth, we humbly implore Thee to bestow Thy spiritual blessing on this convocation, and grant that the Brother who now seeks to participate in the light of our mysteries may be endued with a portion of Thy divine Spirit ; may he not enter our Order lightly, nor recede from it hastily, but pursue it steadfastly ; and may he ever remember that the object of our Institution is the welfare of our fellow-creatures, but, above all, the honour and glory of Thy most Holy Name.

All   So mote it be.

Z.   Bro. A. B., in all cases of difficulty and danger, in whom do you put your trust ?

Can.   In the True and Living God Most High.

Z.   Glad are we to find your faith continued on so firm a basis. You rise and follow your conductor.

(Four knocks. Candidate rises). Companions, take notice that Bro. A. B., who has been regularly initiated into Freemasonry, passed to the Degree of a

Z.   Fellow-Craft, and in due time raised to the Sublime Degree of a Master Mason, is about to pass in view before you, to show that he is a Candidate properly prepared to be exalted into Royal Arch Masonry.
(The Principal Sojourner, walking backwards, leads the Candidate round the Chapter ending in the West, facing the East. There is no ' squaring' in the Royal Arch).

Z.   Bro. A. B., as you seek to participate in the light of our mysteries, we must call upon you to advance towards the Sacred Shrine, in which they are deposited, by seven steps, halting and bowing at the third, fifth, and seventh, for at each step you will approach nearer to the Sacred and Mysterious Name of the True and Living God Most High.
(The Principal Sojourner instructs the Candidate to take three steps, commencing with the left foot, halt, and bow ; take two steps commencing with the right foot, halt and bow ; take two more commencing with the right foot, halt and bow. The Principal Sojurner then stands on the Candidate's right, facing East).

Z.   You have now arrived at the crown of a vaulted chamber, into which it is necessary that you should descend. You will therefore figuratively wrench forth two or the Arch-stones.
(The Principal Sojourner takes up the crow-bar from the floor-cloth and places it in the Candidate's hands, which he guides into making two levering motions. He then replaces the crow-bar on the floor-cloth).

Z.   Let the Candidate be duly lowered into the Vault, and attend to a portion of the writings of our Grand Master King Solomon.
(The Principal Sojourner instructs the Candidate to kneel on the kneeling-stool before him. The Principals knock, the Companions stand to order with the sign of Reverence.[1] Joshua reads Proverbs II, 1-9, and III, 13-20).

J.   " My son, if thou wilt receive my words, and hide my commandments with thee ;
So that thou incline thine ear unto wisdom, and apply thy heart to understanding ;
Yea, if thou criest after knowledge, and liftest up thy voice for understanding ;
If thou seekest her as silver, and searchest for her as for hid treasures :
Then shalt thou understand the fear of the Lord, and find the knowledge of God.

1. In some workings the Companions sit for the Scripture readings.

J.   For the Lord giveth wisdom : out of His mouth cometh knowledge and understanding.

He layeth up sound wisdom for the righteous : He is a buckler to them that walk uprightly.

He keepeth the paths of judgment, and preserveth the way of His saints.

Then shalt thou understand righteousness, and judgment, and equity : yea, every good path."

" Happy is the man that findeth wisdom, and the man that getteth understanding.

For the merchandise of it is better than the merchandise of silver, and the gain thereof than fine gold.

She is more precious than rubies ; and all the things thou canst desire are not to be compared unto her.

Length of days is in her right hand ; and in her left hand riches and honour.

Her ways are ways of pleasantness, and all her paths are peace.

She is a tree of life to them that lay hold upon her : and happy is every one that retaineth her.

The Lord by wisdom hath founded the earth ; by understanding hath He established the Heavens.

By His knowledge the depths are broken up, and the clouds drop down the dew."

Z.   You will now endeavour to find something within the vault.

(*The Principal Sojourner guides the Candidate's right hand to grope on the floor-cloth by the kneeling-stool, and places a scroll in his hand. He prompts the Candidate's next answers*).

Can.   It is found.

Z.   What is found ?

Can.   Something like a scroll of vellum or parchment.

Z.   What are its contents ?

Can.   For the want of light I am unable to discover.

(*Principal Sojourner lodges the scroll in the candidate's bosom*).[1]

Z.   Let that want of light remind you that man by nature is the child of ignorance and error, and would ever have remained in a state of darkness, had it not pleased the Almighty to call him to light and immortality by the revelations of His Holy Will and Word. Rise, wrench forth the Key-stone, and prepare to receive the light of the Holy Word.

(*The Principal Sojourner assists the Candidate to rise, again places the crow-bar in his hands, and*

1. This can be extremely awkward, and in many workings the scroll is at this point replaced on the floor-cloth.

guides him to make one levering motion).

Z.   Let the Candidate be again lowered into the Vault, and attend to a portion of the writings of the prophet Haggai.

(The Principal Sojourner instructs the Candidate to kneel, and the Companions stand to order with sign of Reverence. The Principals give four knocks, and Haggai reads Haggai II, 1-9).

H.   " In the seventh month, in the one and twentieth day of the month, came the word of the Lord by the prophet Haggai, saying,

Speak now to Zerubbabel, the son of Shealtiel, governor of Judah, and to Joshua, the son of Josedech, the High Priest, and to the residue of the people, saying, Who is left among you that saw this house in her first glory ? And how do you see it now ? Is it not in your eyes in comparison of it as nothing ?

Yet now be strong, O Zerubbabel, saith the Lord; and be strong, O Joshua, son of Josedech, the high priest; and be strong, all ye people of the land, saith the Lord, and work; for I am with you, saith the Lord of Hosts.

According to the word that I covenanted with you when ye came out of Egypt, so My Spirit remaineth among you : fear ye not.

For thus saith the Lord of Hosts : Yet once, it is a little while, and I will shake the heavens, and the earth, and the sea, and the dry land.

And I will shake all nations, and the desire of all nations shall come : and I will fill this house with glory, saith the Lord of Hosts.

The silver is mine, and the gold is mine, saith the Lord of Hosts.

The glory of this latter house shall be greater than of the former, saith the Lord of Hosts : and in this place will I give peace, said the Lord of Hosts."

Z.   You will now prepare yourself to take the sacred and Solemn Obligation, without which none can be exalted into this Supreme Degree.

(The Principals give the knocks, and then leave their chairs and proceed to the Altar. The Companions gather round the Ensigns and stand to order with the sign of Fidelity.[1] The Principal Sojourner brings a small Bible to the Candidate).

1. The sign of Reverence is used here in many workings which take the line that Craft signs should never be used in the Royal Arch. The difference lies merely in the position of the thumb, which is squared upwards in the sign of Fidelity, closed (and even concealed by the fingers) in the sign of Reverence.

P.S.   Support the Volume of the Sacred Law[1] on your left
         hand, and place your right hand upon it.

Z.   State your names at length, and say after me :—

OBLIGATION

Can.   I, A. B., in the presence of the True and Living God
         Most High, and of this Holy Royal Arch Chap-
         ter, duly constituted, consecrated, and congre-
         gated, of my own free will and accord, do hereby
         and hereon (*Principal Sojourner places his left
         hand on the Candidate's right hand and on the
         Bible*) most solemnly promise and swear that I
         will always hele, conceal, and never divulge any
         of the secrets or mysteries restricted to this
         Supreme Degree, denominated the Holy Royal
         Arch of Jerusalem, to anyone in the world, un-
         less it be a true and lawful Companion of the
         Order whom I shall find to be such after strict
         examination.   I further solemnly promise that I
         will not dare to pronounce that Sacred and
         Mysterious Name which may now for the first
         time be communicated to me, unless in the pres-
         ence and with the assistance of two or more
         Royal Arch Companions, or in the body of a
         lawfully constituted Royal Arch Chapter, whilst
         acting as First Principal.   All these points
         I solemnly swear to observe, without evasion,
         equivocation, or mental reservation of any kind,
         under the no less penalty, on the violation of
         any of them, than that of suffering loss of life by
         having my head struck off. So help me the True
         and Living God Most High, and keep me stead-
         fast in this the Sacred and Solemn Obligation
         of a Royal Arch Mason.

Z.   As a pledge of your fidelity, and to render what you
         have repeated a Solemn Obligation binding on you
         so long as you shall live, you will seal it with your
         lips four times[2] on the Volume of the Sacred Law.
         (*Which the Candidate does*).   Companion Principal
         Sojourner, you will raise the Candidate in due form
         by the grip of a Royal Arch Màson.
         (*The Principal Sojourner raises the Candidate in four
         movements during his following speech*).

P.S.   (*Taking the Candidate's right hand in his*) Brother
         A. B., now (*places left hand, palm upwards, on the*

1. **Domatic workings here depart from the usual Masonic tradition
   and substitute the 'Bible' for the 'Volume of the Sacred Law.'**
2. **In a few earlier workings, five times.**

outside of Candidate's right arm near the wrist) a
Companion (*Principal Sojourner brings his right hand,
palm inwards, up above his left hand, placing it inside
the Candidate's arm*) of our Order, (*he brings his
left hand, palm inwards, up above his right hand,
placing it outside the Candidate's arm just above the
elbow*). Rise. (*He brings his right hand, palm inwards and upwards, up under the Candidate's arm-
pit, and raises him*).

Z.   Having been kept for a considerable time in a state of
darkness, what, in your present condition, is the
predominant wish of your heart?

Can.   Light.

(*The Companions hold the Ensigns tilted forward, on
either side, to form an arch, which the Candidate will
see through when he is restored to light. At the end
of this archway the three Principals hold their sceptres
in the form of a triangle, framing Zerubbabel*).

Z.   Companion Principal Sojourner, let that blessing be
restored to the Candidate. (*Principal Sojourner removes the hoodwink*).

Z.   We congratulate you upon being admitted to the light
of our Order, and it is with satisfaction we express
our confidence that your future conduct will fully
justify our partiality in having exalted you into this
Supreme Degree, so truly denominated the essence of
Freemasonry. You will now read the contents of the
scroll you brought with you out of the Vault.

(*If the Candidate has not got the scroll in his bosom,
the Principal Sojourner hands it to him. He reads
from it Gen. I, 1-3*).

Can.   " In the beginning God created the heaven and the
earth.

And the earth was without form and void; and darkness was upon the face of the deep. And the Spirit
of God moved upon the face of the waters.

And God said, Let there be light, and there was
light."

Z.   Such my newly exalted Companion, are the first
words of that Sacred Volume, which contains the
record of God's revealed will. Let us therefore bless,
praise, and magnify His Holy Name for the knowledge vouchsafed to us, and walk worthily in the light
which shines around.

You are now at liberty to retire in order to restore
your personal comfort, and on your return to the
Chapter the ceremony will be proceeded with.

(*The Sojourners escort the Candidate to the door,*

and the Principals lower their sceptres. The Sojourners return, and remove their collars, surplices, and regalia which they place on their chairs and again retire, saluting with the Reverential or Hailing sign. In the anteroom the Candidate restores his clothing (if he has been prepared as for raising) and both he and the Sojourners wear Master Masons' aprons. When they are ready the Janitor gives the Third Degree knocks).

N.   Most Excellent, there is a report.

Z.   Companion Scribe Nehemiah, see who seeks admission.

N.   *(Opens door)* Whom have you there ?

Jan.   Three Master Masons from Babylon, having heard that you are about to rebuild the Temple to the honour and glory of the Most High, are anxious to sojourn amongst you, and to assist in that great and glorious undertaking.

N.   Wait, while I report to the Most Excellent. *(Shuts door).* Most Excellent, three Master Masons from Babylon, having heard, etc., etc. *(same as Janitor's report).*

Z.   Admit them. *(The two Sojourners and the Candidate enter, and stand in line in the West, facing East).* Strangers, whence come you ?

P.S.   From Babylon, Most Excellent.

Z.   What is your request ?

P.S.   Having heard that you are about to rebuild the Temple to the honour and glory of the Most High, we are anxious to sojourn amongst you and to assist in that great and glorious undertaking.

Z.   As no strangers can be permitted to assist in that holy work, we must first inquire who you are ?

P.S.   Brethren of your own tribes and families, Most Excellent.

Z.   But are you not descended from those who fled when the City and Holy Temple were sorely oppressed, or are you of those left behind by the Babylonish General for the purpose of tilling the land ?

P.S.   We would scorn to be descended from those who basely fled when the City and Holy Temple were sorely oppressed : neither are we of those left behind by the Babylonish General for the purpose of tilling the land; but we are nobly born, and, like yourselves, descended from a race of patriarchs and kings. Abraham, Isaac and Jacob were our forefathers. Most Excellent, we are of the royal line of David and princely tribe of Judah, who for their sins and those of the people

P.S. were led into captivity, with Jehoiakim, their king, by Nebuchadnezzar, King of Babylon, there to remain for seventy years, as was foretold by the prophet Jeremiah. The period of our captivity expired in the first year of the reign of Cyrus, King of Persia, when it pleased the Almighty to inspire that noble prince to issue the following proclamation :—Thus saith Cyrus, King of Persia. All the kingdoms of the earth hath the Lord God of heaven given me ; and He hath charged me to build Him an house in Jerusalem, which is in Judah. Who is there among you of all His people ? The Lord his God be with him, and let him go up.[1] We eagerly availed ourselves of this opportunity of returning to our native land, and have come up accordingly to sojourn amongst you, and to offer our assistance in rebuilding the Temple to the honour and glory of the Most High, who hath promised by the mouth of His holy prophet there to establish His Name for ever, and give peace to the whole earth.

Z. We acknowledge your noble ancestry, and cheerfully admit you as members of our tribes and families. It only remains for us to inquire on what part of the holy work you wish to be employed ?

P.S. Any position to which Your Excellencies may be pleased to appoint us will be deemed an honour conferred.

Z. Humility and docility are sure indications of merit, but, from the lateness of your application, the principal offices are already filled. We will, however, engage you to prepare the ground for the foundation of the second Temple, on the site where the first formerly stood ; for which purpose you will be provided with proper working implements, but we lay this strict injunction upon you, that should you during the progress of your labours make any discovery you deem of importance you will communicate it to none but the Grand Sanhedrim now sitting.

P.S. We humbly thank Your Excellencies for the trust reposed in us, and pledge ourselves to a faithful discharge of the duties thereof.

(Scribes Ezra and Nehemiah take up the working-tools and lifelines from their places on the floor, and distribute them, the crow-bar, scroll, and life-lines to the Principal Sojourner, the pick-axe to the Assistant Sojourner, and the shovel to the Candidate).

1. 2 Chron. XXXVI, 23.

Z. Go, and may the God of your fathers be with you.
(The Sojourners and the Candidate retire. In the anteroom the lifeline is tied round the waist of the Principal Sojourner, small cords are tied round his wrists, the other ends of which, when they have re-entered the Chapter, are held by the Assistant Sojourner and the Candidate. The three carry their working tools which were given them by the Scribes. When all is ready, the Janitor gives four knocks).

N. Most Excellent, there is a report.

Z. Companion Scribe Nehemiah, see who seeks admission.

N. *(Opening the door)* Whom have you there ?

Jan. The three Sojourners who were sent to prepare the ground for the foundation of the second Temple, having made a discovery they deem of importance, are anxious to communicate the same to the Grand Sanhedrim now sitting.

N. Wait, while I report to the Most Excellent. *(Closes door, gives Reverential or Hailing Sign).* Most Excellent, the three Sojourners who were sent to prepare the ground for the foundation of the second Temple, having made a discovery they deem of importance. are anxious to communicate the same to Your Excellencies.

Z. Admit them. *(Scribe Nehemiah opens the door and admits them).* Brethren, we understand that you have made a discovery you deem of importance. It is therefore necessary that you communicate to us the discovery you have made, and the circumstances which led thereto.

P.S. Resuming our labours early this morning we discovered a pair of pillars of exquisite design and workmanship ; proceeding onwards, we found six other pairs of equal symmetry and beauty, which from their position, appeared to have supported the roof of a subterranean passage or gallery leading to where the Most Holy Place formerly stood. Our progress was here impeded by the fragments which had fallen during the conflagration of the former Temple. These we cleared away, and arrived at what appeared to be solid rock ; accidentally striking it with my crow, I remarked a hollow sound. I therefore hailed my companions, when he with the pick loosened the earth which he with the shovel cleared away, when that which at first appeared solid rock proved to be a compact piece of masonry wrought in the form of a dome. Aware of who had been the Architect of the

P.S.

former Temple, and that no part thereof had been constructed in vain, we determined to examine it further, for which purpose we wrenched forth two of the Archstones, when a Vault of considerable magnitude appeared to view. All being anxious to descend, we cast lots. The lot, Most Excellent, was mine.

My Companions then tied this strong cord or lifeline round my body by which to lower me into the vault ; but being apprehensive of dying from damp noxious vapours or other unforeseen causes, I took a smaller cord in each hand by which to give preconcerted signals should I require more liberty, or wish to be drawn up. I was then duly lowered into the Vault. On arriving at the bottom I felt something like the base or pedestal of a column, with certain characters engraven thereon, but for the want of light I was unable to decipher their meanings. I then signalled with my left hand for more liberty, and on exploring the Vault, found this scroll of vellum or parchment, but from the same cause was unable to read its contents. I therefore signalled with my right hand, and my Companions drew me up, bringing the scroll with me. On arriving at the light of day we found from the first words therein recorded that it was a part of the long-lost Sacred Law, promulgated by our Grand Master Moses at the foot of Mount Horeb in the wilderness of Sinai. The possession of this precious treasure stimulated us to further exertions ; we therefore enlarged the aperture by removing the key-stone, and I descended as before. The sun by this time had gained its greatest altitude, and darted its rays with meridian splendour into the Vault, enabling me clearly to distinguish those objects I had before so imperfectly discovered. In the centre of the Vault stood a block of white marble, wrought in the form of the Altar of Incense, a doubled cube. On the front were engraven the initials of the three Grand Masters who presided at the building of the former Temple, that is, Solomon King of Israel, Hiram King of Tyre, and Hiram Abiff—with certain mystic characters, and a veil covered the Altar. Approaching with reverential awe I raised the veil, and there beheld on a plate of gold that which I humbly conceived to be the Sacred and Mysterious Name of the True and Living God Most High. I carefully re-veiled it, retired with all respect and reverence, gave the agreed-on signal, and was again drawn up. With the assistance of my Companions I closed the aperture, and

P.S.	we have hastened hither to communicate to Your Excellencies the discovery we have made, and the circumstances which led thereto.
Z.	Your narrative bears every appearance of truth, but to convince us you must state what you saw on that plate of gold.
P.S.	(*Bowing*) That, Most Excellent, we must humbly beg to decline, for we have heard with our ears, and our fathers have declared unto us, that in their days and the old time before them it was not lawful for anyone to pronounce the Sacred and Mysterious Name of the True and Living God Most High, save the High Priest, nor him but once a year, when he entered the Holy of Holies and stood before the Ark of the Covenant to make propitiation for the sins of the people.
Z.	We admire your pious caution ; and your conduct considerably increases our esteem. We will however depute two of our Companions, Ezra and Nehemiah, to accompany you to the spot, and their report shall determine your reward.
	(*The Principal Sojourner gives his crow-bar and scroll to the Assistant Sojourner, and goes to the North-West of the Chapter with Scribes Ezra and Nehemiah. There he communicates the words JE-HO-VAH and JAH-BUL-ON to them in full form, sotto voce. The Principal Sojourner then returns and takes the crow-bar and scroll from the Assistant Sojourner. Scribes Ezra and Nehemiah then approach the East, Ezra by the North and Nehemiah by the South, with seven steps, halting and bowing at the third, fifth, and seventh. Together they unveil the Altar and examine it, and report with Reverential or Hailing Sign to Zerubbabel*).
E.	Right, Most Excellent, in every particular.
N.	Right, Most Excellent, in every particular. (*They dismiss sign and return to their seats*).
Z.	(*After consulting with Haggai and Joshua*) My colleagues in office concur with me in opinion, that as a reward for your zeal and fidelity in having discovered the long-lost secrets of the Royal Arch you should be at once called to that exalted rank held by your illustrious ancestors. Companions Ezra and Nehemiah, divest those worthy Masons of the implements of labour, clothe them with the robes of innocence, and instruct them to advance hither that they may be further rewarded.
	(*Scribes Ezra and Nehemiah divest the Sojourners*

and the Candidate of their working-tools and Master Masons' aprons, assist the Sojourners in putting on their regalia, and clothe all three with surplices. Scribe Ezra then goes back to his place. Nehemiah instructs the Candidate how to approach the East with seven steps, halting and bowing at the third, fifth, and seventh, and demonstrates these steps, after which he takes his place. The Candidate advances, followed by the Principal Sojourner, who, however, does not take the steps himself, but sees that the Candidate does so correctly. The three Principals stand, and Zerubbabel invests the Candidate during the following speech with the jewel, sash, apron and staff).

Z.   The robes with which you have been invested are emblems of that purity of heart and rectitude of conduct which should at all times actuate those exalted into this Supreme Degree. We reward you with this jewel as a mark of our entire approbation, and admit you Companion amongst us ; we decorate you with this ribbon and badge, the insignia of our Order, and entrust you with this Staff of Office, which you will ever have a right to bear, unless seventy-two of the Elders are present ; and hereby constitute you princes and rulers in the Order ; and should you continue to act in the faithful discharge of your duties, you will by a regular gradation be entitled to full participation of our secrets.

(During this speech Zerubbabel invests the Candidate. The Staff of Office is the first of the Ensigns on the North side, that of Judah. The Principal Sojourner brings it to Zerubbabel and replaces it after it has been put in the Candidate's right hand).

Z.   It is in this part of the ceremony that the Words are communicated. Excellent Companion Haggai, will you please assist. They are given on a series of triangles formed first by the right foot, second with the right knee, third right hand on right elbow, and fourth, left hand grasping left wrist.[1] The Words are JEHOVAH, JAHBULON. They are given in a series of syllables. I will commence and you will follow.

(Haggai assists at the communication of the Words, Zerubbabel, the Candidate, and Haggai reciting the syllables in that order, forming the triangles. The Principal Sojourner stands by the Candidate to assist and prompt in what is at first a very confusing busi-

---

1. Some workings only prescribe *three* triangles.

ness. After this ceremony the Principal Sojourner escorts the Candidate to the West by way of the South and both face East).

P.S. (*With Reverential or Hailing sign*) Thus invested, rewarded, decorated, and entrusted by Your Excellencies, it shall ever be our study to merit a continuance of your approbation by faithfully and assiduously discharging the duties of the high vocation to which you have this day been pleased to call us. (*Dismisses sign*).

Z. We congratulate you on being exalted into Royal Arch Masonry, at once the foundation and keystone of the whole Masonic structure. You may perhaps imagine you have this day taken a Fourth Degree in Freemasonry ; such, however, is not the case.[1] It is the Master Mason's completed, for when you were raised to the Third Degree, you were informed that by the untimely death of our Master Hiram Abiff the secrets of a Master Mason were lost, and that certain substituted secrets were adopted to distinguish all Master Masons until time or circumstances should restore the genuine. These secrets were lost for a period of nearly five hundred years, and were regained in the manner which has just been described to you, somewhat in a dramatic form, the more forcibly to impress on your mind the providential means by which those ancient secrets were regained.

We have now arrived at that part of the ceremony when Excellent Companion Joshua will give the Historical lecture, Excellent Companion Haggai the Symbolical, after which I will explain the Mystical portion of this Supreme Degree. Be seated. (*The Principals give knocks*). Companions, I claim your attention for Excellent Companion Joshua for the Historical Lecture.

1. This distinction may appear almost meaningless, for in practice the Royal Arch *is* a separate degree. The position is a legacy of the compromise arrived at in the union of the Ancients and the Moderns in United Grand Lodge, 1813. The latter claimed that pure and ancient Masonry consisted of three degrees only, whereas the former strove to retain the Royal Arch. Its retention was accomplished through this formula. In every jurisdiction other than England the Royal Arch is listed as a separate degree.

DARKNESS VISIBLE

ADDRESS OF THE THIRD CHAIR
THE HISTORICAL LECTURE

J. Companions, there are three epochs in Freemasonry which particularly merit your attention : they are, the history of the first or Holy Lodge, the second or Sacred Lodge, and the third, or Grand and Royal Lodge.

The first or Holy Lodge was opened Anno Lucis 2515,[1] two years after the exodus of the Israelites from their Egyptian bondage by Moses, Aholiab, and Bezaleel, on consecrated ground at the foot of Mount Horeb in the wilderness of Sinai, where the children of Israel pitched their tents and gathered themselves together to offer up praises and thanksgivings to the Most High for their signal deliverance from the hands of the Egyptians. There, but before that time, the Almighty was pleased to reveal Himself to His faithful servant Moses, and to commission him His high ambassador, of wrath to Pharaoh and his people, but of freedom and salvation to the house of Jacob. There were delivered those mysterious forms and prototypes, the tabernacles, the ark of the covenant, and the tables of the Sacred Law engraven by the finger of the Most High, with sublime and comprehensive precepts of religious and moral duty. There also were dictated, by His unerring wisdom, those peculiar forms of civil and religious polity, which by separating His once favoured people from all other nations, consecrated Israel a chosen vessel to His service. For these reasons it was denoted the first or Holy Lodge. Solomon King of Israel, Hiram King of Tyre, and Hiram Abiff presided over the second or Sacred Lodge, which was opened Anno Lucis 2992, in the bosom of the holy Mount Moriah, on the very centre of the ground where the solemn sanctuary of the Sanhedrim was afterwards erected. On that consecrated spot Abraham proved his intuitive faith by not refusing to offer up his beloved son Isaac, a destined victim on the altar of his God, when it pleased the Almighty to provide a more agreeable sacrifice. There, on the threshing floor of Araunah the Jebusite, David offered up the mediatorial sacrifice by which the plague was stayed. And there, in a vision, were revealed to him the plans of that magnificent Temple afterwards erected by his illustrious son, of whom God

1. For explanation of the Anno Lucis Calendar, see p. 81.

173

J.   said, "He shall build a house for My Name, and I will stablish the throne of his kingdom for ever ";[1] For these reasons this was denominated the second, or Sacred Lodge.

The third, or Grand and Royal Lodge, was holden at Jerusalem and opened Anno Lucis 3469, shortly after the return of the children of Israel from their Babylonish captivity, by Zerubbabel, prince of the people, Haggai the prophet, and Joshua the son of Josedech, the High Priest. Then it was that the kingly power was restored in the person of Zerubbabel to the royal line of David and princely tribe of Judah. Nor was all vestige thereof again effaced until after the destruction of Jerusalem by the Romans under Titus in the seventieth year of the present era. Therefore, to commemorate the restoration, this was called the third, or Grand and Royal Lodge, and we have in the present Chapter a resemblance of those grand originals. In every regular, well-formed and properly constituted Royal Arch Chapter we acknowledge the representation of the Grand and Holy Royal Arch Chapter at Jerusalem. The three Principals represent Zerubbabel, Haggai, and Joshua, whose names they bear, the two Scribes represent Ezra and Nehemiah, Lectors and Expounders of the Sacred Law and attendants on the Grand Sanhedrim. Yourselves represent the Sojourners, who for their zeal and fidelity in having discovered the secrets of the Royal Arch, were rewarded with seats among the princes and rulers of the people, represented by the rest of the Companions.

Z.   (*Principals give four knocks*) I now claim your attention to Excellent Companion Haggai for the Symbolical Lecture.

ADDRESS OF THE SECOND CHAIR

SYMBOLICAL LECTURE

H.   Companions, the forms, symbols, and ornaments of Royal Arch Masonry, together with the rites and ceremonies at present in use among us, were adopted by our predecessors at the building of the second Temple, as well to preserve in our minds the providential means by which those ancient secrets were regained, as to impress on our hearts those exalted lessons of morality which we, as members of this

1. Samuel, VII, 13.

H.   Supreme Degree, are bound to practise.

The form of a Royal Arch Chapter, when properly arranged, approaches, as nearly as circumstances will permit, that of a Catenarian Arch ; thus we preserve a memorial of the vaulted shrine in which the Sacred Word was deposited, whilst from the impenetrable nature of this the strongest of all architectural forms we learn the necessity of guarding our mysteries from profanation by the most inviolable secrecy. It also strongly typifies that invariable adherence to social order and spirit of fraternal union, which have given energy and permanency to the whole constitution of Freemasonry, thus enabling it to survive the wreck of mighty empires, and resist the destroying hand of time. And as the subordinate members of the Catenarian Arch naturally gravitate towards the centre, or keystone, which compresses and binds the whole structure together, are we taught to look up with reverence and submit with cheerfulness, to every lawfully constituted authority, whether it be of civil or Masonic regulation.

The keystone of the Arch is represented by the three Principals of the Chapter. For as the secrets of the Royal Arch were only regained by wrenching forth the keystone thereof, so a perfect knowledge of this Supreme Degree can no otherwise be obtained than by passing through those several Chairs.

In Royal Arch Masonry we acknowledge six lights, three lesser, and three greater ; the three lesser represent the light of the law and the prophets, and by their number allude to the Patriarchal, Mosaical, and Prophetical dispensations ; the three greater represent the Sacred Word itself, and are emblematical of the creative, preservative, and annihilative[1] powers of the Deity. These lights are arranged in the form of an equilateral triangle, each of the lesser bisecting the line formed by two of the greater, thus geometrically dividing the greater triangle into three lesser triangles at the extremities, and forming a fourth in the centre, all equal and equilateral. This symbolical arrangement corresponds to the mysterious triple tau which has two right angles at each of the exterior lines, and two in the centre, in all eight right angles corresponding in number with those contained in the four

1. This purely Hindu conception proved offensive to many and has been revised in Metropolitan workings to *re-creative*. The Complete workings have *de-creative* in place of *annihilative*, which is nonsense.

H.   triangles, for the three angles of every triangle are together equal to two right angles. It also serves to illustrate the jewel worn by the Companions, which forms by its intersections a given number of angles ; these may be taken in five several combinations, and when reduced to their amount in right angles, will be found equal to the five regular Platonic bodies, representing the four elements and the sphere of the Universe.

The ribbon worn by the Companions is a sacred emblem, denoting light, being composed of two of the principal colours with which the veils of the Temple and Tabernacle were interwoven. Its sacredness is further signified by its irradiated form ; it has even been considered an emblem of regal dignity and power.

The ensigns on the staves borne by the Companions are the distinctive bearings of the twelve tribes of Israel, and are figurative of a peculiar blessing bequeathed to each by the patriarch Jacob, who, shortly before his death, assembled his sons together for that purpose, as we find recorded in the forty-ninth chapter of Genesis ; the tribes are further pointed out in the second chapter of the Book of Numbers. The four principal banners represent the leading standards of the four divisions of the army of Israel. They bear devices of a man, a lion, an ox, and an eagle : a man, to personify intelligence and understanding ; a lion, to represent strength and power ; an ox, to denote the ministration of patience and assiduity ; and an eagle to indicate the promptness and celerity with which the will and pleasure of the great I AM are ever executed. The bearings on the sceptres denote the regal, prophetical, and sacerdotal offices, all of which ever were, and still ought to be, conferred in a peculiar manner, accompanied by the communication of particular secrets.[1]

The Bible, Square, and Compasses are the appropriate emblems of the three Grand Masters who presided at the building of the former Temple : the Bible denotes the wisdom of King Solomon ; the Square the strength of King Hiram ; and the Compasses the exquisite skill of Hiram Abiff ; but the truly speculative Mason regards them as the unerring standards of the wisdom, truth and justice of the Most High, His wisdom is amply exemplified in the Volume of the Sacred Law, which contains the record of His

1. See pp. 184-6 for these specific secrets of the Chairs.

H.   mighty acts, and is the register of His revealed will. His truth is justly depicted by the Square, that being the acknowledged symbol of strength and criterion of perfection, while His unerring and impartial justice in having defined for our instruction the limits of good and evil, assigning to each his due proportion of pleasure and pain, is elucidated by the Compasses, by which instrument we are enabled to ascertain and determine the limits and proportions of all geometrical figures, and reduce our ideas of their proportion and equality to a given standard.

The Sword and Trowel were adopted by Royal Arch Masons to commemorate the valour of those worthy men who assisted at the building of the second Temple, who with Trowel in their hand and Sword by their side were ever ready to defend the City and holy sanctuary against the unprovoked attacks of their enemies, thereby leaving an impressive lesson to future ages, that next to implicit obedience to all lawfully constituted authority, a manly and determined resistance to lawless violence is the first of social duties. The Pickaxe, Crowbar, and Shovel were the implements made use of by the Sojourners who were sent to prepare the ground for the foundation of the second Temple. The Pick to loosen the ground, the Crow to take purchases, and the Shovel to clear away the rubbish and loose earth. These we symbolise : the stroke of the Pick reminds us of the sound of the last trumpet, when the ground shall be shaken, loosened, and the graves deliver up their dead ; the Crow being an emblem of uprightness, points to the erect manner in which the body shall arise on that awful day to meet its tremendous though merciful Judge ; while the manner in which the body is laid in the grave is fully depicted by the work of the Shovel, and we with humble but holy confidence hope that when these earthly remains have been properly disposed of, the spirit will arise to immortal life and everlasting bliss.

Z.   (*The Principals give the four knocks*) I shall now proceed to give you the Mystical Lecture.

ADDRESS OF THE FIRST CHAIR
MYSTICAL LECTURE

Z.   Companions, the mystical knowledge of this Supreme Degree comprehends the forms and explanation of the Sacred Signs, the nature and import of the Holy Words, and the traditional ceremonies to be observed in sharing and communicating our secrets. In Royal Arch Masonry we acknowledge five signs, corresponding in number with the Five Points of Fellowship, in which the Master Mason has already been instructed ; and as these point out the relative duties we owe to each other, so do the Royal Arch signs mark in a peculiar manner the relation we bear to the Most High as creatures offending against His mighty will and power, yet still the adopted children of His mercy.

I will now go through the signs, and you, my newly exalted Companion, will rise and copy me. This is the Penal sign, the only perfect sign in Freemasonry given with the left hand. This is the Reverential or Hailing sign, and is to be used on all occasions when entering or retiring from the Chapter, or when addressing the Principals. This is the Penitential or Supplicatory sign, on bended knees and with uplifted hands. This is the Monitorial, hands girding the loins, thumbs in front, and this the Fiducial sign. You will now resume your seats, and I will explain them at greater length.[1]

The Penal sign marks the penalty of our Obligation, and alludes to the fall of Adam, and the dreadful penalty entailed thereby on his sinful posterity, no less than death. It intimates by the very act that the stiff-necked and disobedient shall be cut off from the land of the living by the judgment of God, even as the head is severed from the body by the sword of human justice.

To avert which, we are taught by the Reverential or Hailing Sign to bend with humility and resignation beneath the chastening hand of the Almighty, at the same time to engraft His laws on our hearts. In this expressive form did the father of the human race present himself before the Most High, to receive the enunciation of his just though terrible doom, and this sign was afterwards adopted by our Grand Master Moses, who, when the Lord appeared to him in the burning bush, at the foot of Mount Horeb in

---

1. See p. 153 for descriptions of these signs.

Z. the wilderness of Sinai, thus shaded his eyes from the brightness of the Divine presence, and placed his hand on his heart in token of obedience, and this sign was afterwards accounted unto him for righteousness.

The Reverential or Hailing sign may justly be deemed the parent of the Penitential or Supplicatory sign, since it so truly denotes that frame of heart and mind without which our prayers and oblations of praise cannot find acceptance at the throne of grace, before which how should a frail and erring creature of the dust present himself but on bended knees and with uplifted hands, at once betokening his humility and contrition? Thus did Adam kneel to God, and bless the Author of his being ; thus too did he bend with contrite awe before the face of his offended Judge, to avert His wrath and conciliate His mercy, and has transmitted this outward form of humility and contrition to his posterity for ever.

The Monitorial sign reminds us of the weakness of human nature, unable of itself to resist the powers of darkness, unless assisted by that light which is from above. By this defenceless posture we acknowledge our whole frailty, and confess that we can do no manner of good or acceptable service except through Him from whom all good counsels and just works do proceed, and without whose Divine and special favour we must ever have remained unprofitable servants in His sight.

Therefore, after the manner of our holy ancestors, the atoning priests by this outward form of faith and dependence, the Fiducial sign, we show that we would prostrate ourselves with our faces to the dust. Thus must we throw ourselves on the mercy of our Divine Creator and Judge, looking forward with humble but holy confidence to His blessed promises, by which means alone we hope to pass through the ark of redemption into the mansions of eternal bliss and glory, into the presence of Him who is the great I AM, the Alpha and Omega, the beginning and the ending, the first and the last.

At the building of King Solomon's Temple, a vast number of Masons were employed, and their names or marks were found engraven on some part or other of the building, but the names of the three Grand Masters who presided were nowhere found, until they were discovered in the Royal Arch by the Sojourners, who were sent to prepare the ground for the founda-

Z.   tion of the second Temple. In the centre of the Vault stood a block of white marble, wrought in the form of the Altar of Incense, a double cube, on the top of which was a plate of gold, white being an emblem of innocence, and gold of purity.

On the front were engraven the initials of the three Grand Masters who presided at the building of the former Temple, that is, Solomon King of Israel, Hiram King of Tyre, and Hiram Abiff, and meant to perpetuate their names as well as to commemorate the circumstance and proceedings attending the erection of that structure. There was likewise the mysterious triple tau, a mark or character affixed to the summonses of Royal Arch Masons, on occasions of more than usual importance. The tau is taken from the Hebrew, and is that mark or sign spoken of by the angel whom Ezekiel saw in spirit, when it was said to the man with the writer's inkhorn: "Go through the midst of the city, through the midst of Jerusalem, and set a mark upon the foreheads of the men that sign and that cry for all the abominations that be done in the midst thereof," by which mark they were saved from among those who were slain for their idolatry by the wrathful displeasure of the Most High.[1] In ancient times, this mark was placed upon those who were acquitted by their judges in proof of their innocence, and military commanders caused it to be set on the foreheads of the men who returned unhurt from the field of battle, denoting that they were in perfect life. For these reasons it has ever been considered a mark or sign of life. The union of the taus here depicted alludes to the Deity, by whom the gloomy, horrific, and unshapen chaos was changed into regular form and peaceful existence.

On this plate of gold are a circle and a triangle ; these mathematical figures have ever been selected as referring to the Deity or some Divine attribute. The circle is an emblem of eternity, for as it has neither beginning nor end it may justly be deemed a type of God, without beginning of days or end of years, and it continually reminds us of that great hereafter, when we hope to enjoy endless life, and everlasting bliss.

The word on the circle is JEHOVAH, that great,

---

1. The most cursory reading of Ezekiel, however, suggests that Royal Arch devotees of Jah-Bul-On would have been classed with the idolators, and would fail to receive this mark !

Z.

awful, tremendous and incomprehensible Name of the Most High. It signifies I Am that I Am, the Alpha and Omega, the beginning and the end, the first and the last, who was, and is, and is to come, the Almighty. It is the name of the actual, future, eternal, unchangeable, and all-sufficient God, who alone has His being in and from Himself, and gives to all others their being ; so that He is what He was, was what He is, and will remain both what He was, and what He is, from everlasting to everlasting, all creatures being dependent on His mighty will and power.

In times of antiquity, names of God and symbols of divinity were always enclosed in triangular figures. In the days of Pythagoras, the triangle was considered the most sacred of emblems, and when any obligation of more than usual importance was to be administered, it was invariably given on the Triangle, and when so taken, none were ever known to violate it. The Egyptians termed it the sacred number, or number of perfection, and so highly was it prized by the ancients, that it became amongst them an object of worship. They gave it the sacred name of God, affirming that it represented the animal, mineral, and vegetable kingdoms ; they also called it Abroeth, which signifies Soul of Nature. This Sacred Delta is usually enclosed with a square and circle, thereby expressing its vivifying influence, extending its ramification through all created nature ; for these reasons it has ever been considered the Great All, the *Summum Bonum.*

The word on the triangle is that Sacred and Mysterious Name you have just solemnly engaged yourself never to pronounce, unless in the presence and with the assistance of two or more Royal Arch Companions, or in the body of a lawfully-constituted Royal Arch Chapter, whilst acting as First Principal. It is a compound word, and the combination forms the word JAH-BUL-ON.[1] It is in four languages, Chaldee, Hebrew, Syriac, and Egyptian. JAH is the Chaldee name of God, signifying " His Essence and Majesty Incomprehensible." It is also a Hebrew word, signifying " I am and shall be," thereby expressing the actual, future, and eternal existence of the Most High. BUL is a Syriac word denoting Lord or Powerful, it is in itself a compound word, being

1. Although Masonry claims to be founded on the Word of God, this syncretism is as blasphemous in an Old Testament setting as, say JESUS-MOLOCH-PAN would be to the Christian.

181

Z.   formed from the preposition Beth, in or on, and Ul, Heaven, or on High ; therefore the meaning of the word is Lord in Heaven, or on High. ON is an Egyptian word, signifying Father of all, thereby expressing the Omnipotence of the Father of All, as in that well-known prayer, Our Father, which art in Heaven.[1] The various significations of the words may be thus collected : I am and shall be ; Lord in Heaven or on High ;

    " Father of All ! In every age,
       In every clime adored
       By saint, by savage, and by sage,
       Jehovah, Jove, or Lord."

The characters at the angles of the Triangle are of exceeding importance, though it is immaterial where the combination is commenced, as each has reference to the Deity or some Divine attribute. They are the Aleph, the Beth, and the Lamed of the Hebrew, corresponding with the A., B., and L. of the English alphabet. Take the Aleph and the Beth, they form AB, which is Father ; take the Beth, the Aleph, and the Lamed, they form BAL, which is Lord ; take the Aleph and the Lamed, they form AL, which means Word ; take the Lamed, the Aleph, and the Beth, they form LAB, which signifies Heart or Spirit. Take each combination with the whole, and it will read thus : AB BAL, Father, Lord ; AL BAL, Word, Lord ; LAB BAL, Spirit, Lord.[2]

Such, my newly exalted Companion, is the best explanation I can give of those sacred words and characters ; it proves the Royal Arch to be the climax of Freemasonry, and is intimately blended with all that is nearest and dearest to us in a future state of existence ; Divine and human affairs are interwoven so awfully and minutely in all its disquisitions. It has virtue for its aim, the glory of God for its object, and the eternal welfare of man is considered in every

---

1. The Oxford ritual adds at this point " Joseph in Egypt married the daughter of Potiphera, Priest of On "—thereby making it quite clear than an actual Egyptian God is referred to, and not merely an attribute of the Godhead.

2. The Rev. F. de P. Castells in *The Antiquity of the Holy Royal Arch* (A. Lewis, London) points out at some length the crude nonsensicalities of the Hebrew exegesis in the Mystical Lecture. The main thesis of his book, that the Royal Arch derived much of its philosophy and symbolism from the Jewish Kabbala and can be paralleled in the *Zohar*, seems indubitably true, but the eighteenth century was not an age of Hebrew scholarship as far as Masonry was concerned, and whatever the primitive inspiration it is difficult to prove an earlier origin for this degree.

Z.   part, point, and letter of its ineffable mysteries. Suffice it to say, it is founded on the Sacred Name, Jehovah, who was from all beginning, is now, and will remain one and the same for ever, the Being necessarily existing in and from Himself in all actual perfection, original in His essence.

Companions, I charge you, should you ever be about to mention that Sacred and Mysterious Name lightly or irreverently, pause, place your finger on your lips, and remember the penalty of your Obligation.

This Supreme Degree inspires its members with the most exalted ideas of God, it leads to the exercise of the purest and most devout piety, a reverence for the incomprehensible JEHOVAH, the eternal Ruler of the Universe, the elemental life and primordial source of all its principles, the very spring and fount of all its virtues.[1]

AN EXPLANATION OF THE JEWEL

(*This is not given as a lecture, but is frequently included in printed rituals. Only the opening and the concluding paragraphs are given here ; the remainder is a wearisome disquisition of mystical geometry in an idiom incomprehensible save to the student of Plato as interpreted by the Jewish Kabbalists*).

The Companion's Jewel of the Royal Arch is a double triangle, sometimes called the Seal of Solomon, within a circle of gold ; at the bottom is a scroll bearing the words *nil nisi clavis deest* (nothing is wanting but the key); and on the circle appears the legend *Si talia jungere possis sit tibi scire satis* (if thou canst comprehend these things, thou knowest enough). On the triangle is inscribed EYPHKAMEN (EUREKAMEN) *Invenimus cultor dei civis mundi* (we have found the worship of God, O citizen of the world.)[2] On the reverse of the circle are engraven the words *Deo, regi, et fratribus ; honor, fidelitas, benevolentia* (for God, king, and the brethren ; honour, fidelity, and benevolence) ; and on the reverse of the triangles, *Wisdom, Strength, Beauty, Peace, Concord, Truth*. Within these is another triangle, with sun in the centre, irradiated ; a pair of compasses issue from the sun, suspending a globe representing

1. In Complete and Metropolitan workings the Candidate, Nehemiah, and Zerubbabel again share the Word at the close of the Lecture. This is usually followed by showing the Candidate the Chapter warrant, and presenting him with its Regulations and By-laws.

2. This translation is of course ludicrous. The only possible rendering that makes sense would be *We have found, O worshipper of God, O citizen of the World*. But see note, p. 224.

the earth, beneath these is a triple tau, signifying among other occult things, *Templum Hierosolyma*, the Temple at Jerusalem. It also means *Clavis ad Thesaurum* (a key to a treasure), and *Theca ubi res pretiosa deponitur* (a place where a precious thing is concealed), or *Res ipsa pretiosa* (the precious thing itself). It is usual to add on the scroll the date of the exaltation of the wearer.

This jewel, by its intersections, forms a given number of angles, to be taken in five several combinations, which, being reduced to their amounts in right-angles, will be found equal to the five regular Platonic bodies, representing the four elements, and the Universal Sphere. These combinations will be found respectively to correspond in geometrical value with the five regular solids contained under equal and equilateral triangles, equal squares, and equal and equilateral pentagons, that is, the Tetrahedron, Octohedron, Cube, Icosahedron, and Dodecahedron, which were used by the Platonist to express the four elements and the sphere of the Universe.

* * * *

In conclusion, let our attention be directed to the fact that the Royal Arch Jewel thus presents us with an emblem of those great attributes of the Deity, His eternity and triunessence. The former is represented by the circle which surrounds the Jewel, the latter by the relation which its component parts bear to the triple tau ; while by the equivalent we find in those parts for the five solids expressing the four elements and the sphere of the Universe, we are further reminded of His Omnipotence and Creative power, Who first formed the elements out of nothing, and from them constituted that mighty frame within whose comprehensive sphere are included myriads of worlds, each containing millions of animated beings dependent on His will and mercy. The Jewel which every Companion wears on his breast should inspire him with profound veneration for that Incomprehensible Being at whose command the world burst forth from chaos into light, and all created matter had its birth ; whose Infinite Wisdom directs, and whose unspeakable Goodness preserves and blesses every work that has proceeded from His Hands.

THE INSTALLATION OF THE PRINCIPALS

The order in which the Principals are installed varies, some workings give precedence to Zerubbabel, then Haggai, and lastly Joshua, others instal them in reverse order. There are arguments to justify both procedures, but most printed rituals (whatever the working order) begin with Joshua and end with Zerubbabel, and this was probably the earlier practice.

Each Chair (or Principal) is in a sense equivalent to a separate degree in that it has its own secrets reserved to it which are unknown to the Principals of lesser rank. Joshua, for instance, does not know the word and sign of Haggai or Zerubbabel ; Haggai knows Joshua's (the Chair he presumably occupied himself the previous year) but not Zerubbabel's. Only when in this third year of office, on being installed to the First Chair of Zerubbabel does a Principal learn the secrets of all three Chairs. There is, then, a separate Conclave for each of the three Principals, in which all below the rank of the particular Conclave must retire.

If Joshua is to be installed first (and the ceremonies are much the same in whichever order they are taken) a Conclave of Installed Principals is declared by Zerubbabel, in which all Principals and Past Principals of the Chapter may be present. The Joshua-Elect is placed in the West, and is presented by a Past Zerubbabel to the Installing Principal, who in some workings (including Metropolitan) is Zerubbabel ; in others each Principal instals his successor before himself being installed to the chair above.

As no one can become a Principal unless he is past the Chair in the Craft, the sign and word of an Installed Master (GIBLUM) are demanded of the Joshua-Elect. Then may come a ceremony of ablution or feet-washing (often omitted) which is intended to remind him that " all who were about to enter the priesthood had to undergo a series of purifications and anointing, that they might enter the service of God undefiled both in body and mind ". After a series of questions inquiring into his fitness for his office and willingness faithfully to discharge the same, he takes his Obligation of fidelity and secrecy, under the penalties of his former Obligations.

He then kneels before his chair of office while certain passages of Scripture are read to him. These are Leviticus, VIII, 1-12 ; Numbers, XVI, 46-48 ; and Genesis XXXIII, 20. During the appropriate verse from Leviticus (" And he poured of the anointing oil upon Aaron's head, and anointed him to sanctify him ") the Joshua-Elect is sometimes anointed with oil, though this again is very commonly dropped in some workings.

The priestly significance of these Scriptural passages is then pointed out, and solemn prayer is offered for him. He rises from his knees, and is entrusted with the secrets. The sign is an alleged action of Aaron's when he " stood between the dead and the living " (Numbers XVI, 48) and placed his left hand to his nose and swung a censer with his right. The word is EL-ELOHE-(ISRAEL), which occurs in his concluding verse, Genesis XXXIII, 20. He is invested with his collar, robe, and sceptre (which he is told to salute with the mental repetition of his word) ; their symbolism and significance are pointed out to him, he takes his chair, and is saluted by the Principals.

Haggai's installation is similar in most particulars. A Conclave of Second Principals is declared, and all below that rank withdraw. The pass-word is BERITH, meaning a covenant. His Scripture readings are I Samuel III, 1-21 ; Exodus VI, 6, and XIV, 21-27 ; Genesis XVII, 1, and XXXV, 11. As Joshua's Scriptures emphasised his priestly office, so do Haggai's the prophetical. His sign is an inverted tau-cross made with the right hand—down, left, right—symbolising the dividing of the Red Sea, and his words are EL SHADDAI, which occur in the Hebrew of his concluding verse, Genesis XXXV, 11.

The installation of Zerubbabel, which takes place in a Conclave of First Principals, again follows the same pattern. The pass-word is NEDER, the import of which is a vow. The readings are I Samuel XVI, 1-13 ; Exodus III, 6 and 14, and VI, 3 ; and Psalm LXVIII, 4. He may be anointed during I Samuel XVI, 13. The kingly office is explained to him. His sign is to make a triangle against his face, the thumbs forming the base, and the forefingers the sides, through which he looks down on the Altar. His word is JAH, from Psalm LXVIII, 4. The final exhortation expresses the hope that he will be inspired by his " illustrious predecessors in the Grand Chapter of Jerusalem " to a faithful discharge of his duties.

Incense is not infrequently used in these ceremonies.

When the installations are at an end, the Companions are admitted, and the new Zerubbabel invests the other officers, Scribes Ezra and Nehemiah, the Sojourners, the Treasurer, the Director of Ceremonies, the Stewards, and the Janitor.

APPENDIX A

RITUAL VARIATIONS

IN SCOTLAND, IRELAND & AMERICA

It is impossible to consider all the trifling variations (which in any case are not important) in the workings of the sister Grand Lodges in English-speaking countries. Within these jurisdictions there is no more absolute uniformity than there is in England, though the general structure, the words, grips, and for the most part the signs remain constant.

A unique feature of English Masonry, however, is the position of the Royal Arch as the completion and fulfilment of the Third Degree. In Scotland, Ireland, and America it is one of several higher degrees under different jurisdiction, and separated from the Third by other intermediate degrees. This position is explained in Appendix B, where the arrangement of these other degrees is described.

SCOTLAND

I have seen rituals published (and obviously used) in Scotland which retain certain quaint archaisms not found South of the Border since the eighteenth-century expose, except perhaps in local unprinted Northern Provincial workings unknown to me. On the other hand, I have seen rituals from recognised Masonic publishers which purport to give Scottish workings that differ very little from the English. The tentative conclusion may be drawn, therefore, that there is considerable diversity in non-essentials, and that there has been a certain amount of Anglicising which has in places modified earlier usages.

Scottish Lodges are as a rule numerically larger than English ones, and it is now permissible to initiate, pass, or raise as many as five at a time, to keep pace with increasing numbers. In England the maximum is two per ceremony.

A ritual appearing under the name of a Past Provincial Grand Master of Forfarshire, the twelfth edition of which was published in 1950, contains many interesting features of undoubted antiquity not appearing in other Scottish rituals which I have seen.

In taking the First Degree Obligation, for instance, the Candidate removes his left shoe and hands it to the Master in reference to a Biblical custom when taking an oath. This appears to duplicate the symbolism of the slip-shod to which a similar meaning is attached. An old catch question of the eighteenth century is introduced into the ritual—" What did you pay for Masonry ? " " An old shoe, an old shoe of my Mother's."

The Due-Guard is preserved (though not under that name) as a first part of the Entered Apprentice sign, in which the hands are held horizontally in front of the body, palms apart and facing each other, the right hand above and the left beneath, representing the position of the hands on and under the Bible when taking the oath.

The Obligation itself contains certain archaic features. The one-time almost universal dedication of the Lodge " regularly assembled, properly constituted, and dedicated to the memory of the holy St. John " is preserved, which appears to have almost vanished in England when the Craft was de-Christianised. Another early survival is the clause " I will not be at the making of the following persons as Freemasons : a young man of nonage, an old man of dotage, a madman, a fool, an atheist, a person under the influence of liquor, and a woman under no pretence whatever."

In the preparation for the Second Degree the Candidate is ' partially hoodwinked,' and the right breast is bared—not the left as in most English workings.

Instead of the ' proper steps ' to the East in approaching the Pedestal, one, two, and three single steps are taken, bringing the heels together in a square, in the three degrees respectively. In the Second Degree, however, steps are taken ' as if ascending a winding staircase ' consisting of three, five, and seven steps, but this is after the conferment of the secrets, to bring the Candidate into the South-East corner where the Charge is given him.

There is some diversity in the Fellow-Craft signs. In the Hailing sign, for instance, the right fist may support the left elbow, and in the Penal sign, instead of drawing the right hand across the breast and dropping it to the side, a gesture is sometimes made as if tearing out the heart and casting it over the shoulder.

The chief characteristic of most Scottish workings, however, is the more dramatic ceremony of raising to the Third Degree. Although this extended working may be abbreviated or omitted, it appears to be of some antiquity, and must surely make a more vivid impression on the Candidate's mind. The ceremony proceeds as in other workings as far as the symbolical slaying by the Right Worshipful Master, only the

lights are not dimmed, and the Candidate is not at this point
' slain.' The ceremony thus far is so to speak only an explanatory
prologue. Then may follow a drama on the following
lines :—

R.W.M. The Candidate will now retire to prepare for a further
portion of the Ceremony.
(*While the Candidate is outside the Lodge the grave-
cloth is spread and the lights are turned down. He
may be hoodwinked. On his re-entry he is conducted
by the Deacons to the Junior Warden*).

J.W.   (*Loudly*) Who goes there ?

S.D.   Hiram Abiff.

J.W.   The very man. Give me the secrets of a Master
Mason, or—

S.D.   (*Interrupting quickly*) I would rather suffer death
than disclose the secrets entrusted to me.

J.W.   Then—(*knocks loudly with his gavel*)
(*The Deacons hurry the Candidate to the Senior
Warden, with whom this ceremony is repeated. Then
to the Right Worshipful Master, where it is repeated
again, only this time the Candidate is ' slain ' in the
usual manner, and his body covered over*).

R.W.M. The Brethren will take notice that in the recent ceremony, as well as in his present situation, our Brother
has been made to represent one of the brightest
characters recorded in the annals of Freemasonry,
namely Hiram Abiff, who lost his life from his unshaken fidelity to the sacred trust reposed in him.
This, I trust, will make such an impression on his
and your minds as to cause you to act with similar
fortitude, should you ever be placed in a similar
state of trial.
(*A funeral march or some other solemn music is
played, and a gong strikes twelve*).

R.W.M. Bro. Junior Warden, 'tis past high time, and the
Brethren have not resumed their labour ! Why is
this ?

J.W.   Owing to the mysterious disappearance of our Master
there are no working plans on the trestle board, and
the work is at a standstill.

R.W.M. Have proper inquiries been made, Bro. Senior
Warden ?

S.W.   They have been made ; but from current rumours,
and especially the absence of three of our number, we
fear that some heavy calamity has befallen him.

R.W.M. What are these rumours, Bro. Junior Warden ?

J.W.   Fifteen Fellow Crafts of that superior class of
workmen who were appointed to preside over the rest,

J.W.   seeing that the Temple was nearly completed, and
         that they were not yet in possession of the secrets
         of the Third Degree, conspired together to obtain
         them by any means ; and even, if necessary, to have
         recourse to violence. On the eve, however, of carry-
         ing their scheme into execution, twelve of them
         recanted ; but three, of more determined and atrocious
         character than the rest, still persisted in their impious
         design.

R.W.M.   Let strict search be made.
         (*Accompanied by some of the Brethren they walk
         slowly once round the grave, with the sign of Fidelity.
         Solemn Music. When the perambulation is complete,
         the Right Worshipful Master stamps, and the music
         ceases*).

R.W.M.   Any tidings, Bro. Junior Warden ?
J.W.   No tidings whatever.
R.W.M.   Then let further search be made.
         (*They go once again round the grave as before, this
         time with the sign of Sympathy*).

R.W.M.   Any tidings, Bro. Senior Warden ?
S.W.   After much fruitless search, one party has returned
         without making discovery ; but a second party
         has been more fortunate, for on the evening of a
         certain day, after having suffered many privations
         and much personal fatigue, one of the Brethren who
         had rested himself in a reclining posture, in order
         to assist his rising caught hold of a shrub that
         grew near, which, to his surprise, came easily out
         of the ground. On close examination he found that
         the earth had been recently disturbed ; he therefore
         hailed his Brethren and with their assistance succeeded
         in re-opening the ground, and there found the body
         of our Master very indecently interred. They covered
         it again with all respect and reverence, and placed
         a sprig of acacia at the head of the grave to mark
         the spot. They have hastened hither to impart the
         afflicting intelligence.

R.W.M.   Have you any tidings of the three missing Fellow
         Crafts, Bro. Senior Warden ?
S.W.   The third party pursued their researches in the
         direction of Joppa, and were meditating their return
         to Jerusalem, when accidentally passing the mouth of
         a cavern, they heard issuing therefrom sounds of
         deep lamentation and regret. One voice exclaimed,
         " O that my throat had been cut across, rather than
         I should have been accessory to the death of our
         good Master." Then another dolefully exclaimed,

DARKNESS VISIBLE

S.W.   " O that my breast had been torn open rather than I should have assisted in the death of our innocent Master." And then a third most lamentably exclaimed, " O that my body had been severed in two, rather than I should have smitten and killed our sublime Master." The search party then entered the cave, seized the three missing Fellow Crafts, bound them, and have brought them to Jerusalem.

R.W.M. Let them receive the punishment due to their horrid crime !
(*Solemn pause*).

R.W.M. Let us proceed to the grave of our Master.
(*They again circle round the grave, this time with the sign of Horror*).

J.W.   This looks like a new-made grave.

S.W.   Behold the sprig of Acacia !

R.W.M. Fit emblem of so innocent a man ! Bro. Deacons, remove the rubbish.
(*The body of the Candidate is uncovered*).

R.W.M. (*Sorrowfully*) Alas ! 'tis he !
(*All make the Scottish Grand Hailing sign of Grief, and repeat in unison with the Right Worshipful Master the accompanying words*, "O Lord my God, O Lord my God, O Lord my God, is there no help for the Widow's Son ? " *The Brethren not required for further help now resume their seats*).

R.W.M. Brother Junior Warden, you will try to raise the representative of our Master with the Entered Apprentice grip

The ritual is continued from this point as on p. 139, though a lengthy and solemn funeral prayer is sometimes offered over the grave after the two unsuccessful attempts to raise the body.

Some of the older Scottish Lodges have even longer and more dramatic presentations of this ceremony.

IRELAND

The Grand Lodge of Ireland is unusual in that, unlike those of England and Scotland, it has an authorised ritual and a Grand Lodge Chapter of Improvement to promulgate it. A greater measure of uniformity prevails, though this is far from complete. There are differences to be noted between the Dublin Lodges and those, say of Cork. Although an alleged ' Irish Working ' is printed by a Masonic publisher in London, it is not verbally accurate. It appears to follow a hybrid Northern Ireland form of working. But for the most part Ireland continues to eschew the use of a printed ritual altogether.

Tracing-Boards are not found in Irish Lodges, nor (at least in the Temples of Freemasons Hall in Dublin) is the emblem with the letter G displayed.

191

The more significant differences between the Irish and English workings may be tabulated as follows :

I. *Methods of Preparation.* For the First Degree these are the same as in England, except that the cable-tow is wound three times round the neck. For the Second Degree he is again deprived of money and metals, for it is in this degree, not the first, that the 'charity test' takes place.[1] The cable-tow is wound twice around his neck. For the Third Degree he is again deprived of metals, and the cable-tow is wound once round his neck. A lecture on the symbolical reasons for the preparation is provided, but not always given.

II. *The Pass Words.* Ireland has not only the usual pass words between the Degrees but has pass-words to the First Degree as well, which all Brethren may be required to give in proving themselves. They are given on behalf of the Initiate by his Conductor (a Brother who in Ireland accompanies the Candidate, and plays the part in making the responses which the Deacons perform in England). These pass words are " By the help of God, and the Tongue of Good Report." There are reasons to suppose that this is an ancient usage formerly prevailing but now extinct in England. It may still be found in a few Lodges in Scotland.

III. *The Solemn Obligations.* In all three Degrees the Candidate pledges himself " bearing in mind the Ancient Penalty of. . . etc. and binding myself under the real Penalty of being branded deservedly as a wretch, base, faithless and unworthy. . . " which is far less objectionable.

IV. *The Ceremony of Raising.* There are significant differences in the Hiramic legend. In the usual form the Three Grand Masters alone were in possession of the genuine secrets of the Master Mason ; in Irish workings, however, there was already, before the completion of the Temple, a class of Master Masons in possession of them, even though they could be conferred only by the Grand Masters. This weakens the drama. It makes the murder less plausible, for the three assassins could have assaulted any Master Mason for the betrayal of the secrets with less danger to themselves. It also makes the loss of those secrets far less dramatically catastrophic and significant. Thousands still knew them, and the loss, due to the death of one of the three officers necessary to confer them on others, seems a technicality rather than a tragedy. This, however, may have been the legend of the " Ancients," often similar to Irish workings. The words " it is thus that all Master Masons are raised from a dead level to a living upright " (which seem to give a quasi-sacramental

1. See p. 105.

significance to the rite) appear actually in the Ritual, and not merely in the Lectures.

There are other trifling variants. The apocryphal text " In strength will I establish this Mine house, to stand firm for ever," is dropped entirely. An extra question and answer are inserted when the Candidate is being tested by the Officers referring to the Irish custom of placing the left hand over the ' grip ' to conceal its nature :—" What is the use of a Freemason's left hand ? " " To hele the grip," or, " To cover the work."

The Royal Arch workings in Ireland are quite independent of the Craft, and totally different from English Chapter workings in legend, yet similar in meaning and symbolism. They are based, not on the re-building of the Temple by Zerubbabel after the Edict of Cyrus, but on the repair of the Temple under King Josiah, and the discovery of the Book of the Law (II Kings XXII, 3-13, and II Chronicles XXXIV, 8-21). The Principals of this Degree in Ireland, therefore, are not Zerubbabel, Haggai, and Joshua, but Josiah, Shaphan, and Hilkiah. In spite of the fact that Holy Writ expressly informs us that the historical Josiah spent no little time and energy in breaking down the altars of Baalim and burning the bones of idolatrous priests, the Word of this degree with all its Baal associations is retained.

THE UNITED STATES

Although the general structure and legend of the three Craft Degrees is retained, the wording in America is very different and on the whole more colloquial and garrulous. The impression is left that American workings in general have rather less dignity than their British counterparts. In many respects it appears as if Scottish and Irish rather than English traditions are followed ; this is probably because these workings retain certain features which were also in the English workings when Masonry was first established in the New World, but which have since been revised in England after the Union. For instance, a pass-word is sometimes required for the First Degree, as in Ireland, and the Master wears a hat in the Lodge when it is open, removing it for the prayers ; this was certainly the earlier practice in Great Britain.

The full American ritual, however, especially in the Third Degree, appears to be so lengthy that it is difficult to believe that it is not, in practice, abbreviated.[1] And there is no

---

1. At a demonstration in England of the American Third Degree workings (Minnesota jurisdiction) before the Jubilee Masters Lodge (2712) in November, 1951, the ceremony, slightly abbreviated and omitting the Charges, took the best part of two hours.

uniformity between State and State. In these circumstances only the more important differences can be noted here.

I. *Preparation.* The usual methods of preparation appear to be as follows. In the First Degree the Candidate is divested of metals, blindfolded, and a cable-tow is placed once around his neck. The left arm, left breast, and left knee and left foot are bare, and the right foot slippered. In the Second Degree he is again blindfolded, and the cable-tow is apparently (though not always) wound twice around his right arm above the elbow, which is bare. The right knee and foot and the right breast are also bared, and the left foot slippered. In the Third Degree he is again blindfolded and the cable-tow is wound three times around his body. Both breasts, both arms, both knees and feet are bare—there is therefore no ' slipshod ' or slipper.

II. *The Signs.* A somewhat different system prevails in America, each degree having its due-guard and its sign. The due-guard is a sort of preliminary or precautionary sign which is given before the sign, and relates to the position of the hands when taking the Obligation. In the First Degree this is taken with the right hand on and the left hand under the Bible ; the due-guard is therefore given by holding out the hands horizontally in front of the body on a line approximately with the stomach with the palms facing each other, about three inches apart, left below, right above. The sign is the usual Penal sign of the Entered Apprentice.

In the Second Degree Obligation the right hand rests on the Bible, and the left (as in England) is supported in the angle of the square. The due-guard therefore is given with the left hand similar to the Hailing sign of the Fellow-Craft, with the right hand held horizontally in front of the body with the palm facing downwards, on a level with the bottom waistcoat button. The sign is the same as the Fellow-Craft Penal sign.

The Third Degree Obligation is taken with both hands on the Bible, and the due-guard represents this position, both hands held out horizontally at waist level with the palm downwards. Some workings direct that the right hand should be parallel with the body, and left at right angles to it. The left hand is then dropped, and the Penal sign is given in the same way as in Great Britain. The two Casual signs of horror and of sympathy seem unknown in America, and the only other sign given is the Grand Hailing sign of Distress, with its accompanying exclamation.[1]

The grips and pass-grips are identical with our own.

III. *The Words.* The words are the same, except that only one word (Mahabone, variously pronounced) is given in the

1. See p. 148. This sign is also given in English Lodges as the form known to Scotland, Ireland and America.

Third Degree on the Five Points of Fellowship, but the context and the meaning of the word do not seem to be very clearly explained.

IV. *Proper Steps.* The Proper Steps to the East are simpler than in England. There is no winding staircase to ascend nor open grave to step over. In the First Degree one step only is taken, with left foot, bringing up the right heel to its hollow, forming the tau-cross. In the Second Degree a second step is added to this, leading off with the right foot, and bringing up the left into its hollow. In the Third Degree a third step is added to these two, stepping off with the left foot and bringing up the right heel to heel in the form of a square.

V. *The Ceremony of Raising.* This, if worked in full, is extremely lengthy and dramatic. It appears to be based on the extended Scottish workings, but with a great deal more added.

The structure of the rite, however, is slightly different in that the Candidate is first entrusted with the due-guard and sign and invested with the apron, restores himself to his proper clothing, and only then (when he may well think that the ceremony is over) is there any hint of the death-and-raising rite.

The Candidate is again blindfolded (which must make the actual 'slaying' all the more terrifying) and is conducted through his part of the drama by the Senior Deacon, who makes his responses for him. Three of the Brethren represent the ruffians (Jubela, Jubelo, and Jubelum), who with much loquacious dialogue set about the Candidate in turn, demanding the secrets from him, and eventually slay him by knocking him backwards by a blow with a rubber mallet on to a canvas sheet held securely (one hopes !) by certain other brethren. He is laid on the floor and covered up with the canvas, then the three ruffians 'bury' him by piling a few chairs and so on over the body. At this point the Lodge is darkened and a gong sounds with twelve strokes. In the full workings, the ruffians then attempt to escape by sea from Joppa, but are turned back for not having a pass. They flee into some corner (or into the ante-room) to hide. In the meantime the absence of Hiram Abiff has been noticed, and the Worshipful Master (as King Solomon) orders a roll-call, in which the names of Jubela, Jubelo, and Jubelum are not answered to. The twelve Fellow-Crafts who withdrew from the conspiracy then confess what they know, and a search is made for the body and for the ruffians. Both are found according to the usual Masonic tradition ; the latter (as in the extended Scottish workings) by their cries of remorse being heard issuing from a cave. They are taken back to King Solomon and executed with the Masonic penalties to which their cries gave origin.

Then the Officers and some of the Brethren proceed to the grave and march three times round it, singing a funeral hymn. The body is uncovered, and after the traditional attempts with the First and Second Degree grips the Candidate is raised on the Five Points of Fellowship. A charge or lecture follows.

The entire ceremony is given in dialogue.

As in Scotland and Ireland, the Holy Royal Arch is merely one of many higher degrees, and is not regarded as the completion or fulfilment of the Craft. There is accordingly less emphasis on the secrets of the Royal Arch being the ' genuine secrets of a Master Mason ' lost to the Craft at the untimely death. There are however several interesting variants between English and American Chapter workings ; in the latter the First Principal is not Zerubbabel the King, but the Excellent High Priest who represents Joshua. The ceremony of passing the veils, practically extinct in England, is retained. The symbols and words of the degree are inscribed on the Ark of the Covenant which the Candidate discovers in the Vault. Upon three sides of it are the initials of the Three Grand Masters Solomon King of Israel, Hiram King of Tyre, and Hiram Abiff, and on top of the Ark is the equilateral triangle (not in a circle) on the three sides of which are the syllables of the word, Jah-Bel-On, or Jah-Buh-Lun. These initials and syllables are usually written, not in English or Hebrew letters, but in the Masonic cypher (extremely simple) made up on the noughts and crosses formula supplemented by the St. Andrew's cross. Within the triangle are the Hebrew characters representing Jahweh. There is no Aleph, Beth, or Lamed at the triangle's extremities.

APPENDIX B

OTHER MASONIC DEGREES

ENGLAND

The three Craft degrees form the basis of the whole Masonic system as practised in English-speaking countries. Together with the Royal Arch, they form the sum total of Freemasonry as *officially* recognised by English Grand Lodge, and the majority of Masons go no further. Indeed there is a strong tendency amongst some to look down on the so-called ' higher degrees ' as modern fancy innovations which are no part of pure and ancient Masonry. And for the most part these other degrees are probably of more recent origin.

Of these degrees the most popular in England seem to be Mark Masonry, the Knights Templar, and the Rose Croix, which the the 18th Degree of the Ancient and Accepted rite. A Master Mason's certificate in a jurisdiction recognised by Grand Lodge is essential for advancement into any of these systems.

MARK MASONRY

The legend of the Mark Master Degree, which is dramatically enacted at the advancement of a Candidate, is as follows.

Mark Masons correspond to the Menatschim or Overseers who superintended and marked with their approval the stones brought to them by the Fellow-Craft Masons at the building of the Temple. Every week these overseers would wait upon Hiram Abiff to receive their plans and instructions for the work; on one occasion, however, part of the plans was lost, but an ingenious and intelligent Fellow-Craftsman either having seen the complete plan or else forming a good idea of it from the nature of the work, perceived that a stone of peculiar shape was required to finish the design. After spending much time and labour he completed such a stone, put his mark upon it, and brought it to the overseers. As this stone was neither oblong nor square, and as no place was found for it in the imperfect working plans, it was ordered to be thrown away amongst the rubbish. Later on, however, work was held up because the key-stone to the arch was missing. Hiram Abiff remembered drawing up the design for such a stone, but the Overseers had no recollection of having seen any such plans. Finally the Overseer at the quarries remembered that such a stone had been brought to him, and that he had ordered it to be thrown away. Diligent search was made for it, and it was finally discovered in perfect condition. The Fellow-Craftsman who had shaped it was rewarded with promotion to the Degree of Mark Master.

The Candidate for advancement, of course, plays the part of the Fellow-Craftsman in the dramatic re-enactment of this legend. The pass-word to the Degree is JOPPA. The words are MARK WELL (Ezekiel XLIV, 5), but the "ancient word" KEB RAIOTH or rarely KYROCK (Companions of the Mark) is also given. The pass-grip is given by locking the fingers (as one would naturally do when pulling another up a steep place) and bringing the tips of the thumbs together "so as to form a cramp." The grip is given by linking the little fingers, closing the other fingers with their backs to each other each to each, the thumbs touching as before. The semi-secret motto, which appears on the keystone jewel of the degree, is represented by the letters H.T.W.S.S.T.K.S. (Hiram Tyrian Widow's Son, Sent To King Solomon). God is entitled in this degree as the "Great Overseer of the Universe." Each Mark Master chooses his mark, which is duly registered in his name.

Connected with Mark Master Masonry in somewhat the same way that the Royal Arch is connected with the Craft (though the analogy is not perfect) is the Royal Ark Mariner Degree, which commemorates the salvation of the human race through Noah and the Ark. The ritual is distinguished only by its trivial silliness.

KNIGHTS TEMPLAR AND KNIGHTS OF MALTA

The Orders of Knight Templar and of St. John of Jersualem, Palestine, Rhodes and Malta (this second Order being usually known simply as the Knights of Malta) are controlled by the Great Priory, which operates from Mark Masons' Hall. To be installed as a Knight Templar one must be a Master Mason of at least one year's standing, a member of the Royal Arch, and furthermore, must profess belief in the Holy and Un-divided Trinity. The Order of Knights of Malta is only open to Templars.

The 'Templar transmission,' theory is an extremely fascinat-ing subject on which there is still room for research. Did Knights Templarism become extinct after the suppression of the Order and the death of de Molay, or did it continue in a state of underground existence, surviving and re-emerging in Freemasonry ? This is not the place to discuss or evaluate the evidence; suffice it to say that it is not in these orders of chivalry or in the higher degrees of the Ancient and Accepted Rite in which this continuity should be sought, despite their outward resemblance to Templarism and their use of Templar legend and phraseology. For these orders and degrees are more modern in origin ; few if any can trace an authentic ancestry earlier than the eighteenth century. It is the Craft degrees that should be studied in so far as they developed from the medieval guilds of stonemasons ; these may in turn have become increasingly ' speculative' partly as a result of an infiltration of Templarism.[1] But the subject is shrouded in mystery, and the theory is, on the whole, unlikely.

The ritual of the Masonic Knights Templar was revised in 1873, and certainly in this country at any rate the more gruesome ceremonies connected with the skull and the more horrifying of the imprecations found in foreign workings have been toned down or eliminated. What is left is less picturesque, but comparatively innocuous and boy-scoutish. The Candidate is first dressed as a pilgrim, then after various perambulations symbolic of spiritual warfare and of penance, he is habited as a Knight. The Grand Pass-Word is the tongue-twister Maher-shalal-hash-baz (Isaiah VIII, 1), the Grand Word is Jesus Emmanuel, and the sign is an imitation of Our Lord hanging on the cross, with the arms outstretched, the feet crossed, and the head bent to one side. The Libations are toasts, and in no sense quasi-sacramental.

The Knight Templar and the other chivalric orders of Masonry are concerned supposedly with the defence of the Christian faith as already delivered. They are therefore free from the highly objectionable characteristics of the Rose Croix de Heredom in that they are not concerned with the origins or with the nature of the Christian faith, nor do they regard Our Lord as a symbolic figure in a mystery-cult.

THE ALLIED DEGREES

There are five degrees under the jurisdiction of the Grand Council of the Allied Masonic Degrees, which also operates from Mark Masons' Hall. They are open only to those who have taken the Mark Master Degree, and are as follows:—

> St. Lawrence the Martyr,
> The Knights of Constantinople,
> The Grand Tyler of King Solomon,
> The Red Cross of Babylon,
> The Grand High Priest.[2]

1. It has been suggested, for instance, that the ' regular step ' in Masonry, in which a tau cross is made with the feet, is a survival, and perhaps even the explanation of the accusation that the Knights Templar defiled the cross by treading on it.

2. There are also some thirty extinct or nearly extinct degrees formerly registered under the Allied Council. The intention appears to be to keep them in cold storage to prevent their unauthorised revival. Some, like the Order of the Scarlet Cord are extremely silly and futile, a few, like the Heroines of Jericho, are androgynous.

Other chivalric orders are :—
> Red Cross of Constantine,
> Holy Sepulchre and St. John the Evangelist.

THE CRYPTIC DEGREES

Also administered from Mark Masons' Hall is the Cryptic series of four degrees ; to take these one must be a Mark and Royal Arch Mason. The four are progressive, and are bestowed in order as follows :—

> Most Excellent Master,
> Royal Master,
> Select Master,
> Super-Excellent Master.

These degrees are termed 'cryptic' because their legend deals further with the crypt or vault beneath King Solomon's Temple in which Masonic secrets were concealed. They are, therefore, supposed to shed further light on the Royal Arch Degree.

THE SECRET MONITOR

The Secret Monitor Degree was formerly listed as fourth in the series of Allied Degrees. Now there is also a separate and independent organization or Conclave which works almost this identical degree as the first of its series of three, the third being the Chair Degree. It is known variously as the Brotherhood of David and Jonathan (on whom the legend of the ritual is based) and as a Trading degree, and it exists for mutual protection and fellowship. Much innocent amusement is to be had by shooting arrows down the Lodge. Its origin is American, where it probably dates back no further than the early days of the Civil War.

THE ANCIENT AND ACCEPTED RITE

The Ancient and Accepted (still commonly known as the Scottish) Rite, which consists of thirty-three degrees, is governed by the Supreme Council (10 Duke Street, St. James's, London, S.W.1). Only a few of these degrees, however, are worked in full in this country, though the corresponding system in America is more complete.

The degrees are as follows :—
(1) Entered Apprentice.
(2) Fellow Craft.
(3) Master Mason.
(4) Secret Master.
(5) Perfect Master.
(6) Intimate Secretary.
(7) Provost and Judge.

(8) Intendant of the Buildings.
(9) Elect of Nine.
(10) Elect of Fifteen.
(11) Sublime Elect.
(12) Grand Master Architect.
(13) Royal Arch (of Enoch).
(14) Scotch Knight of Perfection.
(15) Knight of the Sword or of the East.
(16) Prince of Jerusalem.
(17) Knight of the East and West.
(18) Knight of the Pelican and Eagle, the Sovereign Prince Rose Croix of Heredom.
(19) Grand Pontiff.
(20) Venerable Grand Master.
(21) Patriarch Noachite.
(22) Prince of Libanus.
(23) Chief of the Tabernacle.
(24) Prince of the Tabernacle.
(25) Knight of the Brazen Serpent.
(26) Prince of Mercy.
(27) Commander of the Temple.
(28) Knight of the Sun.
(29) Knight of St Andrew.
(30) Grand Elected Knight Kadosh, Knight of the Black and White Eagle.
(31) Grand Inspector Inquisitor Commander.
(32) Sublime Prince of the Royal Secret.
(33) Grand Inspector General.

The first three degrees are not worked at all by the Supreme Council; the Candidate must take them in a Craft Lodge in any jurisdiction recognised by the Grand Lodge of England. The Royal Arch, incidentally, is not a prerequisite for admission into the Ancient and Accepted Rite.[1]

Degrees 4-14 inclusive are conferred titularly by the Supreme Council in a Lodge of Perfection ; that is, they are conferred one after another by name only, with no words or signs.[2] An Obligation of secrecy is required which covers degrees 4-17 inclusive. The Lodge of Perfection is then closed, and a Council of Princes of Jerusalem is opened which confers

1. The 13th Degree (Royal Arch of Enoch) is not to be confused with the Royal Arch, although the degrees have a certain resemblance. The former is based on the legend that Enoch, anticipating the destruction of mankind in the flood, concealed certain secrets and mysteries in an arched vault which was subsequently discovered.

2. These " Intermediate Degrees " are, however, presented (usually one or two each year at an Annual Festival) as museum pieces for the edification of those who have been perfected to the Eighteenth Degree.

degrees 15 and 16 titularly, and is closed. A separate Lodge of Knights of East and West is then opened to confer a little more fully the 17th Degree. Signs are given, and the two words ABADDON and JAHABULON. The former, qualified by the words " the evil one," appears to reek of sulphur and satanism, but the context (were the degree worked in full) is the Apocalypse of St. John. The latter is a variation of the Royal Arch word, so altered, apparently, in order that a Royal Arch Mason may pronounce the whole word without violating his Obligation to give it only in a certain manner.

The 18th Degree, the Rose Croix of Heredom, is worked in full, and indeed is one of the most popular of all the ' other degrees.' Among its sixteen thousand Excellent Perfect Princes the 1950 Handbook lists some four hundred and seventy-five clergymen, including seventeen bishops[1] and a Kelham Father, who subscribe to its nauseating mixture of macabre sentimentality and heresy with a stupefaction of conscience or blindness of theological perception which is extremely difficult to understand. The Craft degrees, however objectionable, are based on comparatively harmless fables in an Old Testament context; the Rose Croix bases its workings on the Crucifixion of Our Lord Himself. As this degree is particularly obnoxious and worthy of ecclesiastical condemnation, a fuller account of it will be given.

Three rooms are required for this degree (apart from the preparation room). First there is the Black Room, in which is an altar hung with black over which are represented three crosses; the centre one with the Mystic Rose (in black) on its limbs, surrounded by the crown of thorns; the other two have the skull and crossbones depicted at their feet. On the Altar are the Holy Scriptures, an unsheathed sword, and a pair of compasses. On the floor are depicted seven concentric white circles on a black ground, with the emblem of the pelican in the centre. In the North, West, and South there are three pillars surmounted by lights; suspended from these pillars are cards or tins on which are painted respectively the letters F, H, and C, standing for Faith, Hope, and Charity.

The Black Room should open into the Chamber of Death, containing skull and crossbones, and even a figure in a winding-sheet laid out as a corpse; a lamp of spirits of wine and salt is placed behind these emblems, and the chamber may be further illuminated by transparencies representing skulls, crossbones, etc., or by flambeaux fixed in skulls.

The third, or Red Room, is brilliantly illuminated and hung with red. The altar in this room has a super-altar of eight steps with thirty-three lights. On the fourth step is

1. Some of these are overseas members throughout the Dominions (Canada excepted) and Dependencies of the Crown.

the Cubic Stone,[1] which opens with a red rose in the centre. The altar is profusely decorated with roses.[2] In the centre of the room is a representation of the Mysterious Ladder of Seven Steps with the movable letters F. H. and C. and I.N.R.I. (the word of this degree) one on each step, with a rose on each.

The Opening ceremony contains the following passage :—

Most Wise Sovereign. Excellent and Perfect First General, what is the hour ?

1st General. The ninth hour of the day.

Most Wise Sovereign. Then it is the hour when the Veil of the Temple was rent in twain and darkness overspread the earth, when the true Light departed from us, the Altar was thrown down, the Blazing Star was eclipsed, the Cubic Stone poured forth Blood and Water, the Word was lost, and despair and tribulation sat heavily upon us. (*A solemn pause*). Since Masonry has experienced such dire calamities it is our duty, Princes, to endeavour, by renewed labours, to retrieve our loss. May the benign influence of Faith, Hope, and Charity prosper our endeavours to recover the lost Word; for which purpose I declare this Chapter of Princes Rose Croix of Heredom duly open, in the Name of the Great Emmanuel.

For any Christian to declare that Masonry experienced a " dire calamity " at the Crucifixion, or that Masons suffered a " loss " in the triumphant redemptive death of Our Saviour on the Cross which the Excellent and Perfect Princes of the Rose Croix of Heredom can by their own labours " retrieve " seems not only heretical but actually blasphemous. The only interpretation which makes sense of this passage would appear to be that it is not the death of Our Lord which is mourned, *but the defeat of Satan.*

The Candidate for perfection enters the Chapter in the Black Room while it is thus plunged in gloom, and after giving the word of the previous degree (Abaddon) and his age (whatever it may be) as thirty-three, is told that " consternation spreads horror over our brows, the earth quakes, the

1. The Cubic Stone is apparently a recurrence of the Perfect Ashlar symbol of Craft Masonry (here applied to Christ), and has no connection with the Philosophers' Stone of the early Rosicrucians.

2. An earlier ritual (1891) directs that the Altar must also be " perfumed with attar of roses."

rocks are rent, the veil of the Temple is rent asunder " etc.
He is welcomed, however, in hopes that his courage may
assist them to retrieve the lost word. Prayer is offered for
him, and the Excellent and Perfect Marshal escorts him in a
mystic travel of thirty-three days to the three pillars in turn
(accompanied by solemn music) where he detaches the three
letters F. H. and C, which are presented to the Most Wise
Sovereign. The Candidate is congratulated on his success
thus far in discovering the initials of those virtues by whose
assistance he may discover the lost word, and the curtains con-
cealing the Altar are drawn apart. He then takes his Obligation
on the New Testament, swearing both secrecy and allegiance
to the Supreme Chapter.[1]

The Candidate now withdraws for a brief period of medi-
tation. On his re-entry a procession is formed which passes
round the Black Room (all bowing to the Cross in passing) and
all except the Marshal and the Candidate pass direct into the
Red Room. The Candidate finds his way thither barred,
because he is unable to give the word. He is told that his
attire is incompatible with that humility necessary for those who
wish to recover the word, and he is accordingly veiled in black
crêpe. He then enters the dimly-lit Chamber of Death,[2] and in
his stumblings over the skulls and other grotesqueries is assisted
by Raphael, who conducts him to the solemn rendering of a
funeral march through the Chamber to the brilliantly illuminated Red Room.

Here he symbolically ascends the mystic ladder " which leads
from darkness to glory and perfection ", picking up the letters
from each step. After Faith, Hope and Charity are disposed of,
the word is triumphantly found, as follows :—

Most Wise Sovereign	Whence come you?
Raphael (for Candidate)	From Judea.
M.W.S.	By what village did you pass ?
R.	Nazareth.
M.W.S.	Who conducted you ?
R.	Raphael.
M.W.S.	Of what tribe are you ?
R.	Judah.[3]
M.W.S.	Give me the initials of the last four steps. (*Raphael hands them to*

1. When Clerics take this oath, it would seem that they deliberately
   enter into a dual allegiance by pledging their fidelity to a religious
   and ' Christian ' body other than, and unknown to, the Church.
2. If three rooms are not available, the Black Room may be prepared
   as the Chamber of Death during the Candidate's withdrawal.
3. Scripture readings are interspersed by the Prelate in explanation of
   these words.

M.W.S.
him). Worthy Knights, by the aid of Faith, Hope and Charity you have indeed succeeded in finding the Lost Word.........taking the initials of the last four steps of your journey, and putting them together, you have found the Name of him who is the Word ;.........

These four letters I.N.R.I. forming the word are placed on the Cubic Stone on the altar; the Candidate is presented with a rose, invested with the collar and jewel of the Order, and sealed with the " seal of perfection "—symbols of the " hidden truths known only to the perfect Mason." The signs are given,[1] and the Herald proclaims the Candidate King of the Pelican and Eagle and a Prefect and Puissant Prince of the Rose Croix of Heredom.

The concluding ceremony is the Third Point, or " Feast of Fraternal Affection ", which though outwardly professing to be a mere *agape* or love-feast, has in its close context with Calvary a possible interpretation far more sinister. A wafer is first consumed. The Most Wise Sovereign presents a piece to the Prelate, both dip their fragments into salt and eat them. The Prelate then communicates his next neighbour in like manner, and so on. The Most Wise Sovereign then partakes of the chalice of wine with the Prelate, who replies with the sign of the Good Shepherd, exchanging the words. The second part of this sign accompanied by the words *pax vobiscum*, it may be noted, is not unlike the Pax ceremony in the Latin Mass but given with the arms crossed. The Prelate then drinks with his neighbour on his left, accompanied by the same exchange of signs and words, and so on till all have

1. There are three signs, and although there is some variation in them in different chapters, the following is a recognised form :—
   (i) The Sign of Adoration, which consists of raising the eyes to heaven and at the same time clasping the hands turned palms outwards, and fingers interlaced with their backs to the forehead, and from thence letting them drop upon the body, exclaiming " Hosanna."
   (ii) The right hand is lifted to the forehead with the fingers closed except for the index finger, saying " He ascended ". This is answered by pointing downwards with the right hand and saying " He descended."
   (iii) The Sign of the Good Shepherd (the usual salute on entering the Chapter or addressing the Most Wise Sovereign) is given by crossing the arms on the breast with the left uppermost. It is answered in the same manner. When this sign is given mutually, the two approach each other and reciprocally cross their arms and hands on each other's breasts, thus forming two crosses, and the letters I.N. and R.I. are exchanged. The password " Emmanuel " is given with the sign of the Good Shepherd, and is answered by " Pax Vobiscum " given with the same sign.

communicated. The Most Wise Sovereign then says " All is consumed ", to which reply is made *Gloria in excelsis Deo et in terra pax hominibus bonae voluntatis.*

The four cards on which the letters of the word are inscribed are then removed from the Altar, " that it be not exposed to the eyes of the profane but be consumed according to ancient custom ", and the Prelate burns them in a second chalice which the 1891 edition of the ritual specifies should contain " spirits of wine with chloride of strontian ",[1] and pronounces the words *consummatum est.* Strontium compounds are used, as every pyrotechnician knows, in rockets and other fireworks where a vivid rose-red flame is required. Its use at this culminating point in a solemn religious ceremony is dramatic and doubtless (to a certain type) emotionally impressive. Indeed only the most captious of critics would venture to suggest that these red flames might in themselves be a Masonic symbol of the origins of this strange parody of Christian worship.[2]

The most deadly heresy of this degree lies in the fact that it is the Candidate himself who symbolically achieves both light and perfection by his own efforts, not in Christ or Christ for him. It is the Candidate who gives his age as thirty-three who journeys for thirty-three days, passing through the Black Room and the Chamber of Death to his mystical resurrection in the Red Room. The prayer in the Black Room until recently contained the phrase " grant that we, being solely occupied with the work of our redemption......" And the Resurrection in the Closing ceremonies is defined significantly as the " hour of a Perfect Mason ". Our Lord's redemptive death is treated as a type and an allegory of the experiences which a Mason must undergo in his quest for light, not as a unique and objective act of redemption wrought for him by God. This is, of course, a purely Gnostic conception.

An address on this degree explains that " the Rose is an emblem of secrecy and silence ; in the Song of Solomon we find

1. Most recent editions of the ritual make no mention of the contents of the cup. Whether this omission is due to the fact that an ordinary flame is now considered sufficient, or whether it is intended to heighten the mystery of the red flames by withholding their chemical origin from the rank and file of the Puissant Princes I have no idea.

2. Dr. H. S. Box pointed out in a letter to the *Church Times* (April 13, 1951) a striking resemblance between the " quasi-Eucharist of this degree " and " the description of the Valentinian Eucharist that occurs in the Gnostic work *Pistis Sophia* (see C. Bigg *The Church's Task under the Roman Empire*)." The less theological will also discover a quite extraordinary parallel between these grotesque rites and the religious ceremonies described in Ngaio Marsh's popular thriller *Death in Ecstasy.* A certain scene in *Macbeth* also comes to mind.

reference to the Saviour under the mystical title of The Rose of Sharon." Here indeed, in this direct association of Christ with an emblem which (according to Masonry, not the Bible) significies secrecy, is a further admission that this degree interprets Christianity in the light of a mystery-religion of the type abhorred and anathematized by the early Church.

" May we henceforth treasure up the sacred doctrines of the Order in the secret repository of our hearts " proclaims the Most Wise Sovereign after the Feast of Fraternal Affection. If the " sacred doctrines " of this Order are Christian and orthodox as is so often maintained[1] it is wholly false, immoral, and ridiculous to keep them in a " secret repository ". If they are other than the teachings of the Church, and therefore not orthodox, the Church has every right and indeed the duty to tear off the tawdry veil of bogus mysticism and inquire into these " sacred doctrines " to which a group of her Bishops, hundreds of her clergy, and thousands of her laity have sworn allegiance and secrecy.

Degrees of the Ancient and Accepted Rite higher than the 18th are mainly honorary or administrative. There is a second gap ; the degrees from the 19th to the 29th inclusive are not worked in England, but are again conferred titularly. The 30th Degree (Knights Kadosh) is open only to Past Most Wise Sovereigns who have been members of the 18th Degree for at least three years, and who have been recommended for the honour by their local Chapters. This degree was originally based on revenge for the death of Jacocus Burgundus Molay, the last Commander of the Knights Templar who was executed In 1312 under Pope Clement V and Phillppe le Bel of France ; these two were regarded as symbols respectively of ecclesiastical and political despotism. In recent years, however, the shadow of Molay has receded, and the degree as worked in England has become more purely philosophical.

The 31st and 32nd Degrees are conferred for merit by the Supreme Council. The former is strictly limited to four hundred members, the latter to one hundred and eighty (both exclusive of promotions in the Dominions and Colonies). The 33rd and last degree (from which of course the Supreme Council is drawn) was traditionally limited to thirty-three

1. The Rev. J. L. C. Dart who as a Grand Elected Knight Kadosh (30th Degree) is also a Past Most Wise Sovereign of the Rose Croix wrote in *Theology* (April 1951) " The Higher Degrees are completely Christian and orthodox." Rather more officially the Rev. Arnold Whitaker Oxford, Grand Chaplain of the Rite, wrote " Its object is the same as that of the Church, to make men Christlike ; but it differs from the Church in its pageantry. It views things from a different standpoint and with a larger freedom. Its members......have a deeper realization of the togetherness of man." (*Origin and Progress of the Supreme Council* 33, 1933).

members ; the Year-Book (1950) appears to include a greater number, but it is not altogether clear how many are overseas members.

THE SOCIETAS ROSICRUCIANA IN ANGLIA

Although open only to Master Masons these degrees are really quasi-Masonic, and are completely different in tone from any regular Masonic system. The rituals of the various degrees are frankly theosophical and pseudo-rosicrucian, and are an extraordinary hotch-potch of high-sounding oriental mysticism and sham occultism. Very surprisingly, these degrees are alleged to be for Christians only.

The nine degrees are arranged in three orders, as follows :—

1st Order,	I.	Zelator,
	II.	Theoricus,
	III.	Practicus,
	IV.	Philosophus.
2nd Order,	V.	Adeptus Junior,
	VI.	Adeptus Major,
	VII.	Adeptus Exemptus.
3rd Order,	VIII.	Magister,
	IX.	Magus.

Closely associated with the S.R.I.A. is the Order of Eri, which is usually conferred only on those who have taken the fifth grade. Its symbolism has a strong Irish flavour.

'OPERATIVE MASONRY

There are still a few lodges of self-styled Operative Masons, not recognised by Grand Lodge. Known as the Worshipful Society of Operative Freemasons, they have, apparently, a supreme Lodge in London which exercises a certain jurisdiction, though they are mainly governed by the traditions of the individual Lodge. Their numbers appear to be small and dwindling. Were their claims to represent a medieval tradition and to have a ritual derived from the ancient York workings older than that of Grand Lodge Masonry capable of being substantiated, they would of course have attracted far more interest from Masonic scholars, but there is no conclusive evidence that they ante-date the 19th century, or that their ritual is not a spurious compilation from other sources including illicit exposures, largely the work of a certain Clement E. Stretton. Their signs differ from those of regular Masons. Regular Masons, including officers of Grand Rank, have, however, joined their Lodges, which are open to all who have taken the Mark Degree.

There are seven degrees, as follows :—

1. Apprentice,
2. Fellow,
3. Super-Fellow, Fitter, and Marker,
4. Super-Fellow, Setter, and Erector,
5. Intendant and Superintendent,
6. Certified Masters or Harodim,
7. Grand Master or Three Ruling Masters.

* * * *

Every degree that has been listed in these pages, although not officially recognised by Grand Lodge, is open to the Regular Freemason, and requires a Masonic qualification. In another category altogether (and outside the scope of this book) are the Co-Masonic bodies for men and women, or for women only, to attend whose Lodges carries, for the Regular Mason, the threat of discipline or even expulsion. There are four such organizations operating in Great Britain.

1. The Order of Universal Co-Masonry (ruled from France),
2. The Honourable Fraternity of Ancient Masonry,
3. The Honourable Fraternity of Ancient Freemasons,
4. The Order of Ancient, Free, and Accepted Masonry.

In addition there is the Order of the Eastern Star, whose ritual and secrets are entirely different from normal Masonic traditions.

The predominantly working-class secret societies popularly known as " poor man's Masonry " (Oddfellows, Buffaloes, Foresters, and the like) are completely ignored by Grand Lodge, and in practice there is very little overlap. It may perhaps be mentioned in passing that these organizations are almost entirely convivial, partly moral, but devoid, to the best of my knowledge, of any speculative, philosophical, Biblical, or religious content.[1] Some of them, however, claim a considerable antiquity.

1. Some idea of the harmless and whimsical nature of these societies may be gathered from the following particulars of the Ancient and Antediluvian Order of Buffaloes. There are three Degrees, (1) Kangaroo, (2) Primo, (3) Knight of Honour. Their Words are Shake-Speare, At-Las (given in alternate syllables) and R-E-X.

SCOTLAND

The grouping and jurisdiction of the various Masonic degrees differs considerably in Scotland. The most striking deviation lies in the position of the Royal Arch which is entirely separate from and independent of the Craft degrees controlled by Scottish Grand Lodge. To take it one must first be advanced as a Mark Master (which can be done either in a Craft Lodge or in a Royal Arch Chapter) and also take the degree, unknown in England, of Excellent Master.[1]

The Grand Chapter of Royal Arch Freemasons of Scotland, then, controls the following degrees :—

Mark Master,
Excellent Master,
Royal Arch,
Third Principal, ⎫
Second Principal, ⎬ Chair Degrees of the Royal Arch.
First Principal, ⎭
Right Worshipful Mark Master.

These degrees are progressive and must be taken in this order. One practical result of this difference in grouping is that an English Royal Arch Companion (even if he happens to have the Mark degree) cannot visit a Scottish Royal Arch Chapter because he has not taken the Excellent Master's degree.

Also under the jurisdiction of the Supreme Grand Chapter of Scotland are the following degrees, known as the Lodge and Council series :—

Royal Ark Mariner,
Commander Noah (its Chair degree),
Babylonian Pass or Red Cross,
Knight of the Sword,
Knight of the East,
Knight of the East and West,
Chief and President (a Chair degree).

And again under the same jurisdiction is the Cryptic Rite series with the following Royal and Select degrees :—

Royal Master,
Select Master,
Super Excellent Master,
Thrice Illustrious Master.

Thus it will be seen that the Scottish Grand Chapter controls altogether eighteen degrees.

---

1. This degree is not to be confused with the first degree in the Cryptic series in England. It includes a version of the " Passing of the Veils " ceremony which used to be part of the Royal Arch working in England, and is still so in Ireland and America.

There is a Scottish Supreme Council for the Ancient and Accepted Rite, whose thirty-three degrees are (with slight verbal variations in title) similar to the English series, and worked in similar groupings.

Scotland also has its independent Great Priory for the Religious and Military Orders of Knights Templar and Knights of Malta.

Peculiar to this country, however, is the Royal Order of Scotland.[1] This may be of some antiquity. Its ritual is unique among Masonic workings in that it is written in a rhyming doggerel which suggests an eighteenth-century origin ; its legend contains many features found in other degrees such as the Royal Arch, the Rose Croix de Heredom, the Knights Kadosh, and the Allied Degree of the Red Cross of Babylon. There are two degrees in this Order, the Harodim and the Rosy Cross. It is open only to Christians.

In general, Freemasonry in Scotland is more popular and relatively far more numerous than in England, partly because it tends to be cheaper, and because austere Presbyterianism has eliminated most of the colour, glamour, and ceremonial from Christian worship. When the soul is starved of these elements in religion, it will naturally tend to compensate itself in less desirable ways. It is not only the hostility of Rome that has left Masonry weak in Catholic countries.

IRELAND

From the Masonic point of view Ireland remains a single jurisdiction. Although its strength is mainly from Ulster, the headquarters are in Dublin. As might be expected, it is more firmly Protestant in membership than in England, and enjoys even greater support from the non-Roman Churches.

Masonry in Ireland may be grouped into six grades, as follows :—

1. The Craft degrees, controlled by the Grand Lodge of Free and Accepted Masons of Ireland :—

> Entered Apprentice,
> Fellow-Craft,
> Master Mason,
> Installed Master (the Chair degree).

II. The Supreme Grand Royal Arch Chapter of Ireland, which, as in Scotland, is distinct from and independent of the Craft, and which also controls the Mark degree, an essential pre-liminary to the Royal Arch. The Chapter degrees are :—

---

1. The Royal Order of Scotland has its Lodges in England, the Empire, and even in America, supposedly for those of Scottish origin or parentage, but these are ' provincial '; the governing body is in Edinburgh.

Mark Master,
Royal Arch,
Chief Scribe,
High Priest,
Very Worshipful Mark Master,
Excellent King.

Chief Scribe, High Priest, and Excellent King are Chair degrees of the Royal Arch (which, as noted in Appendix A, has a rather different legend from the English Royal Arch). The Very Worshipful Mark Master degree is only conferred prior to an installation as Excellent King.

III. The Grand Council of the Degrees of Knight of the Sword, Knight of the East, and Knight of the East and West, controlling the chivalric degrees of

Knight of the Sword,
Knight of the East,
Knight of the East and West,
Excellent Chief (a Chair degree).

IV. The Order of the Temple and Great Priory of Ireland, controlling the chivalric degrees of

Knight Templar,
Mediterranean Pass,
Knight of Malta,
Eminent Preceptor (a Chair degree).

V. The Grand Chapter of Prince Masons of Ireland, which controls :—

Knight of the Eagle and Pelican and Prince Grand Rose Croix,
Most Wise Sovereign (its Chair degree).

This is the same as the Eighteenth Degree of the Ancient and Accepted Rite, and is indeed acknowledged as such, but in Ireland it is worked as a separate degree under a separate jurisdiction. It is significant and indeed paradoxical that the good Irish Protestant is not after all invariably averse to an elaborate ' Christian ' ritual with plenty of candles on the Altar as long as such things are rigidly kept out of Church. He will reverence an altar cross provided it is adorned with a rose and not with the figure of Christ crucified.

VI. The Supreme Council for the 33rd Degree, Ancient and Accepted Rite for Ireland, controls only the following degrees out of the thirty-three :—

28. Chevalier du Soleil, or Knight of the Sun,
30. Philosophical Mason Knight Kadosh,
31. Grand Inspector Inquisitor Commander,
32. Prince of the Royal Secret,
33. Sovereign Grand Inspector General.

The Lodge and Council series of Scotland, the Cryptic Degrees, and the Secret Monitor are apparently unknown in Ireland.

The so-called Orange Lodges are quasi-Masonic only, and although there is a considerable overlap they have no official connection with regular Irish Masonry.

THE UNITED STATES

There is in the United States of America no supreme Grand Lodge or centralised Masonic authority. Each State is sovereign and independent. Each State, too, has its own Grand Chapter, Grand Council, and Grand Encampment. There is a General Grand Chapter, and a Grand Encampment claiming the allegiance of most (but not all) of the local State bodies, but these represent federations rather than central authorities.

The American system of Freemasonry may be tabulated under the following groups.

I. The three symbolic degrees :—
    Entered Apprentice,
    Fellow-Craft,
    Master Mason.

These are conferred by the Lodges under the control of the Grand Lodges of their respective States, and as in Great Britain form the basis of the whole Masonic system.

II. Chapter Masonry, corresponding in its degrees approximately to the Scottish Royal Arch system :—
    Mark Master,
    Past Master,
    Most Excellent Master,
    Royal Arch.

The Past Master is not a mere Chair degree, but is conferred independently of ruling a Lodge as it is a pre-requisite for exaltation to the Royal Arch. American Lodges tend to be so large (sometimes numbering several hundred) that the average Mason has little more chance of ruling one than the average citizen has of becoming mayor of his town, hence the necessity for a separate degree.

III. Council Masonry, corresponding to the Cryptic Degrees :
    Royal Master,
    Select Master,
    Super-Excellent Master.

These degrees are progressive, and are conferred in local Councils under the control of the State Grand Councils.

IV. The Commandery :—
    Knights of the Red Cross,
    Knights Templar,
    Knights of Malta.

These degrees or orders, conferred by Commanderies under the control of the Grand Commanderies of the various States, are theoretically open only to professing Christians.

V. The Ancient and Accepted Rite.

This has the thirty-three degrees as in England and Scotland, but (apart from the first three which again are taken in Craft or Blue Lodges) each degree is worked progressively and in full. America is divided for this Rite into two jurisdictions, the Northern, centred at Boston, and the Southern, which is administered from Washington, D.C. The Rite is not confined, as in England, to professing Christians. The ritual and symbolism of the Rose Croix degree, for instance, although not unlike the English rite, are presented in a rather more general and ' philosophical ' light, and specific references to Our Lord by name, except in the words Emmanuel and I.N.R.I. are deleted. (It would, perhaps, be more accurate to say that the Christian element was inserted in England.) Hence although based on the Crucifixion this degree in America is so universalised that a non-Christian can enter it in the same spirit that a non-Christian or non-Jew can enter into the Craft degrees based on the Old Testament.

VI. Certain independently-worked degrees such as the Secret Monitor.

There are in addition other independent and separate quasi-Masonic systems such as the exclusively Jewish B'nai B'rith, and probably obsolescent traces of the Rites of Mizraim and Memphis, with their multiplicity of degrees based on oriental mysticism and Egyptian mythology.

Co-Masonry flourishes in America more than in any other country. The various quasi-Masonic secret societies (Elks, Buffalos, Knights of Pythias, Riders of the Red Robe, Ku-Klux-Klan, Mystic Shrine, Enchanted Realm, etc.) are, as the sands of the sea, innumerable. The extraordinary popularity of Freemasonry and its imitators in America[1] (whose love of secret societies exceeds that of any other country except perhaps China) may be attributed partly to the fact that Americans are naturally extremely friendly, gregarious, and great ' joiners ' partly to a sub-conscious desire to escape the matriarchal female influence, so much stronger than in Great Britain, and

1. Total number of Masons in the United States, 3,597,810. Royal Arch, 634,000. Royal and Select Masters, 245,000. Knights Templar, 323,000. Ancient and Accepted (Scottish) Rite, Northern Jurisdiction, 378,000 ; Southern Jurisdiction, 340,000. The Mystic Order Veiled Prophets of the Enchanted Realm (104,000) and the Ancient Arabic Order Nobles of the Mystic Shrine (575,000) are independent of Masonic jurisdiction, but like the Societas Rosicruciana in Anglia their membership is composed solely of Masons, ' Shriners ' being limited to those who have reached the 32° in the Ancient and Accepted Rite, or who are Knights Templar.

partly, perhaps, to the absence of the glamour and pageantry of Royalty and hereditary titles, and to their less colourful and historic ceremonial in connection with government, national, and municipal occasions.

APPENDIX C
MASONIC SERVICE IN CHURCHES

It is well known that a Lodge, group of Lodges, or indeed a whole Province, may arrange for a special Masonic service to be held in some Church, Chapel, or Cathedral. Christian Masons will point to these services as proof positive that Masonry and Christianity cannot therefore be incompatible.

This argument, however, should not be taken quite at its face value. The Board of General Purposes, in reply to queries on this subject, have laid down two points of procedure as follows :—

(a) May the form of Masonic Service used at the Royal Albert Hall at the Bicentenary Celebration on June 24, 1917, be departed from?

Where the form of Service used at the Albert Hall be departed from, the form of such Service must be submitted to the Grand Secretary. Before granting a dispensation, the Grand Secretary will satisfy himself, that the occasion is desirable, the accommodation suitable, and the Preacher a Mason.

In Provinces or Districts, the application must be made to the Provincial or District Grand Secretary.

(b) May a Masonic Service be advertised?

A Masonic Service must not be advertised in any way.[1]

The " Albert Hall " form of Masonic service is not Christian, and makes no specific reference whatsoever to the second Person of the Holy Trinity. For a Masonic service in a Christian Church to be a Christian service, therefore, a dispensation is required from the Grand or Provincial Grand Secretary, who of course are laymen, and need not be Christians themselves. The Diocesan or the incumbent of the Church in which the service is to be held have no authority in the matter except to insist that unless a dispensation is granted, such a service cannot be held at all. There is no guarantee that such a dispensation will be granted ; a case arose recently in which a non-Masonic vicar who was asked to lend his

---

1. The *Masonic Year Book* for 1953 has ceased to print this most embarrassing ruling, but I have no evidence that it has been modified or rescinded.

Church for such a service, on being shown the service-form refused to grant permission unless the service were to be Christian. The dispensation was withheld on the grounds that certain Jewish and non-Christian Masons wishing to attend might be offended, and the vicar was of course reproached for being a narrow-minded bigot.

A correspondent in the *Church Times* in 1929, and again in 1951 revealed the fact that the dilution is not always complete, and that Masonic services do sometimes include the name of Christ ; in such cases either the dispensation was given by the Masonic authorities (in deference, perhaps, to an episcopal preacher), or the regulation requiring it was flouted. Yet I have amassed quite a collection of printed Masonic service-papers (including the hymns) by no means all of them sent to me by opponents of Masonry. Only one is Christian. And I have received letters, not only from England, but from India, Africa and Australia, from clergy who have indignantly prohibited these Christless services from their Christian Churches in cases where a dispensation was withheld.

It is indeed baffling to understand the attitude of our episcopate in issuing pastorals and protests in abundance against those clergy who rightly or wrongly approximate their services externally more or less to those of the Church of Rome, or again the attitude of those who rigorously oppose all joint worship with the Nonconformists, and yet remain absolutely mute and complacent over services which are not Christian at all ; which are deliberately non-Christian, in order not to offend Jews and others who reject our Lord.

The prohibition of all advertisement of Masonic services is, in these circumstances, disquieting, but hardly remarkable. Their very existence, and certainly their nature, are unknown to the great bulk of Church people.

The following Order of Service is one that has been used in Canterbury Cathedral, and is typical. Not only is it non-Christian, but the name of Our Lord has been deliberately deleted from the conclusion of the first two familiar Christian prayers.

DARKNESS VISIBLE

ORDER OF SERVICE

MASONIC HYMN
(Tune, " University College ", A. & M. 291)

Hail, Eternal ! by whose aid
All created things were made ;
Heaven and earth Thy vast design
Hear us, Architect Divine.

May our work begun in Thee
Ever blest with order be.
And may we, when labours cease,
Part in harmony and peace.

By Thy glorious Majesty,
By the trust we place in Thee,
By the badge and mystic sign,
Hear us, Architect Divine.[1]

SO MOTE IT BE.

LET US PRAY

Almighty God, unto Whom all hearts be open, all desires
known, and from Whom no secrets are hid ; cleanse the
thoughts of our hearts by the inspiration of Thy Holy Spirit.
that we may perfectly love Thee, and worthily magnify Thy
Holy Name.

SO MOTE IT BE.

THE LORD'S PRAYER

PSALM XV

THE LESSON   (St. James I, 4-27)

Anthem. Yea, though I walk through the valley of the shadow
of death, I will fear no evil : for Thou art with me, Thy rod
and Thy staff comfort me.

LET US PRAY for the Peace of the World

Almighty God, from Whom all thoughts of truth and peace
proceed : kindle, we pray Thee, in the hearts of all men the
true love of peace, and guide with Thy pure and peaceable
wisdom those who take counsel for the nations of the earth :

1. This hymn is a well-known Masonic favourite, often sung before Lodges
    are opened. The " badge " by which God is invoked (verse 3) is of course
    the apron. If the " mystic sign " refers to the Penal sign of cutting
    one's throat, the verse seems not only supremely silly but actually
    profane.

that in tranquillity Thy kingdom may go forward, till the earth is filled with the knowledge of Thy love, to the honour and glory of Thy most Holy Name.

SO MOTE IT BE.

LET US PRAY for the Masonic fraternity.

Almighty and eternal God, Who orderest all things in Heaven and Earth, we humbly implore Thee to pour down upon our Fraternity the continual dew of Thy Blessing. We beseech Thee to guide, support, and strengthen all who are Rulers in the Craft, and to give them a full measure of Thy Divine Wisdom. May brotherly love, relief, and truth be ever upheld and promoted in and through our Lodges. May prudence direct us, Temperance chasten us, Fortitude support us and Justice be the guide of all our actions, so that with one heart and mind we may strive together for the good of all mankind and the honour and glory of Thy Most Holy Name.

SO MOTE IT BE.

LET US PRAY for our Masonic Institutions.

O Lord, our Heavenly Father, Who art the giver of all good things and of old didst lead, protect, and provide for Thy Children, Israel : Bless, we humbly beseech Thee, all efforts we are making for the relief of distress, our care for the orphan, the aged and the sick. Give to each one of us such a measure of Thy Love, that cheerfully and willingly supporting our Masonic Institutions we may effectively relieve necessity and gratefully share the many blessings vouchsafed to us, to the glory of Thy Holy Name.

SO MOTE IT BE.

Let us remember before the Great Architect all our brethren who have passed to the Grand Lodge above.

O Lord of Heaven and Earth Who hast Thy Temple in the Heavens and the Earth for Thy footstool, we remember before Thee those of our brethren who having laboured faithfully here below have been called to Thine Immortal Mansions, Eternal in the Heavens. We bless Thy Holy Name for these Thy servants, beseeching Thee to give us grace so to follow their good example that we, with them, may be counted worthy of The Grand Lodge above where Thou, O Great Architect, livest and reignest for ever.

SO MOTE IT BE.

Let us ascribe to the Most High, Honour, Glory, and Thanksgiving.

Thine, O Lord, is the greatness and the power, and the glory, and the victory, and the majesty : for all that is in the Heaven and in the Earth is Thine. Thine is the Kingdom, O Lord, and Thou art exalted as head above all : both riches and honour come of Thee, and Thou rulest above all : and in Thine hand is power and might, and in Thine hand it is to make great and to give strength unto all. Now therefore, Our God, we thank Thee and praise Thy glorious Name for ever and ever.

SO MOTE IT BE.

HYMN
(Tune, " Strength and Stay ", A. & M. No. 12)

O brother man, fold to thy heart thy brother,
Where pity dwells, the peace of God is there ;
To worship rightly is to love each other,
Each smile a hymn, each kindly deed a prayer.

Follow with reverent steps the great example
Of Him Whose holy work was doing good ;
So shall the wide earth seem our Father's temple,
Each loving life a psalm of gratitude.

Then shall all shackles fall ; the stormy clangour
Of wold war music o'er the earth shall cease ;
Love shall tread out the baleful fire of anger,
And in its ashes plant the tree of peace.

THE SERMON

HYMN
O Worship the King, All glorious above.

NATIONAL ANTHEM

LET US PRAY

We commend, O God, to Thy loving care, all those who are absent from us, and all who have left us. Let Thy fatherly hand ever be over them ; and in Thy mercy keep them in safety. whether in this life or in the life beyond. And grant that we and they may ever abide in Thy eternal love.

THE BLESSING

CLOSING HYMN
(Tune A. & M. No. 274)

Now the evening shadows closing
Warn from toil to peaceful rest.

Mystic arts and rites reposing
Sacred in each faithful breast.

God of Light, Whose Love unceasing
Doth to all Thy Works extend,
Crown our Order with Thy blessing,
Build, sustain us to the end.

Humbly now we bow before Thee,
Grateful for Thine aid divine ;
Everlasting power and glory,
Mighty Architect, be Thine.[1]

SO MOTE IT BE.

1. This is the popular Masonic ode sung after closing the Lodge.

APPENDIX D

LIGHT INVISIBLE

In October 1952 appeared an answer to this book called *Light Invisible*, of which the author ("Vindex"), who claims to be a Freemason and a clergyman of the Church of England, prefers not to reveal his name. And, incidentally, an analysis of the correspondence columns devoted to Masonry during 1951-2 in the three Church papers, the *Church Times*, the *Church of England Newspaper*, and the *English Churchman*, reveals that of the letters written by or in defence of Freemasons some 70% are signed pseudonymously, whereas of those written in criticism only 12% failed to sign their real names.

Obviously written in great haste and bad temper, but here and there with devastating candour, *Light Invisible*, if genuine, is extremely disquieting. It presents Freemasonry in a rather worse light from the point of view of orthodox Christianity than does *Darkness Visible*. In the rare lucid intervals between passages of scurrilous abuse and deplorably bad history, when "Vindex" makes some attempt to come to grips with the theological argument he not only agrees with but underlines my main contentions. He accuses me of misrepresenting Christianity rather than Freemasonry. "If a Christian and a Hindoo meet together in a Lodge," maintains the author (p. 59) "and pray together to God, it is surely axiomatic....that the Christian must acknowledge that the Hindoo's God is ultimately the same as his own." If Christianity is an exclusive faith, if the Incarnation was God's full and final revelation of Himself, it is frankly admitted many times that Freemasonry is incompatible with it. But several quotations are adduced from certain extreme and unrepresentative Anglican modernists to prove that such is not the position of the Church of England, and that those who hold it are narrow-minded intolerant bigots. The passage (p. 56) where ' natural ' religion is contrasted, not with the supernatural but with the unnatural is only one of many indications, however, that the author is very nearly theologically illiterate.

Light Invisible deals with many criticisms of Freemasonry which I personally have never made. It makes a candid admission that although Masons do not enter the Craft for any material advantages, and indeed give a solemn undertaking before initiation that they are "uninfluenced by mercenary or other unworthy motive" in certain circumstances they are under oath to favour each other. Usually this is hotly denied, but technically "Vindex" is right. The Third Degree Obligation pledges the Mason to uphold the Five Points of Fellowship, and when these are fully explained later in the ceremony, the second Point includes an undertaking to support a brother Mason in all his laudable undertakings. Assuming then that business and professional promotion is indeed laudable, the Freemason appears bound to favour a fellow-Mason, other qualifications being equal.

The suggestion that *Darkness Visible* was intended to have any bearing on inter-Church relationships in either a Catholic or Protestant direction, or that it was inspired by any personal bitterness or animosities is, I can truthfully assert, ludicrous. It is "Vindex," not myself, who indulges in embarrassing personalities. I am not concerned with individuals, but with a principle relevant to *all* Christians—the vindication of the Incarnation of Our Lord and Saviour in the face of the religious or quasi-religious substitutes which it is my conviction Freemasonry secretly provides.

It is only fair to add, however, that the average Freemason will regard *Light Invisible* as a major blunder and indiscretion. Both in its discourtesy and in its outspokenness it is far from typical of the attitude of the majority of the Brethren as I know it. But it is disquieting to find an editorial review of this damaging book in the *Freemasons Magazine*, No. 677, (published from Great Queen Street and styled "The Organ of the Craft") referring to it as an "authoritative" statement of Masonic principles.

NOTE TO THIRD EDITION
(See pp. 37 and 183)

I have been taken to task for my version (p. 183) of the inscription of the Royal Arch Jewel, *Invenimus cultor dei civis mundi*, We have found the worship of God, O citizen of the world. As this motto is very damaging from the Christian point of view, the objections in all fairness merit attention.

On the Jewel itself, the upright of the interlacing triangles bears on its three sides EYPHKAMEN—INVENIMUS—WE HAVE FOUND. The downward triangle has CULTOR DEI —CIVIS MUNDI. The third is blank.

The Masonic authority E. H. Cartwright, in a letter quoted by Dr. Ross Hepburn in a lecture to a research Lodge in New Zealand (No. 130), accused me of combining two sets of Latin words on two separate triangles which appear to have no connection. He appears to ignore the fact that they are so combined exactly as I give them in the Aldersgate, Metropolitan, Perfect, Complete, and Sussex rituals, also in Herbert F. Inman's *Royal Arch Working Explained* and in A. Holmes-Dallimore's *Supreme Order of the Holy Royal Arch.*

The lecture on the Royal Arch Jewel in the Hornsey ritual to which Mr. Cartwright called attention in his letter, however, more logically separates the words CULTOR DEI—CIVIS MUNDI from INVENIMUS. Early Royal Arch Jewels carry the companion's name on the blank side of the downward triangle ; e.g. John Smith—cultor dei—civis mundi (a worshipper of God, a citizen of the world). *Invenimus* presumably refers to the finding of the secrets. A printed ritual of the Midland workings also has this rendering.

This is logical, avoids the howler, and is undoubtedly the correct version. Hornsey Chapter of Improvement is to be congratulated on preserving it. But the corrupt version is certainly more widespread, and if I have blundered in following it, I do so in excellent Masonic company.

BIBLIOGRAPHY

The literature of Freemasonry is considerable, and this bibliography is deliberately selective rather than comprehensive. I have included, however, not only books that are relevant to the theological issues dealt with in these pages, but also some on the history and origins of the Fraternity and its ritual workings, to give guidance for further reading to those whose interest has been aroused.

No reference is made to manuscript rituals or other unpublished sources of information, nor have I included much material relating exclusively to the ' higher degrees ' or to Continental Masonry.

1. RITUALS AND CEREMONIAL GUIDES

(Printed in a manner supposedly " intelligible only to the Craft ").

Craft Rituals :— ' Claret ' (1865),
Emulation,
Stability,
Oxford,
Ritus Oxoniensis
Revised,
Complete,
' English,'
Scottish,
Irish,
Nigerian,
Lectures of the Three Degrees,
' Ecce Orienti ' (American. Each State has its own version).
' Taylor,'
' William Harvey ' (Scottish).

Royal Arch :— Aldersgate,
Metropolitan,
Domatic,
' Adam Brown ' (1834),
' Claret ' (1866),
Complete,
Oxford,
Perfect,
' Taylor,'
Midland.

GUIDES :—

Cartwright, E. H., *A Commentary on the Free Masonic Ritual*, Hepworth, Tunbridge Wells.

A Drill Book of Craft Masonry, A. Lewis, London.

Hobbs, J. Walter, *Masonic Ritual*, Masonic Record, London.

Inman, Herbert F., *Emulation Working Explained*, A. Lewis,

London. *Royal Arch Working Explained*, Spencer & Co.,
London.
Sanderson, Maj. Meredith, *An Examination of the Masonic
Ritual.* Baskerville Press, London.
The Royal Arch Work, A. Lewis, London.
Your Lodge Work, Masonic Record, London.

(These books are of little interest except to the Mason, yet
together with the rubrics in the rituals they enable the inquirer
to reconstruct the ceremonial in its entirety).

II. MASONIC EXPOSURES.

(Invariably but disingenuously referred to by Masons as
'supposed' or 'alleged' exposures).
(a) 18th Century.
Prichard, Samuel. *Masonry Dissected.* 1730.
Three Distinct Knocks. 1760.
Jachin and Boaz. 1762.
Mahhabone, or The Grand Lodge Door Open'd, 2nd
Edition, 1766.
Wilson, Thomas. *Solomon In All His Glory, Or, The
Master-Mason.* 1768.
*Hiram, or The Grand Master Key To The Door Of Both
Ancient and Modern Freemasonry*, 1776.
(These early exposures are of historical interest in giving
a picture of Grand Lodge workings before the Union of
the Ancients and Moderns in 1813. They are described
and evaluated in a most interesting article by Com-
mander Smith entitled *So-Called Exposures of Freemasonry of the Mid-Eighteenth Century* which appeared
in *Ars Quatuor Coronatorum*, Vol. 56).
(b) Post-Union Exposures.
Carlile, Richard. *Manual of Freemasonry.* 1825. Now
published by Wm. Reeves, London.
(This is the earliest post-Union ritual in existence, and
is still substantially accurate in the Craft Degrees).

A Ritual and Illustrations of Freemasonry. London, C.1850.
(Written from material supplied by Avery Allyn, this is
really an exposure of American Freemasonry. Quaintly
illustrated).
Went, K. P., *Freemasons' Own Ritual.* Wm. Reeves, London.
(Undated, but fairly recent. It contains the three Craft
Degrees only, and although far more up-to-date than
Carlile it is not completely reliable).
(c) American Exposures.
Bernard, David. *Light on Masonry.* Utica, U.S.A. 1829.
(This includes most of Morgan's material with some
additional matter).

Blanchard, J., *Standard Freemasonry Illustrated.* Ezra Cook, Chicago, U.S.A.

Duncan, Malcolm C. *Masonic Ritual and Monitor.* Ezra Cook, 1951.

Morgan, William. *Freemasonry Exposed and Explained.* New York. 1826.
(This classic exposure which led to the author's murder has been re-printed in many forms and editions, some spurious).

Richardson, Jabez. *Monitor of Freemasonry.* Ezra Cook, Chicago, C.1861.

Ronayne, Edmund. *Hand Book of Freemasonry.* Ezra Cook, Chicago, U.S.A. 1904.
(Under the title *Blue Lodge and Chapter Masonry* this contains the full workings of Craft and Chapter degrees in America. The Craft portion alone, with identical pagination, is published under the title of *MAH-HAH-BONE.* The work was revised and brought up-to-date in 1917, and is quaintly illustrated. It appears to be substantially accurate).

III. MASONIC MYSTICISM AND SYMBOLISM.

The following books, some of which are extremely popular and have run into many editions and re-prints, interpret Masonry, to a greater or lesser extent, in the light of a pagan and occult mystery-religion. All are written by ' regular ' Masons. They are included in spite of the academic worthlessness of some for the interest of their points of view. These are only a few, but they are typical of many.

Castells, The Rev. F. de P. *The Apocalypse of Freemasonry,* and *The Arithmetic of Freemasonry.* A. Lewis, London.

Cockburn, Sir John. *Freemasonry, What, Whence, Why, Whither.* Masonic Record, Ltd., London.

Lawrence, The Rev. J. T. *Highways and By-Ways of Freemasonry, The Keystone,* and *The Perfect Ashlar.* A. Lewis, London.

Newton, Dr. Joseph Fort. *Brothers and Builders.* London. *The Religion of Masonry.* Washington, 1927.

Runton, P. T. *The Key of Masonic Initiation.* London, 1942.

Steinmetz, G. H. *Freemasonry—Its Hidden Meaning.* (New York, 1948). *The Royal Arch.* (New York, 1946).

Topley, W. H. *The Craft and The Royal Arch.* Masonic Record, Ltd.

Ward, J. S. M. *Freemasonry and The Ancient Gods.* London. *The E.A., The F.C.,* and *The M.M. Handbooks.* London. *An Explanation of the Royal Arch Degree.* London. *Who Was Hiram Abiff?* London.

Wilmshurst, W. L. *The Meaning of Masonry.* London. *The Masonic Initiation.* London.

IV. MASONIC WRITERS AND SOURCES, HISTORICAL AND GENERAL.

Anderson, James. *The Constitutions of The Free-Masons.* Printed by William Hunter. 1723.
> (The original Book of Constitutions of Grand Lodge).

Castells, The Rev. F. de P. *Origin of The Masonic Degrees.* London. *The Antiquity of The Holy Royal Arch.* A. Lewis, London. *Historical Analysis of The Holy Royal Arch Ritual.* A Lewis, London.

Constitutions of The Ancient Fraternity of Free and Accepted Masons. Published for United Grand Lodge. London. 1940.
> (The current edition, presented to every Candidate on initiation. It contains certain of the Ancient Charges, and plates showing officers' jewels, etc.).

Covey-Crump, The Rev. W. W. *The Hiramic Tradition.* London, 1937.

Danes, Gilbert W. *The Birth and Growth of the Grand Lodge of England,* 1717-1926. Masonic Record, Ltd., London.

Gould, R. F. *The History of Freemasonry.* (3 vols.). London, 1884.

Hawkins, E. L. *A Concise Cyclopaedia of Freemasonry.* A. Lewis, London.

Hughan, William J. *Origin of the English Rite of Freemasonry,* edited by John T. Thorp, 1909.

Jones, Bernard E. *Freemasons' Guide and Compendium.* Harraps, 1950.
> (Really first-class, scholarly, and well-documented, attractively illustrated. The latest and by far the best account of Masonry for the general reader).

Knoop, Douglas, and Jones, G. P. *A Short History of Freemasonry to 1730.* Manchester. *The Genesis of Freemasonry.* Manchester, 1947.

Light Invisible : The Freemasons' Answer to Darkness Visible. by "Vindex." Regency Press, London.
> (A pseudonymous indiscretion, scurrilous but unintentionally amusing, which presents Masonry in a rather worse light than *Darkness Visible*).

Lawrence, The Rev. J. T. *Masonic Jurisprudence.* A. Lewis, London.
> (A standard handbook of procedure).

Mackey, A. G. *A Revised Encyclopaedia of Freemasonry.* (3 vols.). Chicago. *Lexicon of Freemasonry.* New York.

Masonic Year Book. Published under the Authority of the United Grand Lodge of England, 1954.

(The official annual containing lists of every Lodge and Chapter, Grand and Provincial Grand Lodge and Chapter officers, etc. The various Provinces have in addition their Provincial Handbooks giving more detailed information. A similar Year Book is published by the Grand Lodges of Scotland, of Ireland, and of the various States of America).

Masonic Enquire Within. Masonic Record Ltd., London.

Pike, Albert. *Morals and Dogma.* Charleston, U.S.A. 1871.

Poole, The Rev. Herbert. *The Old Charges.* Masonic Record Ltd., London.

Preston, Wm. *Illustrations of Masonry.* Printed for the Author, 1772.

Statistics Fraternal Societies, 57th annual edition, 1951 Rochester, U.S.A.

The Freemason's Vade Mecum. A. Lewis, London.

Waite, A. E. *A New Encyclopaedia of Freemasonry.* (2 vols.). London, 1925. *Emblematic Freemasonry,* London, 1925.

Ward, J. S. M. Article *Freemasonry* in Encyclopaedia Britannica.

V. MASONIC PERIODICALS AND REVIEWS.

Ars Quatuor Coronatorum.
(The transactions of the Lodge Quatuor Coronati (No. 2076), a Lodge which is specially devoted to Masonic research, and an invaluable mine of scholarly informa tion on all subjects connected with Masonic history and symbolism. Many articles have been off-printed as separate pamphlets).

Freemason, The.
(A quarterly of very irregular appearance containing articles of general Masonic interest).

Freemasons' Chronicle.
(A weekly paper containing Masonic news and a feature article).

Freemasons' Magazine.
(A beautifully produced quarterly containing news and articles of general and symbolic interest).

Masonic Record.
(An illustrated monthly journal, with articles of historical, symbolical, and ' speculative ' interest).

Miscellanea Latomorum, or Masonic Notes and Queries.
(On something the same lines as *Ars Quatuor Coro-*

natorum, only rather more popular. Its publication has not yet been resumed since the war).

VI. NON-MASONIC WRITINGS.

Box, Dr. Hubert S. *The Nature of Freemasonry.* Augustine Press, 1952.

Cahill, S. J., The Rev. E. *Freemasonry and the Anti-Christian Movement.* Dublin.

Christ or The Lodge? Philadelphia, U.S.A.
(The report of the Orthodox Presbyterian Church of America which condemned Masonry).

Dillon, Mgr. G. E. *Grand Orient Freemasonry Unmasked.* Britons' Publishing Society, London, re-printed 1951.
(The title is misleading, as the book is by no means confined to the Grand Orient).

Fahey, C. S. Sp., The Rev. Denis. *The Kingship of Christ and Organized Naturalism.* Cork, 1943.

Finney. The Rev. Charles G. *Character and Claims of Freemasonry.* National Christian Association, Chicago.
(The testimony of a great American evangelist and educationalist, once a Freemason).

Graebner, Dr. Theodore, *The Secret Empire* (1927), *A Handbook of Organizations* (1948, this has largely superseded the earlier book). *Is Masonry a Religion?* Concordia Publishing, St. Louis, U.S.A.
(These books contain the arguments on which American Lutherans have condemned Freemasonry).

Gruber, S. J., The Rev. Herman. Article *Masonry* in the Catholic Encyclopaedia.

Johnson, The Rev. Humphrey J. T. *Freemasonry, A Short Historical Sketch.* Catholic Truth Society, London.

Keith, P. J. *English Masonic Isolation, A Myth Exploded.* Britons' Publishing Society, London.

Leo XIII, *Humanum Genus*, 1884. (Reprinted from a translation by Fr. Fahey, C.S.Sp., by The Britons' Publishing Society, 1952).

Penney Hunt, The Rev. C. *The Menace of Freemasonry to the Christian Faith.* Freedom Press, Breaston, Derby.
(An overwhelming case against Masonry built up from Masonic authors. This book did much to influence the decision of the Methodist Conference at Bradford, 1927).

Pollock, A. J. *Reasons Why a Christian Should Not Be A Freemason.* Central Bible Truth Depot, London.

Reflections on Freemasonry, by "An Anglo-Catholic." Freedom Press, Breaston, Derby.

Ronayne, Edmond, *The Master's Carpet.* Ezra Cook, Chicago.

McReavy, The Rev. L. L., *Forbidden and Suspect Societies*. Catholic Truth Society, London.

Rumble, Dr. L. *Catholics and Freemasonry*. Catholic Truth Society, London. (This pamphlet reproduces on its cover the top plate of the frontispiece from *Darkness Visible*, by permission of the Augustine Press).

Should A Christian Be A Freemason? S.P.C.K., London. 1951. (The complete controversy on Freemasonry in *Theology* re-printed).

Thurston, S. J., The Rev. H., *Freemasonry*. Catholic Truth Society, London.

Webster, Mrs. Nesta H., *Secret Societies and Subversive Movements*. New and Revised edition, Britons' Publishing Society, 1954.

X-Rays On Freemasonry, by 'A. Cowan' (Lieut.-Col. Gratton). London, 1901.